Communication and Society
Editor: Jeremy Tunstall

Broadcasting in education: an evaluation

Journalists at work
Jeremy Tunstall

The making of a TV series
Philip Elliott

The political impact of mass media
Colin Seymour-Ure

The manufacture of news
Stan Cohen and Jock Young (editors)

Children in front of the small screen
Grant Noble

The Fleet Street disaster
Graham Cleverley

The silent watchdog
David Murphy

The media are American
Jeremy Tunstall

Putting 'reality' together
Philip Schlesinger

Newspaper history
George Boyce, James Curran, Pauline Wingate (editors)

Deciding what's news
Herbert Gans

The international news agencies
Oliver Boyd-Barrett

The bounds of freedom
Brian Lapping (editor)

Inside information
Annabelle May and Kathryn Rowan (editors)

Sound effects
Simon Frith

The Media in Britain
Jeremy Tunstall

This book is the seventeenth volume in a series
edited by Jeremy Tunstall and devoted to
explorations of the interrelationships between
society and all forms of communication media.

A. W. BATES

Broadcasting in education

An evaluation

Constable · London

First published in Great Britain 1984
by Constable and Company Ltd
10 Orange Street London WC2H 7EG
Copyright © 1984 by A. W. Bates
hardback ISBN 0 09 463590 0
paperback ISBN 0 09 463680 X
Set in Linotron Times 10pt by
Rowland Phototypesetting Ltd
Bury St Edmunds, Suffolk
Printed in Great Britain by
St Edmundsbury Press
Bury St Edmunds, Suffolk

DEDICATION

To all Open University students, past, present and future

Contents

Preface   xiii
1 *Setting the scene*   1
   The present structure of British broadcasting   2
   Educational broadcasting in Britain   5
   Assessing the effectiveness of broadcasting in
      education   8

2 *Formal education: strategic roles for broadcasting*   13
   Justifying educational broadcasting: myth and reality   13
   Schools broadcasting   16
   Programmes aimed directly at learners   18
   Programmes aimed at teachers   27

3 *Schools broadcasting: an end of term report*   33
   Is there anyone out there?   33
   The limitations of statistics on utilisation   39
   Enrichment and learning resource: the overseas evidence   41
   Enrichment and learning resource: the British evidence   42
   Enrichment or learning resource?   45
   Meeting special needs and deficiencies: the evidence   48
   Summarising the evidence   64

4 *Non-formal basic education: strategic roles for*
      broadcasting   67
   What is non-formal education?   67
   The needs   68
   Children's programming   73
   Basic adult education   76
   Social action programming   78
   Rural programming   82
   Programming for disadvantaged minorities   91
   Policy issues   94

5 *Getting it right: helping the disadvantaged*   96
   Audience characteristics and education by stealth   96
   Levels of commitment   99
   Getting it wrong   101

'Sesame Street': achievements and critiques   103
The BBC and the Adult Literacy Campaign   108
Common features of success   112
The importance of network policies   115
Summing up   117

6 *Continuing and distance higher education: strategic roles
    for broadcasting*   119
The use of general broadcasting in continuing education   119
Continuing education programmes: the British
    perspective   122
Continuing education: an international perspective   129
Roles in continuing education: some conclusions   135
Television and radio in distance higher education   137
Roles in distance higher education: some conclusions   150

7 *Getting it right: continuing and higher education*   152
Course planning and support services   152
Transmission arrangements   156
Multi-media factors   160
Financial arrangements   168
Programmes   171
Getting it right in continuing and distance higher
    education: conclusions   179

8 *Broadcasters, professionalism and educational
    effectiveness*   181
Unanswered questions   181
Quality in programming   183
Professionalism in broadcasting   192
The limits of professionalism   199

9 *The impact of new technology on educational
    broadcasting*   203
Radio and cassettes   203
Video-cassettes   206
Video-discs and interactive video   216
Cable and satellite   221
Teletext and viewdata   225
Microcomputers and microcomputer developments   227
The key developments   231

10 *The future of educational broadcasting*   232
Variety   232

Successes 232
Weaknesses 233
Broadcasting as a profession 234
Future trends 235
Future advantages of broadcasting 237
Needed improvements 239
The decommitment to public service broadcasting 242

Appendix 244
Appropriate teaching functions for television, radio and
  audio-cassettes in Open University courses 244

Bibliography 250
Index 261

List of tables

1 Strategic roles for television and radio   9
2 Number of school broadcast series nationally networked in Britain (school year 1981–82). (*Source:* Educational Broadcasting Council, 1982)   17
3 Schools television and radio in UK: equipment and programme use. (*Source:* Educational Broadcasting Council, 1982)   35
4 Audiences for selected school radio series (BBC): 1981–82. (*Source:* Educational Broadcasting Council, 1982)   36
5 Audiences for selected school television series (BBC and ITV): 1981–82. (*Source:* Educational Broadcasting Council, 1982)   38
6 Utilisation of television and radio for different secondary school subject areas. (*Source:* Educational Broadcasting Council, 1982)   40
7 Evaluation and progress reports on projects using broadcasting for direct teaching or curriculum reform   57
8 Adult illiteracy rates in a selected number of countries. (*Source:* UNESCO, 1980)   70
9 Levels of audience commitment: two examples. (*Sources:* Horneij, 1975, and Salkeld, 1979)   100
10 BBC adult literacy broadcasts. (*Sources:* Hargreaves, 1980; Jones and Charnley, 1978)   106
11 Numbers of tutors and students in adult literacy tuition: 1976. (*Source:* Jones and Charnley, 1978)   110
12 Total continuing education programming, 1981   123
13 New adult education nationally networked television programmes produced in UK, 1981   124
14 Total output, BBC CE and OU CE, 1981   130
15 Use of audio-visual media in autonomous distance teaching universities. (*Sources:* Bates, 1980; Rumble and Harry, 1983; MacKenzie *et al.*, 1975; and private sources)   142
16 Control characteristics of broadcasts   212
17 Control characteristics of recorded material (cassettes)   213

List of figures

1 Listening rates by transmission week at the Open
      University (1979 and 1980)   153
2 Audiences for BBC foreign language courses   154

(Acknowledgement is due to British Council, for permission to reproduce these figures from *Media in Education and Development,* Vol. 15, No. 3, 1982.)

Preface

This book took me six years to write. Nor is it what I originally intended. During the period 1978 to 1983, major changes were starting to occur in the world of broadcasting and communications. These changes really forced me to go back to basics, to look at the way broadcasting had been used in education, to identify where and why it had been successful, and to analyse its likely role in the immediate future. My original idea was to write a book about the *conditions* needed to make broadcasting successful in education. While I have met this aim to some extent, I found that I also had to map out in detail the various ways in which broadcasting has been used, because the right conditions for successful use depend very much on the *context* of educational broadcasting. I was surprised to find on starting that no comprehensive, general description of educational broadcasting existed. Also, when I began, the pattern of coming changes was not then clear. Over the six years, the likely impact of new technology on broadcasting has become much sharper.

I'm glad I did change my intention, and I am even more grateful for my publisher's patience. It has enabled me to write a much more comprehensive book on educational broadcasting, and one which I hope will fill a big void. Teachers, teacher trainers, educational broadcasters, and politicians concerned with education will I trust find this book a useful source of information, and a stimulus to thinking about what they are doing. My major hope though is that it will prompt a thoughtful debate about the direction of educational broadcasting – even public service broadcasting – over the next decade. I fear that we are going to lose public service broadcasting in Britain, almost by default. This is one cry, I hope not in the wilderness, against such a dismal prospect.

I have drawn very heavily on the work of others. Wherever possible, I have tried to acknowledge this. Special mention though must be made of my colleagues in the Audio-Visual Media Research Group at the Open University. Over a period of ten years I have been blessed with a number of brilliant colleagues who have also been lovely people. Margaret Gallagher and Hans Grundin have made the greatest contribution to anything that may appear new in this book, but significant ideas and research findings have also come from Diana Laurillard, Nicola Durbridge, Duncan Brown, Stephen Brown, Larry Kern and Frances Berrigan. From outside the Open University, Wilbur Schramm, Gavriel Salomon and Neil Postman have been the main giants on whose shoulders I have attempted to climb. David Mathew and Stuart Atkins from the BBC's Educational Broadcasting Council, Charles Mayo from the IBA, Eileen Ware from the Media Project, the Volunteer Centre, Bob Fuller from the University of Nebraska, and Malcolm Parlett have all kindly read and commented on parts of the manuscript. Michael Clarke speedily and accurately typed the draft when it was at last complete. Jeremy Tunstall, the series editor, and Elfreda Powell of Constables have been extremely helpful and encouraging throughout. With so much help, the errors, stupidities, omissions, and biases that remain are clearly my own responsibility.

Lastly, on reading through the final manuscript, I feel I have been over-critical of the shortcomings of educational broadcasting. Measuring educational effectiveness is not easy. Many of the mental processes stimulated by educational broadcasting are not accessible. We cannot climb into people's brains to see what's going on. My belief is that educational broadcasting is no worse, and a good deal better, than most other educational provision. But I could judge it only on the evidence available.

1

Setting the scene

Broadcasting is undergoing fundamental changes. These changes will affect education no less than our leisure viewing. We are entering what has been termed the 'Third Age of Broadcasting' (Wenham, 1982). The first age, from the early 1920s to just after the Second World War, was the age of BBC radio. The second age, from the early 1950s to today, has been the age of 'responsible' national broadcast television. It has been a remarkably stable period, only slightly disturbed in Britain by the advent of commercial television in 1955 and BBC2 in 1964. While the amount of broadcast television has gradually expanded and competition between channels has become quite keen, the basic ideals and ethos of British broadcasting have remained largely unchanged. In particular, British commercial television has if anything strengthened rather than weakened the traditional heritage of the BBC with regard to cultural standards, the concept of public service and provision for minority interests.

But between 1981 and 1986 massive changes to the British broadcasting scene are occurring, characterised by a huge increase in the range of television delivery systems and services, very fierce competition for audiences and revenues, and increasing demands on the public to pay for such services directly. Consider what is happening. In 1981 a fourth national television channel, Channel 4, was created. In 1982 we were blessed with the introduction of not one but two breakfast television services. Video-cassette machines are rapidly becoming standard furniture in many homes; in fact by 1986 half the homes in Britain will be so privileged. Since prerecorded cassettes can be hired for as little as fifty pence (if you don't mind the skull and crossbones on the pirate cassettes), this is already equivalent to the provision of another television channel. Just entering the shops is the video-disc, capable of providing ultra-high-quality pictures, stereo sound, 57,000 still frames, slow motion, and fast search – at a price less than a domestic video-cassette machine. From 1984 – a significant year – cable operators will be allowed to provide as many channels as is economically viable to those households willing to be connected up – with less regulation than in any other country in the world: no need to be balanced or unbiased, no need to be 'responsible', no need to

provide educational or community services or minority programming, no need to encourage British programme production. There
are BBC plans to operate four 'direct broadcast' satellite television
channels from 1986. There is also the possibility of 'international'
channels provided, legally or illegally, by such agencies as Radio
Luxembourg or Rupert Murdoch's Satellite TV Company. Computer programs and video games also use the domestic television set
for display. We are indeed in the third age of broadcasting, at a
speed no less remarkable for the lack of public debate and discussion about the desirability or possible effects of such a headlong
charge into the Tower of Babel.

It is hard to imagine what the cumulative effect of such changes
will be on the services provided currently by BBC1, BBC2 and ITV.
Will it mean 'wall-to-wall Dallas'? Will it mean that at last you can
find out, at the flick of a switch, all you wanted to know about
polynomial equations? There will certainly be increased competition for audiences, and it is quite possible that the long-cherished
ideals of public-service, 'quality' and 'minority' programming will
be early casualties in the battle for ratings. What is certain is that the
changes when they do come are bound to affect the role of television
and radio in education.

This era of uncertainty makes it necessary to reconsider first
principles about educational broadcasting. What *are* its roles? What
can it do better than anything else? How effective is it? What is
needed to make it effective? Will there be a *need* for educational
broadcasting in the future? It is important to ask these questions,
because there is an air of determinism about developments in
television, both technological and political. There is an assumption
that because the technology is coming it must be used, and it must
be used to maximise profits. There is no adequate counter to such a
philosophy if we, the public, are not clear about what we want from
broadcasting now and in the future. Also there is no point in fighting
for something that is not worth keeping; if on the other hand there is
value to be gained from using broadcasting, those with an interest in
education need to ensure that their interests are protected, whatever changes are likely to occur. Before though looking at the
advantages and disadvantages of television and radio in education it
will be helpful to describe the present context of educational
broadcasting in Britain.

THE PRESENT STRUCTURE OF BRITISH BROADCASTING

The BBC is financed from licence revenues collected from owners or renters of television sets. The BBC is, debatably, independent of direct government control through a system of part-time governors appointed by the Queen in Council. Governors advise, warn and are involved in the appointment of the more senior BBC executives, but the day-to-day management of the BBC is firmly in the hands of full-time 'professional' BBC staff. The BBC provides two national TV channels (BBC1 and BBC2) of which BBC2 is slightly more cultural and directed slightly more to covering minority interests than BBC1. The BBC also operates four national radio channels. Radio 1 is made up mainly of pop music; Radio 2 of light entertainment and light music; Radio 3 mainly of classical music, with some 'high-brow' drama, talks and poetry; and Radio 4 of drama, news, documentary, some comedy, and some classical and serious music. All channels provide hourly news bulletins. The BBC operated twenty-five local radio stations in 1982. It has an overseas (external) service and is responsible for its own transmission networks. With the exception of the overseas service, which gets a grant from the Foreign Office, all these services are paid for from the licence fee income, which totalled £563·7 million in 1982.

There are fifteen regional Independent Television (ITV) companies, financed by advertising revenue. Between them, they provide the programming for a national commercial television network, with some regional variations (as with the BBC). Franchises are awarded by the Independent Broadcasting Authority (IBA), which monitors the output of the companies and runs the ITV transmission network. Members of the IBA are also appointed by Parliament. The government raises a levy on profits made by the ITV companies.

The ITV companies also contribute from their revenues to the costs of a fourth national television channel, Channel 4. This company operates differently from the other national broadcasting organisations. It does not have its own production facilities or staff but buys programmes from the ITV companies, independent producers and from overseas. It may also commission productions from other producers. The programmes are broadcast through the IBA network, with each of the ITV companies selling advertising time on Channel 4 in its own area. The programming for Channel 4 caters much more for minority tastes than the other ITV channel. In Wales there is a separate and independent Welsh-language service operating on Channel 4. By the end of 1982, the IBA had awarded franchises to forty-seven local radio stations, which are financed by advertising. Local radio stations, both BBC and IBA, are continuing to be opened. It is anticipated that there will be over a hundred local radio stations by the end of the decade.

A new system of television and radio audience research has recently been established in Britain. One of the recommendations of the Annan Committee on the Future of Broadcasting (Gt Britain: Home Office, 1977) was that there should be one system of audience measurement, rather than the two previously operated by the BBC and ITV companies, which inevitably resulted in different ratings because of the different methods used. The Broadcasters' Audience Research Board (BARB) was established in 1980. It is a limited company jointly owned by the BBC and the Independent Television Companies' Association (ITCA). There is a board of three directors, of whom one is an independent chairman, with one member from each of the BBC and the ITCA. There are two services provided by BARB. The first is audience measurement, and the second is audience reaction. Audience *measurement* is based on a panel of around 2,900 private households. Each set is fitted with a meter which monitors when the set is switched on and the channel being viewed. This is backed up with diaries, plus a larger survey (25,000 households) once a year. This system, currently run under contract by AGB Research Ltd, monitors the size of television audiences for each programme and the amount of viewing, and provides information about the socio-economic background of the audiences. The audience *reaction* service is operated by the BBC's Broadcasting Research Department. Using interviews in people's homes, information is collected daily from around 1,000 people throughout the UK about their reactions to *radio* programmes. They are also left a questionnaire to complete about the *television* programmes they watch over the next five days. Information is collected for all programmes on enjoyment and interest, plus more detailed information on certain selected programmes. However, the sample size is such that information on audiences with less than 500,000 is unreliable by these means, so while this relatively new system provides valuable information for advertisers and programme makers for the bulk of general programming, it is not much help to the many education and social action programmes which appeal to small audiences. Both the BBC and IBA undertake special research studies, through their own research departments, which sometimes include minority programmes (see Ware, 1983, for a more detailed account of audience research).

Although about 2½ million people in Britain already receive television or radio signals relayed to their homes by cable from central receivers, the provision has been limited to relaying the main off-air broadcast channels. In addition, in the 1970s, several small, non-profit-making cable TV experiments were allowed to try out community and local programming. These were strictly controlled and limited by the Home Office, the government department responsible for the regulation of broadcasting in Britain. In 1983, however, the government announced that it would encourage a major expansion of cable television services. Parliament has established a Cable Authority which is to award and monitor franchises. The first eleven cable operators under the new system should be fully operational by the end of 1985, followed by many more over the next few years. Each cable operator will have a cable TV monopoly in its area and will be subject to very light regulation. In particular, there is no legal obligation on cable operators to carry educational or community programming. Cable franchises will be offered on a much more local basis than the thirteen ITV regional franchises.

Lastly, at the time of writing, the BBC was planning to operate two satellite television channels from 1986, when the first United Kingdom Direct Broadcast Satellite (DBS) is due to be launched. One channel will operate on a Pay-TV basis, showing latest film releases. The second channel will be made up of selections of programmes previously shown on BBC1 and BBC2. The aim is to make the satellite service self-financing, separate from the licence revenue, although in the early years it is hard to see how the BBC can avoid using licence revenue money to get the service going.

The government has also announced that the IBA will be able to operate a further two satellite channels from 1986, although it remains to be seen whether commercial companies will come forward to provide sufficient programming for these two channels on a profitable basis.

EDUCATIONAL BROADCASTING IN BRITAIN

In Britain, educational broadcasting is a substantial enterprise, incurring expenditure in 1982 of the order of £100 million. The following gives some indication of the size of the activity during 1982:

(1) More than £50 million was spent by broadcasting organisations on the production and transmission of specifically educational broadcasts;
(2) Over fifteen million individual copies of accompanying publications (pupils' workbooks, teachers' notes, etc.) were sold to schools and colleges;
(3) Over 32,000 schools and 550 colleges of further education

had television sets, i.e. just over 97 per cent of all such
establishments in the United Kingdom;
(4) Over 12,000 schools and over 500 further education colleges
had video-cassette machines (36 per cent and 96 per cent
respectively);
(5) Nearly all schools and further education colleges had radio
sets (99 per cent and 85 per cent respectively);
(6) There was an average of 85 hours a week of specifically
educational broadcasts being transmitted on national networks when schools and colleges were open.

The BBC has four educational broadcasting departments fully
funded from its licence revenue: schools television; schools radio;
continuing education television; and continuing education radio.
The independent television companies are required by the IBA to
provide schools programmes, continuing education programmes
and a specified amount of social purpose programming, funded
from their own revenues. From 1983, another fifteen hours a week
of educational broadcasting – primarily out-of-school and social
purpose programming – is being provided by Channel 4, also funded
from its own revenues.

Both the BBC and the ITV companies – as well as some of the
local radio stations – employ full-time education officers responsible
for liaison with local educational establishments and for providing
feedback on educational programming. Both the BBC and IBA
have appointed their own advisory bodies for educational programming. The BBC has appointed an Educational Broadcasting Council (EBC) which is serviced and financed by the BBC, and which has
a small research department attached to it. This research department provides both the BBC and ITV companies with annual
equipment and utilisation figures for education, based on annual
surveys of schools and further education institutions. The EBC
research department also carries out special studies for the BBC.
The IBA awards fellowships, usually for one year, and many of
these have been used for special studies in the field of educational
broadcasting, but there is no research department specifically
devoted to research into the ITV companies' educational
programmes.

Lastly, the Open University occupies a unique position in British
educational broadcasting. Established as a fully autonomous, de-
gree-awarding institution in 1969, with its own royal charter, the
Open University provides degree-level and continuing education
courses for adults on a part-time basis. Most students are in
employment and study primarily at home. In 1983 the Open Uni-

versity had 85,000 students: 60,000 in the undergraduate programme and 25,000 in the continuing education programme. The
Open University had an annual budget of £60 million in 1983. The
undergraduate programme is financed directly by the Department
of Education and Science (DES – a government ministry), although
students pay fees which amount to about 15 per cent of the
undergraduate budget. The continuing education programme is to
be self-financing. Students study through a mixture of specially-
designed correspondence texts (which provide the core teaching
material), television broadcasts, audio-cassettes, correspondence
and face-to-face tutoring, and on some courses summer schools,
home kits, radio, or computer-aided learning are also available.
Courses are designed by teams made up of academics employed
full-time by the Open University (sometimes assisted by external
subject consultants), educational technologists, editors, course
managers, staff tutors responsible for regional tutorial arrangements, and broadcast producers.

The broadcast producers are employed by the BBC, which has a
unique partnership arrangement with the Open University. The
BBC has established a separate department, BBC/OUP, devoted
entirely to the production of television, radio and audio programmes for the Open University. Each year this department
produces up to 250 television programmes and over 300 radio or
audio programmes. It operates from a £5½ million purpose-built
studio complex on the University campus. In 1983 the BBC/OUP
budget was £10 million. The BBC is paid the full costs of its Open
University operation by the DES. The 1,500 television programmes
and 800 radio programmes are broadcast on national BBC networks, requiring thirty-five hours a week transmission time for
television and fifteen hours a week for radio. The BBC/Open
University partnership is unique in Britain in several ways. It is the
only educational broadcasting service paid for by the government;
the Open University is the only non-broadcasting institution with
guaranteed access to national broadcasting; the programmes are the
result of team decisions involving both producers and academics.

These are the 'formal' structures for educational broadcasting in
Britain. However, general television can also have an 'educative'
effect. People can learn from the news, documentaries, drama,
even comedy programmes. The formal structures are important
because of copyright arrangements – educational programmes (except for the Open University's) can be recorded and kept for one
year for educational purposes without royalty payments. However,
particularly with the advent of Channel 4, which does not publicly
identify its educational programmes, it is becoming more and more

difficult to maintain a distinction between 'educational' and 'educative' programmes, as the book will make clear. It has been generally accepted in Britain that the television service *as a whole* has the obligation to 'educate, inform and entertain'.

This then is the framework of educational broadcasting in Britain. About half the £100 million comes from the broadcasting organisations, primarily for production; the other half comes primarily from local or central government, for purchasing print support materials and for supplying television sets and video equipment for schools and colleges.

ASSESSING THE EFFECTIVENESS OF BROADCASTING IN EDUCATION

There are many ways and many contexts in which broadcasting has been used in education. This book tries to answer the following question: *For what specific purposes, and under what conditions, is broadcasting effective in education?*

To answer this question, I will try to provide a comprehensive overview of the many educational purposes for which broadcasting has been used. A summary of this overview can be found in Table 1 (p. 9). Readers may find this useful as a 'map' when working through this book. Alternatively, Table 1 might be used in conjunction with the index for accessing information about particular uses of broadcasting of special interest to the reader. As well as describing the roles of broadcasting in education, I have evaluated both the appropriateness of the roles assigned to broadcasting and their effects. In so doing, I have also tried to identify the conditions necessary for the successful application of each use of broadcasting. Consequently, Chapters 2 and 3 (covering formal education – the 'in-school' sector), 4 and 5 (covering basic adult education) and 6 and 7 (covering continuing and distance higher education) have been written as pairs. The first chapter in each pair *describes* the way broadcasting has been used in that sector; the second *evaluates* such uses.

To appreciate fully the reasons *why* educational broadcasting has been used in the way that it has, it is necessary to understand the nature of broadcasting organisations. Educational broadcasting is only one, relatively small, part of a much larger organisational output. Broadcasting is a complex technology which has its own impetus and development, its own organisational structures and technical requirements. Educational broadcasters are part of that complex structure, and are therefore very much influenced by the

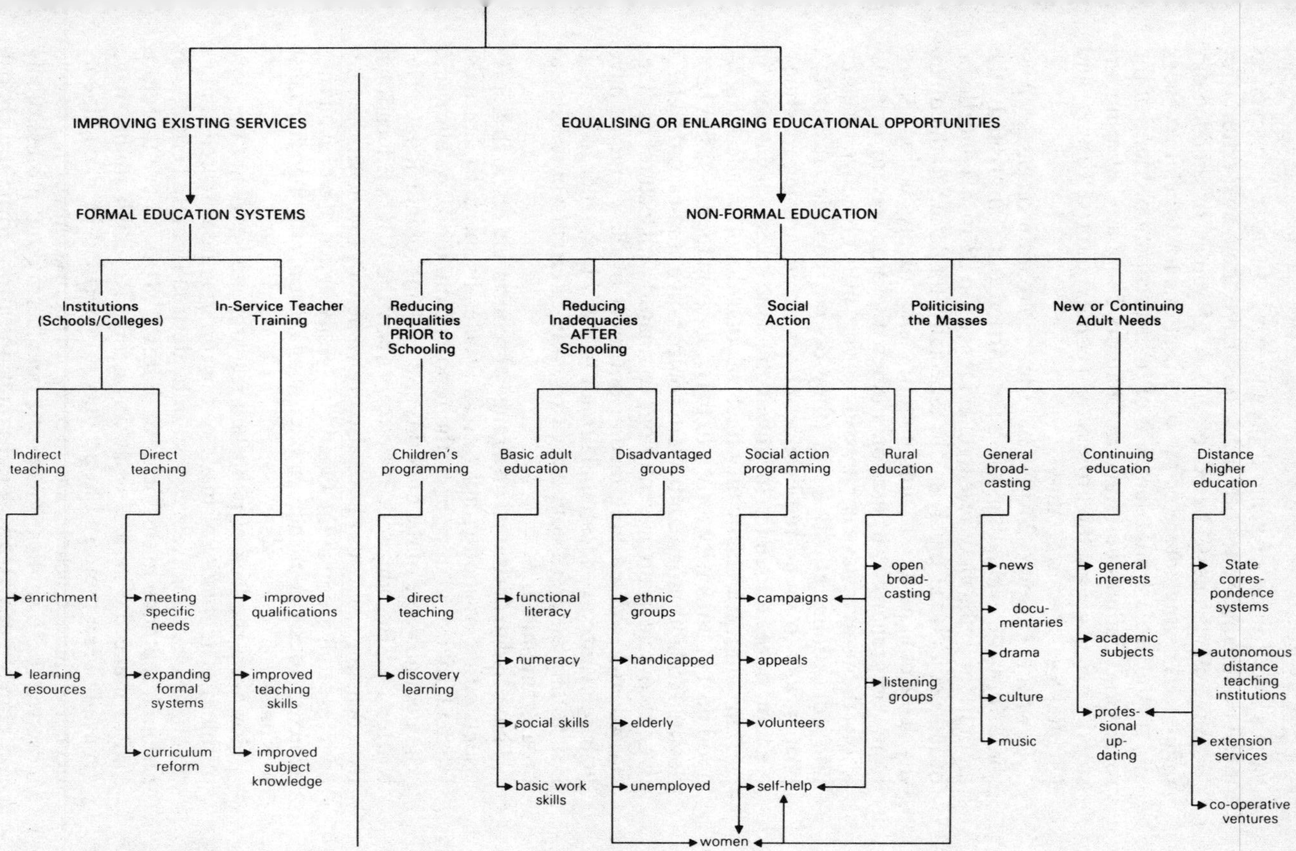
IMPROVING EXISTING SERVICES
EQUALISING OR ENLARGING EDUCATIONAL OPPORTUNITIES
FORMAL EDUCATION SYSTEMS
NON-FORMAL EDUCATION
Institutions (Schools/Colleges)
In-Service Teacher Training
Reducing Inequalities PRIOR to Schooling
Reducing Inadequacies AFTER Schooling
Social Action
Politicising the Masses
New or Continuing Adult Needs
Indirect teaching
Direct teaching
Children's programming
Basic adult education
Disadvantaged groups
Social action programming
Rural education
General broad-casting
Continuing education
Distance higher education
enrichment
learning resources
meeting specific needs
expanding formal systems
curriculum reform
improved qualifications
improved teaching skills
improved subject knowledge
direct teaching
discovery learning
functional literacy
numeracy
social skills
basic work skills
ethnic groups
handicapped
elderly
unemployed
campaigns
appeals
volunteers
self-help
open broad-casting
listening groups
women
news
docu-mentaries
drama
culture
music
general interests
academic subjects
profes-sional up-dating
State corres-pondence systems
autonomous distance teaching institutions
extension services
co-operative ventures

Table 1: Strategic roles for television and radio

values and criteria of general broadcasting. Judging effectiveness means applying values. Broadcasters have their own criteria for judging effectiveness, based on a set of values or an ideology influenced by the nature of the organisations for which they work and by the professional demands of their occupation. Many of the results and findings described in Chapters 2 to 7 are better understood when placed in the professional context of broadcasting, and Chapter 8 sets out to do this.

In writing Chapters 2 to 7, I have tended to draw on cases where some form of evaluation has been carried out. Surprisingly the amount of published research evidence on British educational broadcasting is extremely small, especially in relation to the quantity of output and the amount of money spent on production. Apart from comprehensive utilisation studies, the broadcasting organisations themselves have commissioned very little objective research into educational effectiveness (they do not consider research a proper way to spend the licence money or advertising revenue). Neither have academics in universities shown much interest in carrying out research into the effects of educational broadcasting. A good deal of university research, particularly in the USA, has been devoted to laboratory-controlled, comparative studies of the effectiveness of television presentations compared with lectures or other classroom-based teaching media, but most of these studies have little relevance to educational broadcasting, which tends to be used in a totally different context with totally different approaches to programme-making.

I have had to draw then on a range of reports and research studies issued either as monographs or as articles in specialist journals. Particularly useful have been the reports from the IBA fellowship scheme, and some of the bulletins and accounts of individual series written by BBC education producers or by the BBC's Educational Broadcasting Council. I have also drawn heavily on the work of my own research group at the Open University, much of which has not been previously published, or been available only through specialist journals.

However, the lack of published research studies is not the only problem. The *quality* of many of the reports and research studies that have been done leaves a lot to be desired (for a full critique of research methods in this field see Bates, 1981a). I have therefore had to make the best of what was going. Research studies have generally been preferred to producers' assertions or to comments from individual teachers; and in research reports I have tried to give more weight to studies which have been carried out professionally and competently. However, I could not afford to be too choosy regarding research criteria, and, in all honesty, some of the most valuable sources have been the thoughtful and sometimes painfully frank accounts of their own series written by producers themselves.

Lastly, in Chapter 9, I examine the likely impact of new technology on educational broadcasting, followed in Chapter 10 by a summary of the main points to emerge from this book. The last chapter also looks to the future, suggesting improvements needed to make the use of broadcasting in education more effective and relevant for the last part of this century.

It will quickly become evident that I have drawn heavily on studies carried out overseas. There are obvious dangers in this, but I have done it for two reasons. Firstly, British patterns of broadcasting have heavily influenced many other countries. In addition, for many developing countries in particular, an educational television system is seen as an essential indicator of development. But television demands considerable resources from developing countries, both financially and in terms of scarce, skilled manpower. Particularly in educational broadcasting, the transfer of methods, ideas and approaches from Britain, the USA, and France to developing countries has often been of doubtful benefit. Some of the expectations of earlier projects were, with hindsight and experience, clearly unrealistic. For many developing countries, educational broadcasting has not turned out to be the panacea that some in the developed countries were suggesting in the late 1960s. Because of the difference in ambitions and goals, it is essential to examine similarities and differences in results from different countries, so that some caution can be exercised in the transfer of experience. On the other hand, there have been some notable successes in other countries, and indeed there is much more published research on educational broadcasting in *developing* countries than in Britain. Consequently there is much to be learned from the experiences of such countries, and it is a critical review of the use of educational broadcasting in *developed* countries that is long overdue.

Finally, there is a major omission from this book. I shall not be discussing the impact of general broadcasting on the lives of children or adults, nor how children and adults should be educated to understand better the processes of broadcast television and radio. This is not because I believe these issues to be insignificant. Quite the reverse. Any school today which fails to develop 'media literacy' is as derelict in its duty to children and society as if it omitted to teach them to read and write. Media literacy is too big a subject to be dealt with properly as a small segment of this book, which concentrates on programmes which are deliberately meant to educate. Those interested in teaching media literacy in schools are referred to Masterman (1980) above all, although Postman (1983), Howe (1983), Hunt (1981) and Fiske and Hartley (1978) are also worth reading.

Broadcasting has been used for a wide variety of educational purposes. It has been used to reduce illiteracy, poverty and disease, for national recovery, to create a sense of national identity, and to educate those who otherwise would have received no education at all. It is important then to evaluate its success. This is what this book tries to do.

2

Formal education: strategic roles for broadcasting

One should have no illusions about why educational television or radio systems have sometimes been set up. Such decisions are rarely taken for any one single reason, but, in a number of cases, educational justifications have been clearly subordinate to other pressures. Afghanistan is a case in point, if rather an exotic one.

Shortly before the first of the left-wing revolutions in 1978, the Afghan government, led by President Daoud, had decided to introduce television for the first time. A studio facility was to be built in the capital, Kabul, with a transmitter to cover Kabul and the surrounding areas initially, and an extension planned later to other parts of the country. The new service was to be opened, by the President himself, in March 1978. The decision to introduce television to Afghanistan was made after a visit from a Japanese technical team and an offer from the Japanese government to provide a low-interest loan for the purchase and installation of the basic production and transmission system in Kabul. The main justification for the introduction of television to Afghanistan, which has one of the lowest per-capita income figures for developing countries, was given in the first paragraph of the Japanese International Co-operation Agency's report, proposing in 1975 a television system to the government of Afghanistan: 'Television broadcasting is the most effective media to elevate the level of education to people'.

The transparency of the educational justification became apparent with subsequent events. The facilities covered by the Japanese loan were in fact very limited: the construction of a studio building, the equipment needed for production within that building, the construction of a transmitter covering Kabul and the surrounding area, and a short training programme for Afghan production staff in Japan. It was quite clear to Western experts that a substantial amount of additional equipment would be needed to expand production and transmission beyond the very limited levels covered by the loan agreement. This equipment though would have to be bought at full commercial rates.

The government-controlled national broadcasting organisation, Radio Kabul, was responsible for the planning and introduction of the television service, assisted by Japanese technical consultants. However, according to Radio Kabul's management, the facilities provided under the Japanese loan agreement were insufficient to allow for the production of any schools programmes or any programmes made specifically for government development agencies. The facilities would be fully occupied providing news and general programming (including quiz shows). Therefore the Ministry of Education (which already had a small educational radio department) was instructed to provide a *separate* educational television service. In order to do this, the Ministry of Education had to find additional studio and technical facilities for the production of educational programmes, and train its own production staff, since all the training places under the Japanese loan agreement had been allocated to Radio Kabul producers for the 'main' service. The Ministry of Education also had to find resources for television receivers in schools, since the Japanese loan agreement covered the provision of only 100 receivers, most of which were required by Radio Kabul for technical reasons.

The Japanese refused to extend the loan agreement to include the provision of an educational television production facility, or receivers for school use. The Ministry of Education therefore tried to raise money from international aid agencies, such as the World Bank, the United Nations Development Programme, or from foreign government agencies, such as USAID, since there was no money earmarked by the Ministry of Finance for the development of an educational television service.

There was little enthusiasm though from the various international and foreign aid agencies for such a project because of the high costs and doubts about the likely effectiveness of such a service. Educational television would cover only a limited area around Kabul, which already had better educational provision than the rest of the country. The great majority of the target groups to which the aid agencies were giving priority – the very poor, farmers, children out of school – lived outside the proposed television transmission area.

Nevertheless, the government was still aiming to provide some form of educational television service for the opening day, in March 1978, even if it meant borrowing films from other countries. As it happened, these and all the other plans of President Daoud and his government came to an abrupt end in the bloody revolution of 1978. The final irony was that when the Russians arrived six months later, they promptly put to use the brand new, fully operational studio complex and transmitter to explain to the people why they were there. Subsequently, they have scrapped the Japanese system and installed their own.

The example illustrates that while education and development may be the manifest reasons for establishing a television service, in even the poorest countries in the world commercial and political reasons are more likely to be paramount. Daoud was well aware of his unstable political position and clearly hoped that television would enable him to communicate directly with the people. For the Japanese, the loan agreement was clearly a worthwhile commercial proposition, since, for comparatively little cost, hitherto virgin territory would be opened up for their equipment manufacturers.

Education or development purposes in fact are rarely the main reason for introducing a television service, even in developing countries. Katz and Wedell (1978), after a detailed study of eleven developing countries, conclude:

There is no reason to assume that the introduction of television is automatically equated with development by the leaders of new and developing nations. Typically, it is introduced for a variety of other purposes: as an opiate of the people, as a symbol of nationhood, as a projector of the image of the leadership, as part of a national celebration, to transmit a sporting event, as a result of an attractive proposition by a foreign broadcasting company or set manufacturer, or to meet the cosmopolitan expectations of big-city dwellers demanding to be entertained in the cosmopolitan manner (Katz and Wedell, 1978).

However, whatever the original reasons for setting up a television or radio service, it is not difficult to find valid justifications for using it for educational or development purposes, once it is there. There are three broad political objectives in the use of broadcasting in education (see Table 1, p. 9). The first justifies the use of television and radio by arguing that it can *improve the quality of existing educational provision*. The focus in this approach is on the use of television and radio for improvement *within* the formal education system, the target groups being those already in full-time education at school or college. This will be the focus of this chapter and the next.

The second political perspective justifies the use of television and radio by arguing that it can *equalise or spread more widely educa-*

tional opportunities – what McAnany and Mayo (1979) have called 'the democratization of educational opportunity'. The focus here is on providing educational opportunities beyond the formal school and college system, through part-time, off-campus education for those outside the normal age range or geographical reach of the basic school and college system. This will be the focus of Chapters 4 to 7.

The third is to some extent outside the scope of this book, except that it draws attention to some of the limitations of strictly *educational* television and radio. This justifies the use of television and radio by arguing that they can be used as a revolutionary force, to *bring about radical changes in the social structure* and *in the mobilisation of the poor and oppressed*. The focus here is on wider access to the means of broadcast production and distribution, allowing more extensive community use of media, or the use of media as an organising force for local action. The aim here is to by-pass powerful elites, appealing directly to 'the people'. This will be discussed to some extent in Chapters 4 and 5.

SCHOOLS BROADCASTING

Ask a hundred people in almost any country what they think is meant by educational broadcasting and ninety of them are likely to reply, 'Well, it means those programmes made for schools.' This is certainly the popular view of educational radio and television; and it has been the starting area of most educational (broadcasting) services (Bates and Robinson, 1977).

There has been continuous school broadcasting in several Western European countries for over fifty years. The BBC broadcast the first schools radio programme in 1926, and radio broadcasts to schools began in Sweden shortly afterwards. Ever since, the annual output of schools broadcasts in Western European countries has been substantial. Table 2 shows that altogether there were seventy-six different programme series on radio, and ninety-eight series on television nationally broadcast to schools in Britain during the school year 1981–82 (a series is usually about ten linked programmes of thirty minutes each).

The broadcasting organisations in Britain provide between them a comprehensive range of programmes for schools, offering in any one year programmes of one sort or another for all the age ranges from five to eighteen, and covering most subject areas found in the curriculum of most British schools.

TABLE 2

NUMBER OF SCHOOL BROADCAST SERIES NATIONALLY
NETWORKED IN BRITAIN (SCHOOL YEAR 1981–82)

		No. of different series
RADIO:	BBC network[1]	76
TELEVISION:	BBC	59
	ITV	39
	Total[2]	98

Notes: 1 Figures exclude local broadcasts. Commercial radio stations and BBC local radio stations occasionally offer programmes aimed at school children. For instance, Capital Radio broadcasts drama productions of plays in the General Certificate of Education examination syllabuses. However, local radio programmes are not generally networked, and are rarely intended for direct use in schools.
2 Figures exclude programmes broadcast in one region only.
Source: Educational Broadcasting Council, 1982.

In Britain, the Inner London Education Authority produces its own television programmes for use in schools distributed on videocassettes. In North America, most educational programmes for schools are broadcast, or distributed by cable, usually on a state basis. Programmes are produced by local state educational broadcasting organisations, such as Kentucky Educational Television and the Nebraska Educational Communications Network, by interstate production consortia, such as the Agency for Instructional Television, or by independent local television stations. Consequently in America there is a much greater diversity of educational production than in Britain.

In most developed countries, it has rarely been the intention within the formal education system to use broadcasting to *replace* the teacher, or even to reduce staff–pupil ratios; rather, television and radio are seen as an extra resource on which the schools and colleges can draw if they wish. For this reason, I see school broadcasting as being intended primarily for improving the quality of the existing educational service; certainly, in Britain, it is never seen (rightly or wrongly) by either teachers or broadcasters as a replacement or substitute for basic educational services.

This attitude might be considered to be due to the way school broadcasts are financed in Britain. The production and transmission of programmes is provided without direct cost to the schools (although they have to buy and maintain the reception equipment

and purchase the teacher manuals and supporting print materials
for pupils). However, even in the USA, where school boards pay
directly for production if they opt to join one of the Agency for
Instructional Television's production consortia, the programmes
are still intended as a support to existing basic education services, an
additional resource for improving the *quality* of instruction.

When discussing ways in which television and radio have been
used to improve the quality of instruction, it will be helpful to
distinguish between two rather different ways of generating programme material. One is to make programmes which are directly
aimed at the pupils (even though the programmes may be mediated
by teachers); the second is to aim programmes at the teachers
themselves.

PROGRAMMES AIMED DIRECTLY AT LEARNERS

Programmes aimed directly at pupils and students within the formal
educational system can be considered along a continuum from
'enrichment', through 'learning resource', 'meeting special needs',
to 'direct teaching and curriculum reform'.

Enrichment

This is perhaps the most common term used to describe the use of
schools broadcasting. However, 'enrichment' is rarely clearly defined. I understand enrichment to mean an addition to or a reinforcement of something that the teacher is already trying to do,
but which, in itself, is not essential or crucial to the teaching task.
The aim is to use television or radio to reinforce the content, skills or
attitudes that teachers are already committed to imparting to their
pupils or students. This might be done by increasing motivation to
learn, by making the topic more interesting or relevant, by providing a wider or more realistic context, and so on. The implication
behind such a use is that a topic or subject could still be taught or
learned without the programme being seen or heard, but that such a
programme might increase the chance of learning being more
effective, through its motivational role.

Learning objectives in such programmes tend to be deliberately
vague or diffuse because of the widely varying classroom contexts in
which programmes are likely to be used. In countries like Britain,
where there is no national curriculum, broadcasters face special
difficulties. Below the age at which children begin to follow sylla-

buses which are publicly examined, each school is more or less free to determine its own curriculum. In many primary schools, what is taught, and even more so how it is taught, is very much the choice of individual teachers. Even for the fourteen- to eighteen-year-old age group preparing for public examinations there is no single national syllabus in any subject, since there are several different examination boards and schools are free to choose which they shall follow. Consequently, it is very difficult for educational broadcasters to be sure that their programmes will fit in with the teaching plans of individual classes. It is for this reason that, generally, broadcast producers deliberately avoid teaching 'directly' or 'didactically'. It is certainly true that in the past many programmes went out on a wing and a prayer – with the hope that somehow they would fit in with, or provide some extra dimension to, the children's learning. Such a use of broadcasting leaves a great deal to chance.

Today, though, British broadcasting organisations would consider their programme policies to be more sophisticated, and it probably does them a disservice to describe the programmes as merely enrichment. Through their advisory councils, which include practising teachers, and through their education officers, who have regular contacts with the schools, British broadcasting organisations are able to get a pretty good idea of the needs of schools and the shift of opinions and trends. As a consequence, most British schools broadcasts are seen by the broadcasters themselves as being much more specific in their educational purpose than just providing enrichment material – although no doubt many programmes are still used in that way by teachers in the schools.

Even in developing countries, which generally have centralised, nationally determined curricula, television or radio are still most frequently used as a support to the standard curriculum. The programmes supplement and reinforce the existing curriculum, which is normally determined without any consideration of how television or radio might be integrated with the curriculum. Programme designers therefore have to take the curriculum as given, and design their programmes around that curriculum, although they are often guided or advised by the Ministry's curriculum designers. Thus enrichment is still the most common use for schools radio and television in developing countries also, although the World Bank and United States Agency for International Development (USAID) are increasing pressure on developing countries to use radio in particular for direct teaching. Among countries where radio is used to enrich the national curriculum are Thailand and the Philippines, and television is used in a similar way in Singapore, Mauritius, India and Hong Kong.

Programme styles for enrichment programmes in developed countries are very often similar to the styles of general broadcasts in the documentary and current affairs field. Programmes tend to be loosely structured, sometimes with a magazine format (i.e. a number of separate, short items, but generally linked together) and tend to make use of many of the characteristics of general broadcasting that motivate and hold attention.

Learning resources

One of the main developments in recent years has been to consider television and radio programmes as a learning resource, in that they offer teachers, pupils and students teaching material which would not be easily accessible to them in other ways. A former BBC producer, Richard Hooper, described such a use of television and radio as providing learners with 'primary resource material'. He has argued that until recently teachers have been a 'substitute' source of knowledge and information, storing, transforming and communicating knowledge to those who have not so far had the opportunity to experience such knowledge for themselves. Television and radio provide learners with access to knowledge and information in a more direct and concrete form. Examples of primary resource material are newsreel and historical film, film from foreign countries or different parts of one's own country, interviews with national leaders or other people in positions of authority, interviews with participants in significant events, and so on. Television and radio can also provide learning resources through the construction of physical models, professionally designed graphics and animation, professional performance of dance, drama and music, and foreign languages spoken in context by native speakers. None of this material would otherwise be available in the normal school or college context.

It can be seen that the actual material in programmes used as learning resources is very similar to material found in programmes used for enrichment purposes. The crucial difference is in the way that teachers and curriculum designers use such material, although there are implications also for the way programmes are designed and structured.

The important difference is that with using television or radio as a learning resource, material from the programmes is closely integrated by the teacher or curriculum designer with other teaching material. Only those parts of the television or radio programmes that are relevant to the teaching task, and which provide different experiences from other material available, need be used. Ideally, this would mean that when a syllabus is being planned, the likely availability of suitable television or radio material is taken into account before the teaching programme for the term or year is finalised. Such advanced planning however requires access to television and radio material *before* teaching begins. With the advent of relatively low-cost video and audio cassette recording and replay equipment, this is now much more feasible. It is also feasible in developing countries where there is centralised curriculum planning. Television and radio *could* be closely integrated with the curriculum so that television, radio, textbooks, direct teaching by the teacher, and group and socialising activities are all integrated. However, this could only be done when the curriculum is revised or reformed and, to date, centralised curricula in developing countries have not been designed with integrated television or radio used as a learning resource, as distinct from use for direct teaching.

Nor, of course, is it common for such advanced planning and integration of television and radio to take place in schools in developed countries (although it can be found in distance education). However, there are teachers now who do plan the use of television or radio as a learning resource a few days or a week ahead, either using a cassette recording which is already available, or relying on a forthcoming broadcast whose likely contents are well known, from use in previous years. The distinction here between using television or radio as a learning resource or as enrichment is admittedly rather fine. I believe though that there is an important difference between a teacher planning a specific unit of teaching, within which material from a television programme is deliberately chosen because it complements other resource material that the teacher has chosen, and using a television programme which it is *hoped* will relate to other teaching material, but which neither the teacher, nor probably the children, are sure will be relevant.

There are also implications for the design of programmes, when the purpose from the outset is for the material to be used as primary resource material. A programme made for enrichment tends to have a standard length (in Britain twenty or twenty-five minutes) and a unity which allows the programme to stand alone as a meaningful, comprehensive entity. It tends to have an easily recognisable beginning, middle and end. From a broadcasting organisation's point of view, there is much to be said for the enrichment format, in that it can have a dual function within schools for use either as enrichment, or, if used selectively, as resource material, and at the same time be comprehensible to the substantial number of adults who watch or listen to schools broadcasts out of interest.

Programmes made for use as learning resources, particularly if they are made at the outset for cassette distribution and use, should, however, be structured differently. Since teachers will be selecting segments of material, the segments may vary in length and may not even be linked (for instance, the programme may fade to black before the next segment begins). If made for distribution on cassette, the length of the cassette will be determined by the number and length of the individual segments. Activities may be built in at the end of each segment or edited in such a way that they can be omitted if the teacher chooses. There may be cues in the middle of segments where teachers can stop the programme to ask questions or to allow children to carry out some work before returning to the tape. Commentary is likely to be even less directive or instructional than on enrichment programmes; in some cases there will be no commentary (some cassette machines now have a facility which allows the teacher to add his or her own commentary or comments to a pre-recorded cassette).

The aim behind such material is for it to be integrated by teachers into a wider learning experience, where the learning or teaching of facts or concepts is dealt with not just in the programme material, nor primarily by the teacher 'telling' the students or pupils, but as a result of the full experience provided by a variety of learning materials and experiences.

However, it must be emphasized that the use of television or radio material in such a deliberately planned, integrated manner is still extremely rare in schools and colleges.

Meeting special needs

Even in the best education service, temporary deficiencies can occur in a particular school due to the loss through sickness, transfer or retirement of specialist staff. Even in developed countries like Britain and the USA there can be chronic or permanent shortages of specialist staff, particularly for science or mathematics teaching. Schools television and radio programmes, by using the skills of experienced and able specialist teachers, can make those skills available to all the schools in the country. Such programmes can be particularly useful to otherwise trained staff who may nevertheless be covering areas in which they feel they lack sufficient academic qualifications. Such teachers will be well able to provide suitable follow-up work, to answer questions and to prepare themselves adequately by means of the teachers' handbooks which accompany the series, but the programmes themselves provide valuable guidance and confidence in following a certain approach. Similarly, as well as specialist staff, schools may lack specialist equipment, such as musical instruments. Television and radio can be a useful substitute in such circumstances.

Schools television and radio programmes thus provide extra flexibility in schools, allowing sometimes scarce learning resources to be made available to all schools. Such a role is particularly useful in areas with low population densities, where it would be uneconomical to provide a school with all the facilities found in large urban schools (for instance, in the more remote parts of Australia), in areas such as run-down inner city locations in developed countries, or remote rural areas in developing countries, where it can be particularly difficult to recruit scarce specialist staff.

When television and radio programmes are used to meet such deficiencies, a different style of programming may be required from that most appropriate for use as enrichment or learning resources. Since the teachers whom the programmes are aiming to help are not well qualified in the subject area, the programmes will be more useful if they are more didactic and directive, if teachers' notes that provide reinforcement and further explanation of the subject material are also available, and if clear follow-up activities are firmly suggested.

Direct teaching and curriculum reform

Perhaps the most spectacular use of the media of instruction in developing countries has been to try to accomplish a swift reform of a national or territorial system of education. Time is of the essence in this sort of project; changes that would ordinarily take fifty to one hundred years, at the usual measured pace of education, are projected to be achieved in ten or twenty years (Schramm, 1977).

Television and radio have been used in several developing countries for direct teaching. Both the core content and the style or method of instruction are embodied in the programmes themselves. When television or radio are used in this way within the formal school system there is still a need for adult supervision – although in some projects, unqualified 'monitors' have been used instead of trained teachers – but the role of the teacher or monitor is to supplement and support the television or radio teaching. The adult then becomes a classroom supervisor, organiser and manager but not someone who determines either the content or the method by which the content will be taught. Thus the programmes *are* the curriculum.

Direct teaching through television and radio has been used in the formal school systems of developing countries in three related but slightly different ways:

(1) to *expand* the range of the school system, enabling pupils who would otherwise have had no formal schooling beyond a certain age to continue with their schooling. In such circumstances, the government aims to provide education for all children in the relevant age groups in principle, but in practice it finds it is not possible to provide the necessary facilities for all such pupils. In this situation, lessons based on the standard national curriculum are distributed by television or radio to areas where there is no adequate conventional school provision. Pupils normally follow the programmes in classes, using basic accommodation. There is usually a supervisor or monitor in charge of the group. Examples of such projects are the Radioprimaria and Telesecundaria projects in Mexico, and ETV Maranhão in Brazil. In some cases, as with the Radio Schools of Australia, pupils study at home with one of their parents as the supervisor. In this case, there is the possibility of *two-way* communication, as the pupils can talk back on their own radio sets to the distant teacher;

(2) to *improve the quality of instruction*, where there are schools, but due to the low level of education of the teachers or their lack of training, and the lack of other suitable resources, such as books, the quality of instruction is considered to be poor. Once again, programmes based on an already existing national curriculum are transmitted, but in this case to otherwise conventional schools. An example of this approach is the Radio Mathematics project in Nicaragua. The methods used in this project are being applied also to mathematics teaching in the Philippines and Thailand;

(3) to *reform* the national school curriculum, in such a way that both the subject matter (content) and the method of teaching are radically changed, with television playing the central, direct teaching role. Television is in this situation both the medium and the catalyst for reform. To date, and perhaps surprisingly, radio has not yet been used in this way, and when television and curriculum reform have been introduced together, it has always been in the form of direct teaching. Television has been used for curriculum reform in American Samoa, El Salvador, the Ivory Coast and Niger.

Curriculum reform of course is possible without the introduction of television; television could also be systematically introduced as part of curriculum reform without it necessarily playing a direct teaching role. For instance, only a part of the curriculum need be built around television, or television could be one of several resources available to teachers within a new curriculum. However, there are strong reasons why the introduction of curriculum reform combined with television has resulted in the use of television for direct teaching. A successful reform of a national curriculum through conventional methods requires teachers who are already in service, and used to the 'old' curriculum, to be retrained in the new subject material and new methods of teaching. Conventional retraining methods would require special courses (probably residential), involve travel costs and personal inconvenience to the teachers and may require the withdrawal of teachers from their normal teaching activities. In many developing countries it is the *initial* training of teachers which receives priority. In such countries planners may fear that the retraining of teachers required by a national curriculum reform through conventional methods would take too long, would be impractical on a large scale and would be too expensive. What better then than to use television to by-pass the retraining problem completely by using television to carry the main burden of teaching the new curriculum? Also, combining curriculum reform with the opening of a new television service provides a clear target and stimulus for curriculum reform. The day on which the television service opens provides a deadline for the introduction of a new curriculum, a deadline which it would be embarrassing politically to miss.

It is necessary to have worked on such projects, or at least to have read detailed accounts of them, to comprehend fully their ambition and the difficulties they have had to overcome. The Ivory Coast system required not only the construction of a TV production centre, the training of the staff to run it and the production of 500 hours programming in one year alone, but also the installation and maintenance of battery-operated television sets in over 5,000 classes, many in isolated, humid villages in the bush. As well as a reform of the curriculum, the Ivory Coast project also involved training teachers in the use of television-based education and required the distribution of over 200 tons of support print materials in one year (Kaye, 1976). To provide full coverage of the formal school system in American Samoa, in one year the ETV unit was producing 6,000 programmes (Schramm, 1977). In Nicaragua, the programme designers found it necessary to teach mathematics directly by radio to children in rural and poor urban primary schools, *without* printed support materials for the pupils, as these would have substantially increased project costs. They also managed to continue the project successfully through the major part of a bloody revolution. ETV Maranhão provides secondary education by way of television classes which run semi-autonomously through a system of group activities to pupils from very poor homes in a remote part of the Amazon basin in Brazil. This project is particularly unusual in that it is virtually independent of foreign financial or technical assistance.

In short, the use of television and radio for direct teaching and curriculum reform in developing countries has required – and obtained – a great deal of commitment, hard work, idealism and ingenuity. It has affected large numbers of pupils, teachers and educational planners, and required assistance from foreign consultants, a good deal of foreign financial aid and substantial financial resources from developing countries themselves.

To understand why television and radio have been used in these ways in developing countries – but hardly ever in developed countries – it is necessary to understand the educational needs which led politicians and planners to adopt such radical measures. In Niger, before the introduction of the educational television project, only 7 per cent of school-age children actually attended school. In the Ivory Coast, 25 per cent of children in the target age range (seven years old) attended school in the first grade, but by the fourth grade this figure had dropped to 14 per cent. This was in 1967–68, just before the inception of the television-based reform. At that time, the government's goal was to provide universal primary education (i.e. education for *all* children in the relevant age groups) through the first six grades by 1985. In El Salvador, in 1968, less than 25 per cent of the relevant age ranges were enrolled in Grades 7 to 9 (age range thirteen to fifteen). El Salvador's government, however, considered that it was essential to increase substantially enrolments at this level if its plans for economic growth were to succeed. At the same time, the national curriculum was recognised by the government to be based on values and concepts imported from Europe in the nineteenth century and bore little practical relationship to the needs of the country or individuals. In American Samoa, teachers prior to the introduction of the television system were not generally educated beyond 9th grade (normally completed at the age of around fifteen or sixteen, when their formal school education ceased) and they had little command of English, although this was supposed to be the language of instruction in the schools.

There are certain common characteristics of those countries where direct teaching by television and radio have been used. They are typified by low enrolments in the formal school system; high drop-out by those who do enrol; poorly qualified teachers; lack of adequate buildings, books and other basic educational resources; a rapidly increasing population; an uneven distribution of educational resources, with education being more readily available in urban areas and being taken up more by children from more prosperous families; a need for more skilled and semi-skilled workers; and a low national gross income, resulting in severe shortage of money for educational purposes. Politicians and planners in these countries looked to television and radio as a means to break through these major obstacles to educational and economic progress.

There are also certain common characteristics about the projects themselves where direct teaching has been used:

(1) the decision to use television or radio for national curriculum reform was heavily influenced by the availability of funding or technical assistance from abroad;
(2) all the countries had a centralised, national curriculum;
(3) all the countries had a low educational base before the introduction of television or radio for direct teaching;
(4) most of the countries were relatively small and centralised, so schools could be easily reached by a central TV signal.

The use of television or radio for direct teaching in schools has been restricted to developing countries; there are hardly any examples of its use this way in developed countries.

PROGRAMMES AIMED AT TEACHERS

The use of television and radio for in-service teacher training is widespread. Once again, no two systems are exactly the same, and most projects are a mixture of aims. Nevertheless, there are important differences in emphasis as can be seen from the following examples.

Strengthening general academic qualifications

In many countries, there is a strong belief in the need for the teaching force as a whole to be well-qualified academically – or at least to levels clearly above those at which the teachers themselves are expected to teach. The definition of 'well qualified' varies from country to country depending on the level of education provided in the basic school system.

Very few countries though, even in the developed world, have an all-graduate, university-level teaching force. Television and radio therefore have been used in several countries to assist qualified teachers to go on to university graduate status, without having to give up teaching while studying further. The most ambitious attempt to use television and radio in this way has been in Poland (Puszczewicz, 1977). The Polish government in 1974 introduced a major reform of the educational system. This involved, among other things, a rapid expansion of secondary education and an attempt to modernise teaching methods and techniques. Part of this reform also called for the up-grading of all teachers to graduate status within a ten to twelve-year period. However, at the time, out of a total teaching force of 360,000, 160,000 (44 per cent) were not graduates.

In order to bring these 160,000 teachers up to graduate status, the Ministry of Education created 'The National Radio-Television University for Teachers' (NURT). NURT provides the equivalent of a four-year degree course. No entry qualifications are required, and by 1977, 75,000 teachers had already enrolled. Teachers receive three television and two radio programmes a week, broadcast at the end of the school day. The fortnightly teachers' journal, 'Oświata i Wychowanie', publishes the texts of the television and radio lectures. Recommendations for further reading, exercises and notes on the programmes are also provided. In addition, seminars and tutorials are arranged at local teachers' centres at weekends. The programmes are made and broadcast by the Polish national broadcasting system in consultation with NURT. The curriculum for students following NURT courses is so fully integrated with the curriculum for full-time student teachers at universities and teacher colleges that the NURT programmes are also a compulsory part of the *full-time* student teachers' curriculum.

The British Open University also provides non-graduate, working teachers with the opportunity to achieve graduate status through part-time study, although, unlike NURT, the Open University was not set up specifically for teachers. Nevertheless, it does have a School of Education offering a wide range of courses. Teachers, like other Open University students, can also choose to follow specialist academic courses, in Mathematics, Science, Technology, Social Sciences or Humanities, so that any individual teacher is able to make up a package of credits which best fits his or her own perceived needs and interests. However, television and radio play a somewhat lesser role at the Open University than at NURT. When the Open

University opened in 1971, 40 per cent of the first year intake were teachers, but by 1981 this figure had dropped to 20 per cent of new enrolments. Since a teacher with an Open University degree receives the same graduate salary allowance as any other graduate teacher in Britain, and since teachers are able to graduate more quickly through exemptions from certain credits on account of having already received some form of higher education, it is not surprising that of the first 38,187 Open University graduates, 19,759 (51 per cent) were teachers (Swift, 1980). Similarly, the Allama Iqbal Open University in Pakistan, which is modelled to some extent on the British Open University, and which uses radio and television for some of its courses, is also heavily involved in providing graduate courses for teachers.

For many developing countries, an all-graduate teaching profession is an unrealistic ambition, at least in the short term. Getting teachers up to even secondary school-leaving standard can be a major task. However, although the *level* of qualifications may be different, the general aim is the same. Thus the government of Kenya, for instance, wished to expand primary education to enable all children of the target age to receive full-time education. However, to achieve this quickly meant employing large numbers of teachers without any proper professional training or even the secondary school-leaving certificate. This meant that in 1968, 10,438 of the 37,923 teachers employed in Kenyan primary schools had no professional qualifications. Consequently, the Ministry of Education set up in 1968 a Correspondence Course Unit in the University of Nairobi to provide courses through a combination of correspondence teaching, radio broadcasts and occasional residential seminars. Algeria is another country which has used not only radio but also television in a similar way. Over six years, more than 20,000 teachers at the primary level have been trained, using, as well as television and radio, printed materials and group meetings (Skandar, 1977).

Developing professional skills

As well as contributing towards courses leading to recognised academic qualifications, television and radio have also been used to help teachers further develop their professional skills. Again, though, there is considerable variation in the ways in which this has been done.

As part of the reform of the education system in France in 1977, teacher education was given high priority. Television, radio and printed materials are used in a planned, integrated manner by the Ministry of Education to promote teachers' continuing education. The radio and television broadcasts aim to inform teachers about new teaching content, to encourage teachers to accept changes and innovations and to help teachers overcome difficulties which may arise in their work.

In 1976/77 there were three hours a week of television programmes and four hours a week of radio programmes aimed at teachers in France. However, because of the very high charges made to the Ministry of Education by the television and radio organisations for transmission times, there is a tendency to use television and radio as little as possible. Also, teachers are expected to follow the programmes and related materials on a voluntary basis, in their own time, so the French scheme for using television and radio for teacher education is not without its problems (Bon, 1977).

As well as courses which form an integral part of a degree course, the British Open University also offers single courses, or combinations of courses, which can be taken separately from the full degree programme. Some of these continuing education courses are aimed specifically at teachers. For instance, by combining four of these courses, students can obtain a government-recognised Diploma in Reading Education. These courses also have television and radio components. In 1981, there were 2,000 students enrolled for Open University continuing education courses aimed primarily at teachers.

Such courses in Britain, France, and Funkkolleg in West Germany (see pp. 146–7) tend to be broad in scope, dealing with more general educational issues, and give working teachers the opportunity to continue their professional development after their initial training.

Improving subject teaching

Television and radio have also been used to help teachers improve their teaching of specific subject areas. Sometimes the aim has been to introduce improved methods; sometimes the aim has been to improve teachers' knowledge of the subject material itself. Mathematics and science are two common subject areas for this kind of programming.

The 'Delta' project in Sweden attracted about 50,000 teachers, and used television, radio and printed materials to help teachers understand better the requirements of teaching modern mathematics. Teachers attended local centres for a period of five to six days during the school holidays. Each day was spent viewing and listening to broadcast television and radio programmes, and discussing the programmes and accompanying printed materials. The programmes were recorded for reference purposes and use at home by the teachers. Although the teachers attended on a voluntary basis, those who attended were awarded a certificate, and 80 per cent of the target audience in fact participated (Björkland, 1977). Both NURT in Poland and the Ivory Coast TV project have also produced modern mathematics programmes aimed specifically at teachers.

The most ambitious teacher education project, in technological terms, involved the use of a satellite in an attempt to reach 96,000 teachers in 2,400 villages in less accessible parts of India, as part of a programme to improve the teaching of natural science in primary schools. This project was one of a series in the Satellite Instructional Television Experiment organised by the Indian Space Research Organisation during 1975 and 1976. Each target village was provided with a television set, located in a communal centre in the village, and a dish aerial, which received the transmission direct from the satellite. Most of the programmes in the experiment were directed at the children themselves, but one series on the teaching of natural sciences was a part of a fifteen-day course for elementary teachers, supported by practical handbooks, a teachers' manual and other support material (posters, etc.). The course was designed by the National Centre for Educational Technology in Delhi. The material was produced in the several different languages used in the target areas. One of the advantages of the satellite was that it provided several *audio* channels simultaneously, allowing villagers to choose the appropriate sound channel to accompany the programme according to the language which they spoke. In this particular project, 44,000 teachers participated.

It is probably no coincidence that the same satellite (ATS-6) had been used a year earlier in the USA to provide two courses for in-service teachers as part of the Appalachian Educational Satellite Project. The satellite was able to cover a mountainous area stretching across thirteen states. The area generally had poor communications, isolated rural communities and extreme weather conditions. Many of the communities had one-room schools with one or two teachers. For these reasons, conventional in-service teacher courses at the teachers' colleges in the region were difficult to organise. Consequently, dish aerials were set up at fifteen sites. Teachers came to the sites where the dish aerials were located. The experiment not only enabled the downward transmission of programmes via the satellite link from the production centre at the University of

Kentucky at Lexington, but also included a radio link back from some of the sites via another satellite (ATS-3). Four courses were offered, two on careers education and two on teaching elementary reading. Each course consisted of sixteen television programmes and supporting printed material. Students met in groups of twenty to twenty-five per site. There was a limited form of two-way communication through ground and radio links, and a local seminar after each programme. Just over 1,000 teachers participated in this project (Larimore, 1977).

The last two satellite projects are rather exceptional, however. The main purpose of both projects was to test the technological feasibility of direct broadcasting by satellite in an educational context. Neither project was intended as a long-term solution to the problem of in-service teacher training. Nevertheless, plenty of other examples have been cited where television and radio have been used, on a regular basis, for in-service teacher training, and substantial numbers of teachers have participated in these projects.

In this chapter I have been examining the various ways in which broadcasting has been used in an attempt to improve the quality of existing educational provision through the formal education system. I have tried to show that this has been attempted in several ways:

(1) as enrichment to conventional teaching;
(2) as a unique learning resource;
(3) to meet special needs in the basic educational service;
(4) as a catalyst for curriculum reform;
(5) for expanding opportunities for in-service teacher training.

In all these cases, it could be argued that broadcasting appears to have obvious advantages over more conventional methods. However, it will become clear in the next chapter that not all these various roles have been equally successful. Moreover, the scene is rapidly changing. While schools broadcasting remains the most widespread use of television and radio in education, the advance of video recording and playback facilities are bringing with them the potential for far-reaching changes in the role of television and radio in the formal education system. These changes will affect teachers, broadcasters and children, an issue discussed more fully in Chapter 9. But in the meantime, the next chapter assesses the extent to which broadcasting in the formal school system has been successful so far.

3

Schools broadcasting: an end of term report

There has certainly been a lot of broadcasting directed at formal education. Most countries have a schools broadcasting service, in some cases running continuously for over fifty years. Broadcasts have covered the whole school and in-service teacher training curriculum; every school age range has been served; and broadcasting has been used for a diverse range of teaching approaches. The output of programming for schools is probably greater today than it has ever been. But how effective is all this activity? Do teachers use it? Do pupils learn from it? What do we know about when it works and when it doesn't? What kind of report could we give on schools broadcasting?

IS THERE ANYONE OUT THERE?

The minimum measure of effectiveness is whether or not the programmes are used in schools. No matter what the quality of the programmes, they need to be watched or heard to be effective. Since at least in Britain there is no centralised or 'core' curriculum that schools must follow, and since teachers have a good deal of freedom in how they choose to teach, it seems reasonable to assume that the programmes must have some value if teachers willingly make use of them. Cynics may argue that teachers use broadcasts because they are an 'easy option', avoiding the need for lesson preparation, or because they 'keep the kids quiet'; even when programmes are used in good faith by teachers there is no guarantee that they will be more effective than 'ordinary' lessons. If broadcasting though is extensively used, one must have a pretty jaundiced view of the whole teaching profession to assume that they are all using broadcasts as a soft option; and since most series run for at least two or three years, teachers usually have a pretty good idea of what the programmes are likely to offer. So the extent to which teachers deliberately choose to use broadcasts deserves to be treated as a useful, if crude, criterion of effectiveness.

Unfortunately, though, reliable utilisation figures for schools broadcasts are available from only a few countries. In 1977 the West German International Institute for Educational Broadcasting carried out a survey of schools radio in Europe (Internationales Zentralinstitut für das Jugend- und Bildungsfernsehen, 1979). Questionnaires were returned from 40 broadcasting organisations providing schools radio throughout twenty countries. Of the 40, only 16 had carried out or commissioned some form of audience survey of schools radio within the previous ten years. Only 7 reported regular surveys. As a result, getting an overview of the use of European schools radio is difficult. The same applies to European schools television, and the situation is even more difficult in North America where the organisation of schools television is much more fragmented than in Europe.

Fortunately though, schools broadcasting in Britain is systematically monitored each year by the Educational Broadcasting Council. Table 3 sets out equipment statistics and the number of schools using broadcast services in the United Kingdom during 1981–82. There are several points to note from Table 3. First of all, the information is reliable, being based on a carefully drawn sample of schools with a high response rate (82 per cent). Nearly all schools have radio and television receivers and audio recorders, and most schools make at least some use of schools television and radio. While there was a slight decline in the use of radio in secondary schools from 72 per cent using at least one series in 1978 to 66 per cent in 1982, this was more than balanced by an increasing use of television. The proportion of secondary schools using television rose from 85 per cent in 1978 to 92 per cent in 1982. More significantly, the average number of series taken in each secondary school rose from 8·6 to 13·3 over that period. The increase in secondary schools using ITV series was particularly marked – from 58 per cent in 1978 to 80 per cent in 1982. This, though, did not affect the use of BBC programmes in secondary schools, the proportion of schools using their series also increasing, from 78 per cent to 90 per cent over the same period. It is probably no coincidence that this increased utilisation was paralleled by a similar rate of increase of video-cassette recorders in secondary schools – from 70 per cent in 1978 to 96 per cent in 1982.

Television and radio broadcasts are used extensively in British schools. Schools using radio are likely to take between five or six series each year. Primary schools are likely to take an average of nine television series, and secondary schools an average of thirteen. The equipment statistics are particularly significant because while the programmes are offered without cost to the schools, the schools do have to pay for the equipment and support materials. There was

TABLE 3

SCHOOLS TELEVISION AND RADIO IN UK: EQUIPMENT AND PROGRAMME USE

School Year 1981–82 Radio	% of UK Schools		
	Primary and Middle	Secondary	All Schools
VHF receivers (total)	99%	97%	99%
Average number per school	3	4	
Audio recorders (total)	98%	99%	98%
Average number per school	4	10	
Schools using school radio	95%	66%	90%
Average number of series/ school	6·4	5·1	
Television			
Television receivers (total)	97%	99%	97%
Average number per school	1	3	
Colour television receivers	82%	94%	84%
Average number per school	1	2	
Video recorders	24%	96%	36%
Average number per school	1	2	
Schools using BBC television	95%	90%	94%
Average number of series/ school	5·2	9·4	
Schools using ITV television	85%	80%	84%
Average number of series/ school	3·4	3·7	
Total number of schools	27,993	5,743	33,736

Source: Educational Broadcasting Council, 1982.

a rapid increase in the purchase of colour television receivers, audio recording equipment and video-cassette recorders in schools over the five years 1978–82.

Radio

Table 4 gives some idea of the extent of radio penetration in British schools. From the seventy-six series offered on radio by the BBC, I have chosen six to show a representative range of subjects and age ranges.

TABLE 4

AUDIENCES FOR SELECTED SCHOOL RADIO SERIES (BBC): 1981–82

Name of series	Age range	Est. no. of schools	% of target schools	Est. no. of classes	Live only	Live + recorded	Recorded only
Let's Move	5–6	15,480	55%	34,780	29%	11%	61%
Stories and Rhymes	7–9	7,730	28%	15,210	34%	12%	54%
History: Not so Long Ago	9–12	3,990	13%	8,310	33%	9%	58%
Listening & Writing	11–14	1,510	14%	5,140	4%	1%	95%
Electronics	14–16	1,160	21%	3,230	0%	2%	98%
Voix de France	15–18	860	15%	2,320	0%	0%	100%

Source: Educational Broadcasting Council, 1982.

Music, dance and movement, and drama programmes for primary schools appear to be the most used radio programmes in schools, and although there are exceptions, generally the younger the age range, the greater the number of children listening to a single series. 'Let's Move', a music and movement series for the age range 5 to 6, reaches over a million school children each year, as does 'A Service for Schools' (used primarily for school assemblies). A study by the Schools Broadcasting Council (1979) found that of the primary schools that have religious assemblies, half rely entirely on the BBC radio series. Another two music series, 'Singing Together' and 'Time and Tune', approach the million mark in terms of audiences. These four series have audiences as high as most general radio series in Britain – for instance, the audience for each episode of 'The Archers' (a popular radio serial) averages around 1·5 million.

Radio is much less used at the secondary education level, the average proportion of schools using a radio series being only 10 per cent. Only two series reached more than 20 per cent of secondary schools in 1982, one an advanced studies geography series for sixth formers, the other a series on electronics and micro-electronics for fourteen- to sixteen-year-olds. Of the twenty-nine series made specifically for the secondary age range, only twelve reached more than 50,000 pupils. Almost all secondary schools use only recordings of radio programmes, and even in primary schools in 1982 the majority used recordings rather than live programmes for most series.

Television

The pattern for schools television is a little different from that of radio, as can be seen from Table 5. The series with by far and away the largest schools audience is the BBC series 'Watch!', aimed at the age range 6 to 8, with more than three-quarters of the primary schools in Britain taking the series. As well as 'Watch!', two other BBC series, 'Look and Read' (age range 7 to 9+) and 'Words and Pictures' (age range 5 to 7) have audiences estimated at over one million school children. Another eight series (three BBC and five ITV) have audiences of over half a million, all in the primary age ranges. Schools television series are used by about 25 per cent of secondary schools on average, although three BBC series in 1982 – 'Going to Work', 'Scene', and 'Twentieth-Century History' – each reached over 40 per cent of secondary schools. As with radio, the larger audiences for schools television tend to be found in the lower age ranges, due to a large extent to the increased specialisation of

TABLE 5

AUDIENCES FOR SELECTED SCHOOL TELEVISION SERIES (BBC AND ITV): 1981–82

Name of series	Age range	Est. no. of schools	% of target schools	Est. no. of classes	Live only	Live + recorded	Recorded only
My World (ITV)	4–6	10,410	37%	18,360	92%	1%	7%
Watch! (BBC)	6–8	21,550	77%	45,830	90%	4%	6%
Finding Out (ITV)	7–9	8,010	29%	13,640	82%	8%	10%
Merry-Go-Round (BBC)	8–9	12,070	43%	24,290	84%	5%	11%
How We Used to Live (ITV)	8–12	11,730	42%	22,630	78%	9%	13%
	Sec.	1,520	26%	6,060	11%	3%	86%
Near and Far (BBC)	9–11	8,930	32%	16,730	78%	8%	14%
Alles Klar (BBC)	Sec.	990	17%	2,750	–	1%	97%
The English Programme (ITV)	13–18	1,710	30%	7,320	2%	1%	97%
Going to Work (BBC)	14–16	2,700	47%	15,890	4%	12%	84%
Experiment: Chemistry (ITV)	16–18	1,070	19%	2,500	2%	0%	98%

Source: Educational Broadcasting Council, 1982.

subjects in secondary schools, leading to a greater fragmentation of the target audience.

Nevertheless, at the secondary level there are some interesting differences in the use of television in different subject areas and also between television and radio, as can be seen from Table 6.

There are two points to note from Table 6. Firstly, foreign language series are the least used on television. Even allowing for some of the series being deliberately directed at a minority audience (such as the Spanish series), utilisation is surprisingly low in comparison with other subject areas. For instance, although many of the science series were aimed at sixth forms, their utilisation rate is almost double that of the language series. Even on radio, secondary school language series are used by less than 10 per cent of the schools.

Taking then the audience research figures at their face value, schools television and schools radio in Britain have both cleared the minimum evaluation hurdle: in many schools, for a wide range of subject areas and age groups, extensive use is made of them.

THE LIMITATIONS OF STATISTICS ON UTILISATION

Audience figures are useful for providing a global picture of the success or otherwise of schools broadcasts. They provide useful information to broadcasting organisations on *trends* – whether or not the use of broadcasting is increasing, or even whether a particular series over a number of years has gradually caught the interest of teachers. Audience figures can pick out particular successes or failures for series as a whole. They can be useful for justifying the use of broadcasting for schools *within* a broadcasting organisation if the figures can demonstrate that large numbers of children are watching or listening.

However, such figures do not provide any clear indications of which educational functions or programming strategies are most appropriate for educational broadcasting. From the Educational Broadcasting Council's figures it would appear that most subject areas are suitable for treatment by television or radio. There are successes and failures in each area. What we cannot tell from the audience figures is what learning has taken place, nor which of the various strategies outlined in the previous chapter have proved to be most effective.

TABLE 6

UTILISATION OF TELEVISION AND RADIO FOR DIFFERENT SECONDARY SCHOOL SUBJECT AREAS

Subject	Total	Television No. of series BBC	Television No. of series ITV	Television % of schools using series Mean	Television % of schools using series Range	Radio No. of series BBC	Radio % of schools using series Mean	Radio % of schools using series Range
History	2	2	–	39·00	38–40	2	11·50	8–15
Careers/Guidance	7	4	3	32·14	10–47	2	8·50	7–10
Geography	11	8	3	31·18	21–42	2	18·50	15–22
Science	9	3	6	27·89	19–36	1	21·00	21
English	4	2	2	21·25	14–30	5	8·80	5–12
General Studies	1	–	1	20·00	20	5	4·80	2–9
Languages	11	9	2	14·45	6–26	9	9·76	4–15
Other	3	–	3	21·00	14–27	3	6·33	2–10
Total	48	28	20	24·63	6–47	29	9·41	2–22

Note: This table excludes those series which span the primary and secondary age ranges.
Source: Educational Broadcasting Council, 1982.

ENRICHMENT AND LEARNING RESOURCE:
THE OVERSEAS EVIDENCE

The most comprehensive review of the research into the relative success of different strategies for educational television and radio has been carried out by Schramm (1977). While Schramm was more concerned in that study with differences *between* media than with differences *within* a medium, nevertheless his category 'supplementing the formal school system' closely matches the use of television and radio as a learning resource and as enrichment. His analysis of the effectiveness of these two broad strategies drew on studies of television projects in the USA, Japan, Colombia and India, and of radio in Thailand. In each of these studies there were control groups, i.e. schools or classes matched as carefully as possible, their main difference being whether or not they used the programmes.

Each one of these studies showed that students receiving television or radio as a supplement to normal teaching scored *higher* on the various attainment tests used than students not using the television or radio programmes. Schramm concluded:

> Used as supplements to classroom teaching, the media of instruction are effective. They work as well as other classroom teaching. Used in the right way, in the right place, for an appropriate purpose, they will improve the classroom experience.

A separate Japanese study, carried out by NHK, the Japanese broadcasting authority (NHK, 1969), reviewed the Japanese research on schools radio during the period 1960–68. Again, comparing the performance of children who listened to schools radio with the performance of children who did not hear the programmes, they found that taking the studies as a whole:

> there was little difference between classes which listened to schools radio for only one term, but after two terms or more the performance of classes who listened to the programmes noticeably increased in terms of the ability to read and write in Japanese and English, and in English the effect of listening was higher with students of higher intelligence than with those of lower intelligence . . . the educational effects of the broadcasts were not invariant, but depended on many factors: the quality of the programmes; the varying ability of school teachers to guide students in their use of the broadcast material; students' abilities and interests; and the length of the period of utilisation. Conse-

quently, there were large differences from school to school on the relative effectiveness of schools radio.

Both the Schramm and the NHK studies clearly indicate that television and radio can lead to clear improvements when used as an enrichment or as a learning resource to supplement normal classroom activities. The NHK study, though, highlighted the fact that increased effectiveness depends on certain *conditions* being met, and this factor will gain increasing importance as more evidence is reviewed.

ENRICHMENT AND LEARNING RESOURCE:
THE BRITISH EVIDENCE

There is evidence from several studies that British teachers prefer to use broadcasts as enrichment rather than for direct teaching purposes. Cuff (1976) in a study of the use of a French series, 'Le Nouvel Arrivé', found that teachers specifically requested enrichment material. They were *not* interested in programmes dealing specifically with grammar. Very few teachers wanted the programmes to provide core material in a progressively structured manner throughout the year. The main desire, expressed by 62 per cent of teachers in the sample, was for material which brought the foreign country alive.

Cuff also compared classes that used 'Le Nouvel Arrivé' with similar classes that did not, across six different schools. Since the main reason teachers gave for using the series was to provide background knowledge of France and the French way of life, Cuff tried to test the effects of the programmes in improving pupils' background knowledge of France. She was not able to show statistically significant gains between pupils who saw the programmes and those that did not. She argued that this was partly because pupils generally already often had good background knowledge, and also because there were only eight programmes in the series, thus giving relatively little broadcast exposure compared with other sources of information. As often happens on studies of this kind, the differences in test scores *within* classes were often greater than differences *between* classes, making it very difficult to identify any effects clearly, due to differences in treatment. Nevertheless, combining test scores and her own observation of the classes, Cuff felt confident enough to suggest that it was not so much the programmes themselves but *the role played by the teacher* in exploiting them which was the main determinant of whether pupils derived benefit from them. This again is consistent with the Japanese findings reported earlier. Cuff also found that teachers generally wanted more advice from the broadcasting organisation on how best to use such broadcasts.

Perhaps the most surprising result, though, given the generally poor accents of British foreign language teachers and the lack of direct exposure of British children to foreign languages outside school, was the low priority the teachers gave to the statement: 'Television can provide a wide range of native voices.' Two thirds of the teachers replying gave this statement a *low* priority for language series, and few teachers in the sample looked to television to provide a good basis for linguistic work in the classroom.

Four studies carried out by the Schools Broadcasting Council (1976, 1977, 1978; Educational Broadcasting Council, 1979), one on the teaching of English in primary schools, one on the series 'Merry-Go-Round', one on broadcasts and project work, and one on social studies, all confirmed the preference of British teachers for broadcasting as enrichment rather than for direct teaching, across a range of subject areas and age ranges.

One project however that did come near to direct teaching was the BBC Radio series 'Listening and Reading' (SBC, 1972). These programmes were intended to develop reading skills and an interest in books, particularly for children who came from culturally 'impoverished' home backgrounds, where the ownership and reading of books was uncommon. The broadcast programmes were intended to be taped in the schools and listened to by individual children or small groups of three or four children at the same time as following the story in the accompanying booklets. Multiple repetition was considered important, as the producer hoped that the children would want to hear and read the stories again and again. In this way, the producer hoped that the children would use listening and reading simultaneously.

The stories were read in a straightforward manner by an adult actor, with no sound effects. The undramatic style was meant to approximate to that of an adult reading intimately to a small group of children. The accompanying booklets contained texts of the programmes exactly as they were broadcast, and there was a four-page leaflet for teachers explaining the theory and principles on which the series had been planned.

The first series (aimed at six- to seven-year-old children) was used by 4,736 classes or groups. In terms of school radio for this age range in Britain, this is comparatively low use. More importantly, few classes used the series *in the way intended*. In most schools, teachers used the broadcasts live because at that time 'the majority of infant and junior schools had insufficient recording or replaying apparatus in quantity or kind to make widespread the pioneer type of usage recommended', and consequently teachers were unable to provide any repetitions, or at best only one or two. Teachers found that only the best readers could both follow the text *and* listen at the same time. The rest were likely to distinguish only a few words, lose the place and then give up trying to follow. Booklets were generally in short supply for a whole class and many teachers thought that the language and vocabulary of the stories were too difficult and the reading too undramatic.

One class in each of the two schools, though, was given special treatment. Through the assistance of the National Council for Educational Technology, each school was issued with extra recording equipment and adequate copies of the booklets to enable the programmes to be used in the way intended. These two schools were also frequently visited during the series by a BBC education officer and an officer from NCET. The two teachers involved in the scheme were asked to keep notes of pupils' progress and development over the project. From the teachers' reports based on two terms' work, the bulletin reported that improvements were noted in the structure of the children's language, development of written work, and spelling, and by the end of the second term, according to the bulletin, the children had developed a remarkable increase in reading power. One of the two teachers reported that, by the end of the spring term, all but six of her thirty-eight top infants could read fluently – something which had not happened in her experience in that school before.

It is clear that, when planning this series, the broadcasters did not give enough consideration to the realities of school life. Teachers in 1971 did not have the resources to work in the way intended. When the resources and support were provided, reading skills seem to have improved dramatically, but because of the way the project was set up, it is not possible to determine whether this improvement was due to the special attention given to the two schools or to the technique being tried. Given the importance of what was being attempted and the hint of what might have been achieved, it was a great pity that more consideration was not given at the time to providing support for teachers on a more widespread scale. Closer liaison with local education authority advisers might have substantially increased the success of the project.

A rather similar study, but on a much larger scale, was carried out two years later, this time primarily on television (Hayter, 1974). The main aim was to see what would be the effects if schools were provided with 'a reasonable and adequate level of equipment'.

Special efforts were made by BBC and ITV education officers and LEA advisers to help teachers in selected schools to make more effective use of schools broadcasts. In this study, 118 schools took part, and the evidence was collected in the form of unstructured, open-ended reports from teachers. This evidence, which amounted to more than two million words, was then sifted and analysed by a retired Inspector of Schools. The report suggests that given the right conditions, broadcasts clearly stimulated children's language development, imagination, and enthusiasm for using languages, and this could be reasonably interpreted as further evidence of the value of broadcasts for providing enrichment and assisting teachers in the development of language skills. However, the selection of evidence from the teachers' reports is highly subjective and it is impossible to tell from the report how widespread such effects were, nor is it possible to generalise to the great majority of schools in Britain which had not been provided with extra equipment and intensive contact from broadcast education officers and local advisers. Given the unsatisfactory nature of the enquiry, it is difficult to know how much weight to give to Hayter's conclusions, but they do not seem to be too much at odds with other studies:

> when teachers were given adequate equipment and support from advisers, the value of broadcasts became fully and progressively recognised by the teachers during the course of the study . . . using broadcasts well is no easy task: teachers need to be trained to make better use of broadcasting . . . a 'modest' increase in equipment improves considerably the perceived value of broadcasts . . . the existing copyright laws are a serious obstacle to better use of broadcasts in schools.

ENRICHMENT OR LEARNING RESOURCE?

The 'enrichment' ideology is firmly held by most British educational broadcasters and their advisers. Because schools broadcasts are *not* didactic they allow children and teachers to respond to material in a wide variety of ways, according to the needs of individual classes, teachers and children. Using broadcasting this way enables many of the unique characteristics of television and radio – their entertainment value, their access to places, people, experiences outside the normal range of children – to be best developed and used. Broadcasters provide the resource; teachers and learners choose how to use it. This way, the autonomy of the teacher is protected. He or she is in control and not being dictated to by the broadcasters.

This is an attractive argument but one which I believe needs questioning. The distinction made in the previous chapter between 'enrichment' and 'learning resource' is important. There are quite different teaching strategies underlying these two approaches. Use of broadcasts as a learning resource suggests a more intensive and specific use – a point somewhere between the more casual enrichment approach and the more rigorously didactic approach of direct teaching. Learning resource programmes are less likely to be all things to all men, but, where they are used successfully, their educational benefits are likely to be more profound than those of enrichment programmes.

However, there is evidence that when television or radio have been designed much more deliberately as learning resources (e.g. 'Listening and Reading') there have been real problems. Taking all the studies as a whole, for school broadcasts to be successful, certain conditions must be met, and for learning resource broadcasts, these conditions tend to be more demanding, in that if they are not met, the programmes are more likely to fail completely. If though the conditions *are* met, the educational impact of learning resource programmes can be much greater than that of enrichment programmes.

Some of the necessary conditions for programmes of the enrichment and learning-resource type are indicated by the research studies:

(1) adequate provision of recording and replay equipment;
(2) more direction or suggestions to teachers on how such material might be used, specific to each series;
(3) more initial and in-service training for teachers on the use of broadcasting;
(4) adequate time (at least two terms) to enable the full impact of a series to accumulate.

Unfortunately, there are still major difficulties that teachers often cannot overcome, even when they want to use programmes as a learning resource *and* are provided with adequate equipment for recording and replay. To make the most effective use of television and radio as a resource, the teacher needs to build in such material from the outset, when planning a syllabus or a project. This requires adequate information or advance warning, particularly if the programmes are to be used on transmission and not as recordings.

Secondly, only programmes classified by the broadcasting organisations themselves as educational can be legally recorded off-air in Britain. This can be particularly frustrating since so much of the material that teachers would like to use as resource material comes from general broadcasting. Until the copyright laws are changed the use of television and radio as a learning resource will continue to be limited.

It is now possible to buy or hire video-cassettes of a wide range of BBC general programmes from BBC Enterprises (BBC, 1981). However, it would cost a school about £400 to *hire* for instance the 13 programmes in the BBC 'Life on Earth' series just for one week, and nearly £1500 to buy them! Such pricing puts systematic use of recorded general broadcasts beyond the reach of most schools.

Despite the difficulties, some teachers are still willing to go to considerable trouble to use general broadcasts, so valuable can the material be for them. For instance, when my son was in a middle school, his teacher organised a project around the 'Life on Earth' series. It proved though to be a good example of the difficulties teachers face in using general broadcasts. Because of copying restrictions, the children working on the project were asked to watch the programmes at home – with the inevitable consequence that many children missed the programmes. Although there is an excellent book written to accompany the series, it is expensive, and written at an adult, advanced level. What would have been useful would have been a resource pack with photographs and drawings of animals and plants, and their habitats, together with suggestions for children's activities. This excellent series contains unique film from all over the world of rare creatures and plants in their natural habitats. The programmes though were largely paid for from money raised from the British public through the licence fee. It is absurd that teachers are effectively prevented from using such material in recorded form, because of copyright and cost restrictions, when the children's parents have already paid for the production costs of general programmes, through the licence fee or purchasing advertised products. Broadcasters and performers are inhibiting the use of broadcasting as learning resource material through their greed.

On the other hand, even under good conditions, the educational impact of transmitted programmes used for enrichment seems to be nebulous or marginal. Providing a teacher with an 'enrichment' programme is rather like someone with lung cancer being offered a gold cigarette case. It would be churlish to refuse, but it doesn't help much. It is difficult though to see schools broadcasters themselves moving away from programmes of the enrichment type because they reflect the same styles and approaches to programme-making found in *general* television and radio. Enrichment programmes also reinforce the distinction between the broadcasters' role and the teachers' role. Successful utilisation of enrichment programmes is clearly seen as the responsibility of the teacher, allowing the primary activity of producers to remain making programmes.

Deliberately making educational programmes as a learning resource though requires greater attention to be paid to questions of utilisation, teacher training, linking of programmes to text books, and production styles which encourage programmes to be stopped while activities are carried out. Greater input from teachers in the design of such programmes is necessary. This though would blur the organisational boundary between broadcasting and education, and would require more in the way of resources and producer time on activities which are not so immediately and obviously related to programme-making, such as integration with text books and detailed follow-up activities.

However, the advent of video-cassettes and audio-cassettes now encourages the development of *non-broadcast* audio-visual learning resources. If broadcasters are unable or unwilling to develop materials for use in a learning resource mode, they may find themselves by-passed by other production agencies in the future, a point that will be developed further in Chapter 9.

MEETING SPECIAL NEEDS AND DEFICIENCIES:
THE EVIDENCE

Despite the prevalence of the enrichment approach in British educational broadcasting, there has been very little research into how teachers make use of such material in normal working conditions, nor into its effectiveness. On the other hand, although programming for special needs is far less common, this is one of the better researched areas of British educational broadcasting, thanks largely to the IBA fellowship scheme.

Race relations

Teachers often feel unqualified, or appear to welcome assistance, when dealing with race relations within schools. Many teachers have no formal training in this aspect. Indeed, teachers often live in areas different from those in which they teach and hence have no direct experience of immigrant or ethnic communities except through the teaching context. It is fortunate then that one of the best research studies on British schools television was carried out on a Granada television series, 'Our Neighbours', aimed at the age group ten to thirteen. The researcher was an IBA Research Fellow, Graeme Kemmelfield (1972).

The programme chosen by Kemmelfield for his study was 'Our Neighbours from Pakistan'. This showed children living in Pakistan, and a Pakistani family settling in the United Kingdom. The programme emphasised strongly the influence of the Islamic and indigenous culture on the everyday life of Pakistani families in Britain. Kemmelfield's study aimed to find out whether exposure to the programme promoted more informed understanding and sympathetic appreciation of this ethnic group. The study was as much concerned with attitude changes as with cognitive learning.

Kemmelfield used pupils in four schools in the Manchester area for the study, and there were important differences between the schools. Because previous research had shown that the density of immigrant population within areas of residence was a crucial factor in influencing the racial attitudes of Anglo-Saxon English school children, Kemmelfield used schools from both high and low immigrant population areas. More importantly, one of the two schools located in the high immigrant areas actually had a low proportion of immigrants in its intake. The results from this school were similar to the results from the two schools located in the low immigrant areas, whereas the results from the fourth school, the only one with a high proportion of immigrants in the intake (41 per cent), were quite different. In this last school, 28 per cent of the intake were of Pakistani origin, and this school was the only one which gave specific instruction on the Pakistani way of life and had a Pakistani teacher responsible for special English classes. The results from this school were consistently different from the results from the other three schools.

One result common to all four schools was that 80 per cent of the pupils 'trusted' the programme about Pakistanis, and only a small minority thought the programme was 'manipulative', by trying to change their minds about Pakistanis. In the three schools with low immigrant enrolments, the programme was not only well received by the children but was also highly effective in *conveying information* about Pakistani customs and ways of life. In the fourth school, while some knowledge gains were still found, these were small, since the Anglo-Saxon pupils' initial knowledge of Pakistani customs was already high.

With regard to the impact of 'Our Neighbours from Pakistan' on pupils' *attitudes* towards Pakistanis, the results were more complex but nevertheless important. In general, before exposure to the programme, children in the high immigrant enrolment school were more tolerant towards Pakistanis than children in the other three schools. After the programme, there was a clear increase in more favourable attitudes to Pakistanis in the three low immigrant enrolment schools, but in the fourth school, the programme led to more *uncertainty* in pupils' attitudes. Similarly, the programme resulted in *less* demand for racial conformity in the three schools with low immigrant enrolments, but again caused much more uncertainty about this issue in the fourth school, where pupils had been much more tolerant of different racial customs. Also, in the three low immigrant enrolment schools, there was a tendency after the programme for more pupils to agree with statements which suggested that Pakistani children were as likeable as Anglo-Saxon English children and that the two groups should mix more together. This result was not repeated in the fourth school, where the pupils were already well familiar with Pakistani children and customs, and the programme did not affect their views on this issue one way or the other.

This study shows that programmes can change attitudes and lead to knowledge gains when there is a lack of knowledge to begin with. It also shows the highly complex ways in which pupils can react to the same programme. Kemmelfield commented that pupils responded to the programme in a relatively personal and exploratory manner and not just in terms of stereotyped group feelings and thinking. For instance, while in the three low immigrant enrolment schools there was a general shift towards accepting that cleanliness was important to Pakistanis, the same pupils reacted strongly against Pakistani eating habits, as portrayed in one particular sequence of the programme.

Kemmelfield concluded that such programmes are likely to arouse conflicting feelings and opinions in any group of children, and that, in such circumstances, the classroom teacher needs to respond with skill and sensitivity in order to make creative use of such material. Kemmelfield's research shows quite clearly the tremendous potential of television for dealing with the increasingly critical area of race relations in British schools – and also how essential it is to base such programmes on well-designed research if they are to lead to better rather than worse race relations.

Non-academic school leavers

When the school-leaving age was raised from fifteen to sixteen in Britain in 1973, teachers were faced with the challenge of providing appropriate and relevant teaching for non-academic pupils in their last year at school. The Granada TV series 'Decision' aimed to encourage school-leavers to make active, informed decisions about personal and social 'real-life' issues. Jane Steedman, another IBA

Research Fellow, carried out a study of one programme in this series which dealt with buying a house. This, like Kemmelfield's, is one of the better designed studies on schools television in Britain.

An unusual feature of Steedman's study was a critical analysis of the objectives of the programme and its style in relation to its objectives. Steedman's study in fact turned out to be highly critical of the programme. She found that the programme actually had the opposite effect on those who viewed it from what the programme was intended to do. The programme's overall aim was to help young people to make their own decisions and to see the relevance of certain decisions to their own lives. She found though that those that viewed the programmes tended to greater conformity and accept-ance of the views of 'authority figures' in the programme and to what she called 'restricted decision-making strategies' – i.e. less willingness to consider a wider range of decision options – than those who did not view the programme. For instance, the pro-gramme presented a choice of which three houses to buy – but 70 per cent of the leavers lived in rented accommodation, and for these pupils Steedman claimed that a more realistic decision would have been whether or not to buy at all.

Steedman claimed that the style of the programme – a documentary format, but with an authoritative and advice-giving commentary, using primarily authority figures (solicitor, building society manager, etc.) – led to stereotyped responses to the pro-gramme and to a narrowing of the pupils' decision options. She argued that this discrepancy between programme objectives and outcome was due firstly to the teacher–adviser's original ideas for the programme – a bombardment of competing points of view – not being translated into the actual programme, and secondly to the failure of the producers of the series to analyse carefully enough what is actually involved in 'free' decision-making. She pointed out that if the aim really was to help people make their own decisions, it's best not to tell them what they should do.

Steedman's study is interesting for a number of reasons. One reason why the programme seemed to fail was because of the producer's lack of familiarity both with the target audience and the topic (the complex nature of decision-making), and, related to this, the failure to make the programme in the way proposed by the teacher–adviser. Secondly, the producer was clearly dealing both with a difficult topic and a difficult target group, and, in such a situation, the programme appears to have suffered from a lack of pre-production research, or at least some pre-testing, to identify the audience better and its likely response to certain topics and approaches. Lastly, the study shows the importance of the relationship between production style and programme objectives; in this case, the programme style seemed incompatible with the programme objectives.

Handicapped children

Unfamiliarity of producers with a special-target audience, failure to realise programmes along the lines originally suggested by teacher–advisers and inappropriate production styles, are also features found in some of the research into programmes used for teaching handicapped children.

This is an area fraught with difficulties for broadcasters. 'Handicapped' covers a wide range of disabilities, including severe physical or emotional handicap, children with language disorders and those with low mental abilities. Thus within the heading of 'handicap' or 'special education' lie many sub-groups. Nevertheless, the total numbers are substantial. The Warnock Report (Gt Britain: Department of Education and Science, 1978) on the education of children with special needs estimated that as many as 20 per cent of all school children are in need of special educational help at some stage of their school career.

Despite the difficulties with such specialised, fragmented audiences, British broadcasting organisations have transmitted several series which have been used with handicapped children. Yorkshire TV's 'Insight' was aimed at hearing-impaired and slow-learning children in the middle-school range. BBC's 'Let's Go . . .' was aimed at young mentally-handicapped adults, and BBC's 'Television Club' and 'Capricorn Game' are used with slow-learning children in secondary and primary schools respectively.

There have been several studies (again, nearly all supported by the IBA Fellowship scheme) into the use of television for handicapped children. Edwards (1974) identified which programmes were used with handicapped children and how teachers adapted these programmes for use with their pupils. Porter (1978) studied slow learning children's attention to educational television programmes and the techniques which appeared to hold their attention, and Hill (1981) evaluated the 'Insight' series. Tucker (1979) investigated the perceptual requirements of blind and deaf children when using television and technical ways in which such children may be helped. Finally, Spencer and Clarke (1981), of the University of Hull, evaluated the impact of 'Let's Go . . .'.

These research studies have been well reviewed by Porter (1982), herself a teacher of handicapped children. She argues that from a teacher's point of view, television has tremendous potential for teaching slow-learning and handicapped children. A well-designed programme can provide carefully ordered sequencing of events, controlling and organising information in ways that enable the child to comprehend what is happening, through simplifying what in the 'real' world are often complex events and processes. Similarly, programmes can carefully structure language and reinforce it with appropriate visuals. Television can provide models of how to act in certain common situations, a function particularly important for emotionally disturbed children. For physically handicapped or institutionalised children, television is particularly valuable for providing compensatory and vicarious experiences not otherwise available to them. Some of the more general characteristics of television are also important for handicapped children and carry over to educational programmes. For instance, it is often much easier to gain and hold attention through television than through other means available to the teacher. Porter points to what she calls the 'social inclusiveness' of watching television: for once, handi-capped children can do what everyone else does. Lastly, Porter argues that, for handicapped children, television provides security and confidence: watching the same characters doing the same things each week is reassuring for many such children. It is also non-threatening: it never tells them off!

However, Porter claims that television is not used as much as might be expected by teachers of handicapped children. For in-stance, Hill (1981) found that very few schools for slow-learning children appeared to use the programmes in the 'Insight' series, a fact supported by the Educational Broadcasting Council's Annual Survey, 1979–80. From her review, Porter identified a number of reasons for television not being more heavily used in special schools (apart from the general problems of timetabling, lack of adequate recording equipment and teacher indifference).

Programmes contained *too much information* for the children to assimilate and teachers found follow-up work difficult because individual children had focused on different information. Pro-grammes were *too fast*, with too much happening on the screen and sound-track for the children to pick up the main teaching points. Handicapped children need longer to assimilate and process in-formation than normal children; they also need constant repetition of the main teaching points (Hill, 1981; Spencer and Clarke, 1981). The *language* was too complex for handicapped children to follow and understand. Teachers often had to interpret what was said in the programmes in order to help their children understand (Ed-wards, 1974). There was a *lack of visualisation of ideas*: too often most of the teaching information was given verbally, while the picture shown was actually secondary in terms of context. It should be the other way round given the large proportion of slow-learning children with language difficulties. Similarly, there was often a *lack of co-ordination of sound and visual channels*: frequently, the two channels did not correspond in terms of context. The handicapped child becomes confused if the verbal message does not correspond exactly with the visual information (Porter, 1978). A frequent complaint from teachers was that insufficient care was taken regarding *sequencing*. Edwards (1974) remarked that 'Life does not always happen in orderly sequences, but for their comprehension it needs to be presented so.' Many teachers commented on the lack of any clearly defined sequence or structural logic between the different sections of the same programme.

From her own experience as a teacher adviser to the 'Insight' series, Porter (1982) suggests several reasons for the failure of programmes for handicapped children. Producers have no experience of teaching such children, and this lack of knowledge cannot be compensated for by a few school visits and brief encounters with teacher–advisers. Even when advisers and teachers do have comments to make, these are often not implemented in the programme itself. 'Traditionally it has been the broadcast companies who have had control of ETV production and most educators feel that they can have little real say in what is produced' (Porter, 1982). Lastly, she argues that there is a lack of systematic formative research before programmes are finalised, but pre-testing is essential when dealing with such special-target groups.

With regard to this last point, it is interesting to note that 'Let's Go . . .' was the only one of these series tested before transmission, and pre-testing did lead to major changes in the style and tone of the transmitted programmes (Lee, Croton and Whelan, 1978).

Even allowing for the very special needs of handicapped children, this research identifies perhaps more clearly than any other some of the strengths and weaknesses of broadcasting in education in Britain. It is clear from these studies that British schools broadcasting has in recent years been skilful in identifying areas of special need and has tried to provide useful material for teaching in these areas. Television and radio have been used to help improve racial understanding and to teach non-academic school-leavers and handicapped children of various kinds. In all the cases examined, the studies confirmed the huge *potential* of television and radio for providing substantial help in what teachers themselves recognise to be difficult areas.

The research has also shown that such programmes require great care and preparation. In particular, very accurate knowledge of the target audience is necessary. Kemmelfield highlighted the complex ways in which pupils reacted to a programme and the consequent need for the classroom teacher to respond with skill and sensitivity if the impact of the programme was to be creatively harnessed. Steedman found that the programme she studied failed because the nature of the target audience and how decisions are actually made were not fully understood by the production team. The studies on programmes for handicapped children also suggest more failure than success, again due to inadequate knowledge of the target audience and a failure to take into consideration in the design of programmes the special needs of such children.

It is of course because such areas *are* difficult that television and radio can be so useful to teachers. However, broadcasting will only be useful if the programmes actually help the teacher and tackle the problems *effectively*.

Once a series has been decided on by the Advisory Committee to the various broadcasting organisations, there is a conventional programme-making process. The producer consults with teacher–advisers and education officers working for the broadcasting organisation. He then visits a few schools and talks to a few teachers and possibly consults some books and other programmes. Then the producer, after consultation with other production colleagues, prepares a script and produces the programme. It is then previewed by senior production colleagues and possibly by an education officer, and then transmitted. It seems though that, at least for programmes which are intended to meet special needs, the conventional production process is inadequate. Much closer teacher involvement, and, above all, adequate formative research before finalising the programme, appear to be essential. Programmes aimed at meeting special needs then are likely to require more resources and a longer production period, and to be more demanding on producers than the usual schools broadcast. It is a high-risk area but one where broadcasting could be particularly valuable for education, *provided* that broadcasters are willing to change their current approach.

Direct teaching and curriculum reform:
success at a price

While exhaustive research on educational broadcasting in developed countries is very rare, the use of broadcasting for direct teaching in developing countries has been extensively researched, usually by evaluators from developed countries, as can be seen from Table 7.

Most of these evaluations have been based on comparative measurements of performance, either before and after the introduction of the new system, or between pupils covered by the projects and pupils receiving conventional education. Many of the studies provide detailed cost analyses and general data on the countries' economic, social and educational development problems. Schramm (1977) has collected together and analysed the research evidence from several of these projects, and Arnove (1976) presents an excellent critique of the use of television for educational reform and development in developing countries, drawing on several of these studies. Consequently, I wish here to concentrate on some of the broader issues.

One study not mentioned in the previous chapter but listed in Table 7 was an attempt in South Korea to use tethered communications balloons to provide a cheap substitute for a satellite. Signals were to be bounced off reflectors attached to the balloons, providing national coverage for both educational television and radio programmes which were to be used as the basis of a new, reformed school curriculum. However, the balloons proved to be aerodynamically unstable. The American Westinghouse Corporation, the main contractors, agreed as compensation to provide equipment for a more conventional ground-based system. However, this delayed the opening of the educational radio and television networks from 1976 to 1981. In the meantime, the curriculum reform went ahead, with the result that programmes were made to support or enrich the newly existing curriculum, rather than for direct teaching.

Taking the studies listed in Table 7 as a whole (and ignoring the South Korean debacle), the use of broadcasting for direct teaching and curriculum reform has on balance led to substantial educational improvements in the countries concerned. The improvements took several forms:

(1) increased *enrolment* in the formal school system; for instance, in the El Salvador project, enrolments in grades 7–9 increased from 20,000 at the start of the reform to 65,000 within five years;

(2) *reduced drop-out* after enrolment; for instance, in Niger, those pupils included in the scheme continued their schooling right through the five primary grades, with virtually no drop-outs; in El Salvador, of those who entered the seventh grade in 1970, 91 per cent continued into the ninth grade in 1972, compared with 68 per cent in 1969;

TABLE 7

EVALUATION AND PROGRESS REPORTS ON PROJECTS USING BROADCASTING FOR DIRECT TEACHING OR CURRICULUM REFORM

Project Medium	Country	Type of Project	Evaluation or Progress Report
Radio Taramuhara	Mexico	Direct teaching	Schmelkes de Sotelo, 1977.
Radioprimaria	Mexico	Direct teaching	Spain, 1977.
Telesecundaria	Mexico	Direct teaching	Mayo et al., 1975.
Radio Mathematics	Nicaragua	Direct teaching	Friend et al., 1980
ETV Maranhão	Brazil	Direct teaching	Arena et al., 1977
TV	American Samoa	Curriculum Reform	Schramm et al., 1967; Masland and Masland, 1976; Schramm et al., 1980.
TV	El Salvador	Curriculum Reform	Mayo et al., 1976; Ingle, 1976
TV and Radio	Ivory Coast	Curriculum Reform	Kaye, 1976; Eicher and Orivel, 1980
TV	Niger	Curriculum Reform	Schramm, 1977
TV and Radio	South Korea	Curriculum Reform	Schramm, 1977; Jamison and Yoon Tai Kim, 1977; Hawkridge and Robinson, 1982.

(3) *educational standards*, as measured by objective performance tests, were *raised*; in Nicaragua, at all grades covered by
the scheme, pupils taught mathematics by radio learned more
then pupils taught in traditional classrooms, and these results
were consistent across different types of school and levels of
ability; in ETV Maranhão, ETV students achieved higher
pass rates on public examinations than students from conventional private schools, although students in the ETV schools
generally came from poorer families;

(4) on some projects, *costs* per student for broadcast-based
direct teaching projects were estimated to be *lower* than the
costs for traditional education without deterioration of educational standards; costs for instance for the Telesecundaria
system have been estimated to be 25 per cent less than costs
for an equivalent conventional provision (had it existed); in
El Salvador, by 1973, the cost per student using ETV was
estimated to be about 10 per cent lower than the cost per
student had ETV not been used, class size not increased and
teaching load not changed.

Increased enrolments, longer schooling, improved standards, at
no greater costs than those found in conventional teaching, are
substantial achievements. Such performance would be welcomed
by many governments even in developed countries; given the
difficulties that had to be overcome in the developing countries
where these schemes have been introduced, the achievements are
remarkable. While one can quibble over some of the results, it is
clear that direct teaching through broadcasting has substantially
improved educational provision in several developing countries,
within reasonable cost limits.

Nevertheless, doubts remain. Educational standards in some of
these countries were appallingly low at the time of the introduction
of the television or radio reform. Had the same amount of money
been invested steadily in the conventional education system over a
regular period of time, the need for major reforms might not have
arisen in the first place.

Where foreign aid has been provided through a bilateral agreement (i.e. between two countries, e.g. Japan and Afghanistan) it
usually covered mainly capital costs for buildings and equipment,
such as the construction of a studio complex and transmitters, and
production and transmission equipment. Such bilateral aid was
rarely in the form of an outright grant, so both capital and interest
had to be repaid eventually, even if at less than market rates of
interest. Often such aid was tied to the purchase of equipment and

services from the loaning country. As the example from Afghanistan shows, initial equipment may be purchased at discount prices with the help of low-interest inter-governmental loans. However, the developing country then finds that the initial investment is insufficient to maintain or develop an adequate service; nevertheless, necessary subsequent purchases – often far exceeding the original investment – must be paid for at full cost in scarce foreign currency, usually through further loans negotiated at full market interest rates. Thus the developing country becomes reliant on foreign technology and loans, and the cycle of dependency and debt is strengthened.

International aid agencies, such as the World Bank and the United Nations Development Programme, have generally been cautious in funding educational broadcasting projects, preferring to put their money into agricultural and industrial projects which give the developing country more chance of obtaining direct economic gains from the investment.

Several developed countries (e.g. Britain, Sweden, France, West Germany, USA) run training courses in educational broadcasting for which grants or bursaries are available from these countries and from international aid agencies. Again, though, training in well-maintained, expensive and highly sophisticated Western production centres, in a foreign language, is not always appropriate.

In the projects evaluated, though, the main problems have arisen when the foreign assistance has ended. It has often proved difficult for the developing country to maintain a high standard of teaching and to integrate the projects into the main education system. The running costs of such projects – pupils' worksheets, teachers' manuals, transport costs, salaries for production, technical and administrative staff, the cost of TV or radio receivers, and the maintenance and replacement of equipment – are rarely covered by foreign aid. Running costs for one year's operation alone can far exceed the total of foreign capital aid. The national government then has to find large amounts of money, skilled manpower and administrative effort to continue such projects, and several countries have found it impossible to maintain adequate services over a long period.

Many of the projects (for instance, in Niger, Nicaragua and SITE in India) have been pilots or experiments. In such cases it has been impossible to assess the full economic costs and benefits or the operational difficulties of using broadcasting for direct teaching on a large-scale or continuous basis. Indeed, there is a disturbing tendency for developing countries to be used as test-beds for advanced technological applications that developed countries themselves have not been prepared to use extensively, as witnessed by the South Korean and Indian satellite projects.

There are also doubts about the emphasis placed on television rather than radio on such projects. Two of the three countries that have used television for direct teaching and curriculum reform on a *national* scale, American Samoa and El Salvador, are both small, compact countries, easily covered by a television transmission system, and most schools are within easy reach of highways and electricity supplies. In the third country, the Ivory Coast, considerable efforts had to be made to provide schools with suitable reception equipment. Special battery-operated sets, suitable for the French SECAM system, had to be designed, and a sophisticated and costly maintenance system established. The Indian satellite project was restricted to villages with mains electricity supplies. It is extremely expensive to provide television sets for schools on a national basis, particularly if local generators have to be supplied where there is no mains electricity.

Radio, on the other hand, can operate on low-powered, low-cost batteries. Furthermore, while television is becoming much more widespread in Latin America and some South-East Asian countries, there are still many developing countries where the television signals cover only the main urban areas, whereas medium and short-wave radio transmitters usually give national coverage. It is, though, the poor, rural areas where television does not reach which usually have the most inadequate educational provision. Television production, maintenance and distribution all require greater numbers of higher-qualified staff than radio, providing a drain on scarce technical manpower from other possible development activities. Television, because of the high technical standards demanded, also carries a much greater risk than radio of breakdown or failure. Radio then would appear to have several advantages over television for very poor countries; apart from in Nicaragua, though, radio has not been used for direct teaching and curriculum reform.

The financial implications and the relative value of radio compared to television are general concerns for the use of broadcasting in developing countries. There are also concerns specific to its use for direct teaching. The first concern is a practical one. Direct teaching by television or radio requires large amounts of production and transmission time. At one stage, the American Samoa project, which introduced a whole television-based curriculum for all primary grades in one year and all secondary grades in the next, was producing 6,000 live programmes a year. This meant programme makers were making twenty programmes each per week. It is difficult to disagree with Schramm's comment that 'the enormous load of live programming must have had an effect on the quality of the broadcasts'! In El Salvador, a production team was responsible for making three television programmes a week. This still required two teams a day working a double-shift system over a twelve-hour studio day to get enough programmes made in time. The Nicaraguan project required the production of between three and five radio lessons a week, for one subject alone. Most of the projects introduced direct teaching for one year-level or grade at a time, and, especially when formative evaluation was used, the programmes once finalised were recorded and used again in subsequent years. Even so, production loads still tend to be heavy in comparison with developed countries. For instance, at the Open University, producers make only six to ten educational television programmes a year.

Furthermore, such production requirements, even when spread over one grade per annum, have a cumulative effect on transmission times. Five radio or television programmes a week, each of 30 minutes length, require 2½ hours transmission time for one grade and one subject. To cover six grades, 15 hours a week would be required for one subject. Given that there are limited times during the day when programmes can be broadcast to schools, it would be difficult on one channel to accommodate more than two subjects over six grades.

A different concern is the educational limitation of direct, centralised teaching. While some subjects like mathematics, which may have common, standard learning objectives, may lend themselves more to direct teaching, other subject areas do not. For instance, development of communication skills, such as language and imaginative writing, demands more individual and less 'convergent' responses from learners and, consequently, far greater interaction with the teacher and other children in the class. Above all, though, direct teaching ignores the social role of education. Teaching is not *just* about the transfer of information and the development of common cognitive skills. Many educators see personal relationships and social contact as an integral part of the educational process (e.g. see Champness and Young, 1980). It is a legitimate concern that educational media, and in particular direct teaching through television and radio, could lead to narrow, mechanistic instruction more suited to robots than to children. Furthermore, loading the whole curriculum on to television or radio means that the media cannot be used selectively, concentrating on those teaching functions for which they are more suited and leaving other functions to books or personal interaction between teachers and children.

It will also probably come as no surprise to learn that some of the direct teaching projects ran into trouble with teachers. In El Salvador, after a favourable start, the teachers showed increasing hostility towards the television reform which culminated in a two-month strike; the Telesecundaria teachers in Mexico had a running battle with the educational authorities for a more appropriate job classification and better salaries.

Lastly, Lyle (1982), in looking back on the development of a number of television and radio projects first reported in 1967, noticed the movement of many of the original projects from direct teaching to using television and radio to supplement or enrich the work of the classroom teacher. He also noted that the more control teachers had over how and when to use television material, the greater the chance of its utilisation. He also commented that the provision of material on cassettes greatly increased the control that teachers have, which in turn leads to greater utilisation of television material, a point noted earlier with regard to schools television in Britain.

It is, however, too simple to dismiss direct teaching through broadcast television as an inferior form of education. In many developing countries, *conventional* teaching is mechanical, based on rote-learning and accurate recall of facts or procedures which are often totally irrelevant to the children and the society in which they live. Teachers are often barely more educated than the children they are teaching; the teachers will have received little instruction in either educational theory or practice; they will have very few resources, such as textbooks or equipment, at their disposal. The provision of cassette machines is out of the question for many of the poorer countries. In such circumstances, direct teaching through television and radio may not only be more directly effective but can also provide appropriate models of teaching for the teachers. Teachers' hostility has been due less to direct teaching and more to poor working conditions and low salaries. In El Salvador, teachers had to take larger classes and work longer hours with no increase in salary. In Mexico, the Telesecundaria teachers were drawn from primary schools but, despite teaching at a secondary school level, they were being paid less than conventional secondary school teachers. In other direct teaching projects, such as Nicaragua, more care was taken with the teachers.

Direct teaching in fact does not necessarily mean that social learning and group work are excluded. Most direct teaching by television or radio is followed by periods where pupils and teachers work together in more conventional ways, reinforcing and developing material contained in the programmes. The ETV Maranhão project indeed is structured so that there is a great deal of social interaction, peer-group dynamics and pupil leadership. Each group elects a leader and a rapporteur on a monthly, rotating basis. After each programme, students work individually or in groups of six or seven. Group leaders are expected to pose questions or suggest activities to be carried out by individuals in the group. Although there are monitors, these are not qualified teachers, and each monitor covers several groups. Thus the system depends on a good deal of discipline from the secondary pupils. Oliveira (1979) reports that although discipline problems exist, they are fewer than in conventional schools in Brazil.

One major reservation about this use of broadcasting in education stems from unease about the political motivation behind such projects, rather than from doubts about their educational effectiveness in terms of performance and costs. They can easily be seen as palliatives for problems which need much more radical solutions. It is exceedingly dangerous to think that even a massive injection of external finance and technical assistance for broadcast-based curriculum reform will make much of a dent on the problems of developing countries. For instance, five years after the first group of students had progressed entirely through the new system in El Salvador, I watched on my television set newsfilm of government troops shooting down those very students on the steps of the cathedral in San Salvador. Whatever else the most thoroughgoing attempt to use television for national curriculum reform may have achieved, it did not touch the underlying social and economic problems of El Salvador. Such projects cannot substantially compensate for the problems caused by poverty, inequitable distribution of wealth, oppressive government and unequal international trade relations.

For politicians and administrators though who have to work within the existing socio-economic framework of their country, direct teaching by television – or better still by radio – is still clearly an option worth considering. Direct teaching by television and radio can assist curriculum reform, can increase enrolments and can raise educational standards, at possibly lower cost than conventional alternatives. To do this, however, very demanding conditions have to be met, and the long-term financial implications can be serious. Lastly, adequate long-term national financing is essential, and the teachers ultimately will need to feel that they have control over when and how television and radio are to be used if the innovation is to survive and lead to long-standing educational improvements.

SUMMARISING THE EVIDENCE

Evaluating broadcasting in the formal school system is not helped by the unevenness of research. While there has been extensive evaluation of the use of broadcasting for curriculum reform in developing countries, the vast majority of schools broadcasting in Europe and North America has been unresearched. A good deal of the research that has been carried out on schools broadcasting has been amateurish, or focused on a very narrow range of information, such as providing utilisation statistics or identifying the possible audience for likely new series. There has been very little research into what can best be learned through television or radio, into the most effective ways of designing programmes to meet specific learning objectives, or into the programme design requirements for specialist target audiences. Although formative research is an important component of the Agency for Instructional Television's approach in the USA, this is an exception in schools broadcasting. Many of the programmes in Britain that have been systematically researched after transmission were seen to have suffered from a lack of formative research. There was for instance often inadequate understanding of the abilities or needs of target groups and mistaken assumptions about the likely responses to the programmes. Although again there are exceptions, in most countries the broadcasting organisations are largely responsible for the lack of research. Few have carried out research themselves into the learning impact of schools broadcasts. The main exceptions are AIT in the USA, the Swedish Educational Broadcasting Company and the IBA in Britain, through its fellowship scheme, though even this needs to be strengthened through better research training and supervision for the fellows, most of whom are seconded schoolteachers. Broadcasting organisations have also done little to encourage universities to research into this area. Regular contacts between university departments and broadcasters over a continuous period are needed if university-based research is to be relevant, appropriately designed and useful. Research is needed not only to help broadcasters to make more effective programmes, but also to help teachers and teacher trainers to make better use of broadcasting in the schools.

It is a great pity that more research has not been done. The lack of research makes evaluation difficult but, more importantly, research, when it has been carried out professionally and in collaboration with broadcasters, has often indicated what needs to be done to improve the effectiveness of programmes.

Despite the lack of research, several conclusions can be drawn.

Firstly, broadcasting can be and has been used effectively for a wide range of purposes in the formal education system. Secondly, in Britain at least, school broadcasting is very extensively used by teachers and pupils. Indeed, there is probably greater use today of television broadcasts in British schools than at any time previously. Teachers in Britain clearly prefer programmes that enrich and supplement their teaching. It has been difficult to find evidence in Britain that this kind of programming has had much direct effect on learning, although studies overseas have been more positive.

One reason for the growing use of television in British schools is the increasing availability of video recording and playback facilities. These facilities also make it possible for programme materials to be used much more specifically and effectively as learning resources, more fully integrated with and central to the teaching than enrichment programming. This approach in schools though is still comparatively rare, and requires different programme design strategies, provision of adequate recording and playback equipment, easier access to and better knowledge of pre-recorded material, and better training of teachers in the use of media as learning resources. Copying restrictions on general programming are a major obstacle to greater use of television as a learning resource. These restrictions make it virtually impossible to use general programming legally in schools. Despite a recent report for the government on copyright issues by the Whitfield Committee, the government has chosen to ignore completely the educational issues regarding copyright of broadcast television programmes. It is not surprising therefore that there is a good deal of illegal use of general programmes in schools.

The research indicates that television could also play a vital role in meeting special needs within schools but it rarely manages to do so. Programme strategies are not usually adapted to the learning needs of such special target groups. Formative research, essential to successful programme-making in this area, is usually not done. Producers have often failed to make sufficient and appropriate use of specialist advice. This is a high-risk area, requiring greater skill and resources for often smaller audiences, but an area where broadcasting could make a major contribution to the formal school system.

Direct teaching by broadcasting is found almost exclusively in developing countries. When used in this way, television and radio have been associated with clear improvements in the educational service. However, for such probjects to be successful, very demanding conditions have had to be met. Although direct teaching projects have been successful in performance terms, there are still considerable doubts about their wider educational, economic and political implications.

In contrast, there seems to be less controversy about the value of television and radio for in-service teacher training. Large number of teachers – in both developed and developing countries – have received further education and training through these media. Quite often, though, broadcasting is only a part – and sometimes a minor part – of multi-media courses for teachers. Moreover, teachers are already well-educated and so have probably developed sufficient learning skills to be successful independent learners. They are often also highly motivated to succeed through such courses, since successful completion usually leads to higher qualifications, higher status and higher pay.

It can be seen then that television and radio can be successfully used for a wide variety of purposes, in a wide variety of contexts. However, in order for broadcasting to be used successfully, certain conditions must be met. Many of these conditions – such as the motivation of the target group, training of teachers in the use of media, the availability of equipment – lie outside the programmes themselves. Other conditions – such as the structuring of the programmes, the use made of formative research and specialist advisers – are very much under the direct control of programme producers. There is a good deal of evidence to suggest that the conditions necessary for effective programming in this area are frequently not met, although, in Britain at least, the programmes are heavily used. An end-of-term report on school broadcasting then might be: 'Should not be misled by the apparently good performance so far. Could do *much* better – and will need to, given next term's challenges.'

4

Non-formal basic education: strategic roles for broadcasting

The last two chapters discussed the role of broadcasting in the formal education system. Although there is a great deal of variety in the way television and radio have been used in this sector, formal education is a relatively unified concept. It covers the full-time education of children, adolescents, and young men and women, taught in groups in schools or colleges by trained full-time teaching staff. In contrast, non-formal education is a bit like the old advertisement for a popular British Sunday newspaper: 'All human life is here'!

Non-formal education is concerned with improving the personal, social and work life of individuals. In this sense, non-formal education aims to help individuals make practical changes in their daily life and personal development in terms of their own goals and wishes. This means, as Ingle (1974) has pointed out, being more concerned with helping an individual to solve his or her own problems than with transmitting a particular curriculum content. It is therefore by definition more 'learner-centred' than 'teacher' or 'subject' centred.

Schramm (1977) considers distance learning institutions such as the Open University, and out-of-school programmes which provide school-equivalent qualifications for adults, to be part of the formal education system. I disagree. I believe it is more useful to include these two 'out-of-school' forms of adult education in the non-formal sector because they differ radically in their functions, use of media, structures, age ranges and teaching methods from the formal school or college sector, and share many characteristics with other projects or programmes found in the non-formal sector.

Although non-formal education is 'learner-based', *external organisation* of learning, by others than the learner, is essential to the concept of non-formal education. Some individual or institution provides guidance and a structure to the learning experience. Without such a structure, all human activity becomes part of non-formal education and the definition becomes too broad to be useful. This limitation on the definition is important because there is a great deal of unstructured, incidental learning from the mass media. However, where learning is not organised or structured as part of an externally guided, deliberate learning experience, then it falls outside my definition of non-formal education. This is why this book does not deal with the impact of general broadcasting on social attitudes, people's conception of the world, etc., as important as these influences are.

I also make a distinction between basic and continuing non-formal education. Basic non-formal education depends very little on prior knowledge or skills acquired through the formal education system; continuing education builds upon knowledge and skills acquired at school or college, or seeks to extend the school or college curriculum through non-formal approaches.

Too much importance should not be attached to these labels. Because of the delightful variety and inconsistency of human activities, there is a great deal of overlap and organisational variety in education. Nevertheless, there are clearly major differences between a seven-year-old child watching a maths television programme with other children and a teacher in school, and a forty-year-old peasant farmer listening on his own at home to an early morning radio programme on the use of fertilisers. These differences in context have major implications for the design and likely effectiveness of broadcasting in education, and must be taken into consideration, so some form of classification is essential.

THE NEEDS

There has been a rapid expansion of non-formal and adult education throughout the world in the last twenty years. Indeed, although the scale of the problem differs, the reasons for this expansion are similar for both developed and developing countries.

It can be seen from Table 1 (p. 9) that there are five broad purposes in non-formal education to which broadcasting has, wittingly or unwittingly, been applied. Broadcasting has been used to *reduce* educational *inequalities* existing *prior* to entry to the formal education system; to *reduce inadequacies after* formal education has been completed; to meet *new needs* arising during adult life; to stimulate *social action* and community or national development; and to raise *political consciousness*.

Because there are important differences between these aims, they need more detailed examination before considering the specific role of broadcasting.

Reducing inequalities prior to entry to the formal education system

Children do not start equal in school. Reports by Coleman *et al.* (1966) in the USA and by Plowden (Gt Britain: Department of Education and Science, 1967) in the United Kingdom revealed not only marked differences in pupils' performance on entry to the formal school system but also the influence of extra-school factors such as home background and economic circumstances on children's performance prior to and during school. There is strong evidence from psychological research that the first five years of life – *before* formal schooling begins – are crucial for the intellectual, emotional and social development of children.

In 1966 it was estimated that it would cost US \$2.75 billion a year to provide all American children aged four and five with a school-based education. Although in the United Kingdom about 60 per cent of children aged three and four receive some form of play-group, school or nursery education, there are still many children in Britain who have no prior organised educational experience before their entrance at five to the formal school system. There are, in any case, strong psychological arguments in favour of basing educational activities in the home during these very early years of childhood.

Reducing inadequacies subsequent to the formal education system

In 1979 72 per cent of pupils in the United Kingdom left school at sixteen (the minimum school leaving age). Of those that left school in 1979, 13 per cent left with no educational qualifications whatsoever and 75 per cent left with less than five 'O' level subjects. Less than 7 per cent of an age group go on to study for a degree at a university (Great Britain: DES, 1983). No exact figures exist about the number of adult illiterates in the United Kingdom, but Haviland (1973) estimated that there were about two million adults with a reading age of nine years or less (i.e. either semi-illiterate or illiterate). The Russell report (Great Britain: DES, 1973) estimated that about 60 per cent of all adults in England and Wales had left school at the age of fourteen or earlier. From the same report it can be calculated that in 1970 just under 10 per cent of people aged over fifteen (then the minimum leaving age) were following any form of 'conventional' education after leaving school (i.e. enrolled for full-time or part-time day or evening courses, or attending colleges of education or university). For most people in Britain, 'education' ends the day they leave school.

At the same time, priority in public spending on education in the United Kingdom is heavily biased towards provision of formal education. Furthermore, resources are concentrated on those receiving advanced forms of formal education, namely, those who stay on as long as possible in the formal education system. For instance, in the academic year 1978–79, £370 was spent on each primary school pupil, £511 on each secondary school pupil below the minimum school-leaving age, £889 on each pupil staying on at school and £2,575 on each university student in Britain. Comparison with students in non-formal education is difficult because their study is part-time rather than full-time and can extend over a long period. However, in 1978–79 £115 was spent on each student in further or adult education and £820 on each Open University student. Clearly, a massive increase in numbers taking up adult education as traditionally offered through evening classes would require an equally massive increase in public expenditure or an increase in student-paid fees to impractical levels.

In developing countries, the need for adult and further education beyond school and college is even greater. Despite laws requiring the provision of compulsory education at least at primary level, there are often more children out of school than in. The vast majority of those that do receive any form of school education leave by the age of twelve or thirteen. Even in those countries aiming at universal primary and secondary education, it will take between ten and twenty years before children entering the school system can

TABLE 8

ADULT ILLITERACY RATES IN A SELECTED NUMBER OF COUNTRIES

Country	Age Range	No. of illiterates	% of adult population
Angola	All	4,020,000	97
Brazil	15+	15,645,000	24
Egypt	10+	15,611,000	56
France	15+	1,030,000	2
India	15+	211,639,000	67
Japan	15+	1,426,000	2
Mexico	15+	6,694,000	26
Nigeria	15+	17,980,000	85
Spain	15+	2,413,000	10
USA	14+	1,435,000	1

Source: UNESCO, 1980.

begin to make an impact on society. Education aimed at adults on the other hand can have immediate impact.

The size of the problem can be assessed by Table 8, which gives figures for illiteracy rates for adults and adolescents in a selected number of countries.

For developing countries it is just as important to help adults read and write, improve their crops, introduce better community and domestic health practices and aim at self-reliance, as to provide a formal school system for children.

Meeting new needs in adult life

Even successful full-time formal education systems cannot satisfy fully the demands of modern industrialised societies. Working adults more and more need to keep up with new development in their trade or business and to develop new skills as jobs change or are lost. Secondly, given current prospects for unemployment, early retirement and increased longevity of life, there is a rapid increase in the amount of leisure time – forced or unforced – available to many adults in developed countries.

However, the *demand* for continuing education comes mainly from those who are already well-educated. Rogers (1977) estimated that of those leaving school at the minimum leaving age, 75 per cent have *never* taken up any formal form of adult education (i.e. enrolling for a course of studies) after leaving school.

There are then two distinct target groups for adult education: those already well-qualified, who actively seek out further education opportunities; and those less well-qualified, who might benefit even more but who are turned off by conventional forms of education.

Even though there is a relatively low take-up of conventional further education activities by the less qualified educationally, many are still interested in learning or self-development. Tough (1968) estimated that the average adult (in Canada) spends thirteen hours a week on sustained, deliberate efforts to learn. These activities though are generally outside the conventional further education provision, taking the form of self-directed leisure and hobby activities.

Social action and community development

In recent years, in both developed and developing countries, there has been a growing recognition that education alone is not enough and that there is a need to train or educate people to take direct action themselves to improve their own situation or that of those around them. In this type of activity there is less concern with providing formal education or instruction – although this is often a prerequisite – as with getting people to take appropriate action themselves, or to take advantage of existing services.

Raising political consciousness

Social action and community development programmes tend to aim either at helping people to make the best of their situation or to improve their conditions within the existing social and political framework. However, there are instances – still very rare – of projects that are much more radical in intent. These aim to mobilise the people to change the fabric and structure of their society. Once again, instruction or education is usually a necessary prerequisite for such political activity. Sometimes it is the government itself which aims to mobilise the people by appealing directly to them for action to overcome opposition to government policies from powerful elites, local headmen or landowners. Occasionally, non-governmental agencies attempt to raise political consciousness, such as certain radical Roman Catholic priests who have helped create an organised movement of poor farmers (the campesinos) in Latin American countries. Even more rarely, local communities may themselves be the originators of such programmes, attempting through community action to promote both political awareness and changes in government policies.

The difference between social action and raising political awareness is not a sharp one, except that the latter tends to occur when the former fails. For instance, helping young people to find employment or to use their unemployed time constructively would be social action; getting them to demonstrate or riot for more jobs would be raising political awareness. This distinction will become crucial when considering the role of broadcasting in these areas.

Social action and raising political awareness are more concerned with using education directly as a means of social *change* and development, whereas the other three broad purposes are more concerned with extending education *within* the existing social and political framework. Thus the first three purposes tend towards social *cohesion*, while the latter two tend towards social *change*.

Perhaps because the needs are greater and more difficult to meet through state interventions and financing, broadcasting has been used to reach an extraordinarily wide range of target audiences and subject matter in the non-formal education area. This range can be seen from Table 1 (p. 9). For the rest of this chapter and the next, I will concentrate on broadcasting's role in the more basic forms of non-formal education.

CHILDREN'S PROGRAMMING

Although children's programming, at least in Britain, is administratively separate from educational broadcasting, it often has a strong educational role to play. There are two types of children's programmes relevant to non-formal education. There are programmes with clear and deliberate teaching objectives aimed specifically at out-of-school children; and there are programmes of a more general nature, also aimed at out-of-school children but with indirect educational, social and cultural goals.

The most famous example of the first type is 'Sesame Street'. The main aim of 'Sesame Street' was to 'use popular television techniques to promote the intellectual and cultural growth of pre-schoolers, particularly disadvantaged pre-schoolers' (Cooney, 1968). Children's Television Workshop (CTW) produced several series of 'Sesame Street' programmes aimed at children aged three to five, with special emphasis on four-year-olds. The programmes were designed to be viewed at home or at nursery school, and initially were intended to stand alone without support materials (although subsequently a whole range of educational and commercial products were produced as 'spin-offs' from the programmes). The televised lessons each stood independently, although there was a good deal of deliberate repetition from programme to programme. While the programmes were designed to appeal to a wide variety of children, they were set in an inner-city ghetto and used primarily non-white actors. The programmes thus were meant to appeal particularly to children living in deprived inner-city areas, and to promote a basic philosophy of social and racial integration.

'Sesame Street' has been running now without a break, and in essentially the same format, since 1969 in the United States, receiving national coverage and high penetration of the target audiences. Programmes have been broadcast in more or less the original format in over forty other countries throughout the world. In the United Kingdom they have been transmitted by several of the commercial television companies. In another nineteen countries, at least, foreign language adaptations have been broadcast, either based primarily on the original US material but with a specially dubbed sound-track in the native language, or in a co-production format, with half the material taken from the original US material and the other half specially produced locally in the adapting country (Palmer, Chen and Lesser, 1976). Since its beginning, 'Sesame Street' has been intensively and continuously researched and evaluated.

'Sesame Street' programmes have clearly defined behavioural objectives, a publicly stated social purpose, a deliberate use of commercial television techniques for direct teaching, extensive formative research and summative evaluation and a lavish production budget. All this contrasts sharply with British-produced programmes for this age group, such as 'Listen with Mother' (radio), 'Playschool' and 'Jackanory' (television). The BBC refused to show 'Sesame Street', on the grounds that it was culturally alien and unsuitable for British children. This does not mean though that British-produced programmes for this age group have no educational or cultural objectives, even though such objectives may be indirect and subtle.

For instance, Hall (1982) argues that children's programming is an important 'socialising' agency in that it presents models of social behaviour. For Hall, a significant element in BBC's children's programming is the emphasis in the programmes of belonging to a family; the family is portrayed as the basic unit of social integration. 'Playschool' – a programme for the under-fives – symbolises in its opening sequence of a house with windows the warm and supportive environment of the home, from whose secure base ventures into the outside world, through one of the house's windows, can safely be made. Also, programmes such as 'Playschool' are much closer to the traditional nursery school approach in Britain of discovery learning than the direct teaching approach favoured by 'Sesame Street'. According to Hall, 'Playschool's' predominant model is that of the middle-class family unit. One can summarise the contrasts Hall makes between 'Playschool' and 'Sesame Street' as follows:

'Playschool'	*'Sesame Street'*
Children do not appear in programme	Children active in programme
Rural; home-based	Urban; street-based
Middle-class	Poor urban class
Anglo-Saxon participants	Ethnically mixed
Adults as parent figures	Adults as friends/fantasy figures
Gentle pace	Aggressive/fast moving/jokey
Teaches by stealth	Direct, didactic

Each series, Hall argues, reflects the implicit values of its culture even when not consciously attempting to do so. However, it should be noted that the objectives of the two series are quite different: 'Sesame Street' is deliberately oriented towards the educationally disadvantaged whereas 'Playschool' has no such obvious social purpose.

Hall also argues that BBC children's programming reflects a carefully staged and monitored process of development, of becoming socialised. 'Blue Peter', a programme for children primarily in the five- to eleven-year-old range, places heavy emphasis on caring for others through appeals for underprivileged children in developing countries, love of animals and so on. Heavy emphasis is placed on liberal values of caring, empathy and doing good. By the young teens, though, programmes such as 'Grange Hill' (about youngsters in a state comprehensive school) begin to construct the world as young people see it rather than as adults *hope* they see it. In 'Grange Hill', the conflicts and tensions of the real world that youngsters find themselves in become portrayed, one dimension of which is the tussle between belonging to a family and seeking independence.

If Hall's analysis is correct, children's programming reflects the prevailing 'established' values and mores of a society and does so in a highly structured and subtle manner. That there is a strong educational and socialising motive behind much of children's programming in Britain cannot be denied. Whether such cultural influences are in fact effective, given other commercial and social pressures and the influences of other kinds of broadcasts seen by children, is another matter.

One BBC series, 'You and Me', is aimed at four and five-year-olds. All five-year-olds attend school but nearly a half of four-year-olds do not receive any form of formal education. 'You and Me' was therefore scheduled and designed so that it could be used both in infant and nursery schools and by children watching at home, on their own or with a parent. These programmes did have more specific educational objectives than general children's programming, aiming to introduce early mathematical experiences, and experiences leading to reading readiness, as well as being concerned with the language and social development of young children. Like 'Sesame Street', 'You and Me' also aimed to help children whose backgrounds 'result in a restricted use of language'. The programmes were carefully structured, with frequent repetition of main points and with audience participation. Thus these programmes came somewhere between 'Sesame Street' and 'Playschool' in educational approach and use of television techniques.

BASIC ADULT EDUCATION

Basic adult education is a major field of study in its own right with a great deal of argument and controversy about objectives, target groups and methods, rapidly equalling mediaeval theology in the passionate niceties of its self-analysis. At root, though, basic adult education is about adult literacy, numeracy and social coping skills, although some (like myself) would extend it to include basic school curricula for adults.

Broadcasting has been used extensively in support of adult literacy. One of the first projects to use television for adult literacy was 'Telescuola' in Southern Italy, whose course 'Non e mai troppo tardi' ('It's never too late') began in 1960. UNESCO organised a study of forty countries that were using radio and/or television in support of adult literacy programmes (Maddison, 1974). The study found that there had been a rapid expansion in the use of broadcasting for adult literacy in the 1960s, and even by the mid 1970s this had not yet peaked. The movement spread to Britain when the BBC helped initiate a major adult literacy campaign in Britain between 1974 and 1979, and this campaign and the effectiveness of broadcasting in it will be examined fully in the next chapter.

Links between broadcasting organisations and other organisations working locally have proved to be essential in adult literacy projects. The International Institute for Adult Literacy Methods (1974), based at the time in Iran, compared broadcast-supported literacy projects to:

> a military operation in which radio and television represent the artillery to prepare the ground for advance and the infantry (personal teachers) then move in to consolidate the positions taken.

Programmes on functional numeracy are rarer, more recent and less well supported by the infantry. A Yorkshire Television series, 'Make It Count', was aimed at helping those who did not have even the simplest arithmetical skills, such as being able to check change or calculate the cost of five gallons of petrol (never mind converting it metrically). Stringer (1979) found in a study of the series that there were many people, from all walks of life in Britain, who had extreme difficulties of this kind. Stringer claimed that the demand for numeracy tuition is at least as great as the demand for adult literacy tuition in Britain. However, 'Make It Count' never received the extent of support from central and local government which was given to the adult literacy campaign and consequently there were few links between programmes and courses in local centres, although the project is being revived by Channel 4.

Social coping skills (or life skills) are those basic skills required to deal with the complexities of modern society. They are what one needs to know to seek employment, to claim rights and benefits, and to protect oneself from excessive commercialism and over-zealous, lazy, or bungling bureaucracy. For some adult educators, coping skills include literacy and numeracy; others see coping skills as more than just literacy and numeracy. For instance, some courses aim to improve people's everyday language beyond basic literacy, to help them cope with the more complex language of bureaucracy as a first step towards seeking benefits or obtaining justice. Danish Radio's multi-media project 'Danish for Adults', which used radio, television, course books and group work, is such an example.

During the late 1970s and early 1980s, no doubt as a consequence of economic recession and unemployment, there has been a considerable increase in European projects aimed at helping educationally disadvantaged people to develop coping skills, either directly or indirectly, and television and radio have played a key role in many of these projects. The Dutch Open School project, like 'Danish for Adults', is a complex project, but part of it is built around themes such as home decorating or obtaining a playground for children. One aim is for each group to determine its own themes and priorities for study (which caused difficulties in choosing appropriate topics for the television and radio programmes). The Dutch educational television company TELEAC produces the television programmes. These deal with a common spelling problem each week, information on the different kinds of adult education available, items on politics and justice, and some English-language teaching. NOS, another Dutch broadcasting company, is responsible for the radio programmes (Vellekoop, 1982).

In Britain, there have been several broadcast series dealing with coping skills. One of the first was 'Living Decisions in Family and Community', a BBC radio series of twenty-five programmes launched in 1973 which aimed to 'examine the processes of decision-making in everyday life and to improve students' ability to make appropriate decisions in matters affecting their lives' (Stephens, 1976). This course too was strongly linked with provision from other adult education agencies. 'Living Decisions' was followed by another BBC radio series of a similar kind in 1976, called 'What Right Have You Got?', which aimed to give a broad overview of the main rights and responsibilities of the individual in everyday situations (Salkeld, 1979). All these coping courses and projects have been aimed primarily at those with low levels of education, i.e. below school-leaving qualifications, and all seem to have bent over backwards to avoid an academic approach.

In Northern Europe and North America, broadcast series tend to use topics and approaches specially designed for adults. However, there are series aimed at providing adults with formal school qualifications based on curricula similar to those found in schools. In the 1960s, BBC Radio collaborated with the National Extension College (a non-profit-making correspondence college), to provide broadcast lessons to support adult students taking 'O' and 'A' level English examinations.

While such projects are now pretty unusual in Britain, in Spain and several Latin American countries broadcasting is more commonly aimed at helping adults to acquire basic school qualifications. Radio ECCA, for instance, is based in the Canary Islands, but also, through collaborative arrangements, provides courses in Spain itself and in nine Latin American countries. These courses use a combination of radio, print-materials and face-to-face tuition (Cepeda, 1982). In Brazil, a special examination, the 'Madureza', is available for adults seeking the equivalent of the secondary school-leaving certificate (a qualification essential for many types of employment). The 'Minerva' project was set up in Brazil to produce a radio-based programme of studies leading up to the 'Madureza' (linked again to local face-to-face tuition where this could be provided). These programmes are broadcast throughout the whole of Brazil (Oliveira and Orivel, 1982). Similar uses of broadcasting can be found in Malawi, the Dominican Republic and several other African and Latin American countries.

While the need for a wide variety of basic adult education might be seen as a damning indictment of the formal education system, very large numbers of people are apparently lacking these basic skills, in Britain and most other countries. The broadcast courses provided so far have hardly touched the massive numbers in need of basic educational skills, and broadcasting would seem to have a long-lasting and major role to play in this area.

SOCIAL ACTION PROGRAMMING

As the name suggests, social action programming aims to motivate the viewer or listener into action, or to participate in activities beyond the more conventional study activities of educational broadcasting. Social action broadcasting is characterised by the following features:

(1) use of production techniques from popular television, including drama;
(2) use, wherever possible, of 'peak' or popular viewing and listening times;
(3) provision of telephone numbers or addresses for further contact on transmission;
(4) follow-up contacts handled by a non-broadcasting agency;
(5) recruitment of volunteers for follow-up work;
(6) a wider range of topics or content areas than in conventional educational broadcasting;
(7) programmes often made by other than educational broadcasting departments.

Not all these characteristics are always found, of course, but the essential element is the use of *other* agencies for follow-up work.

The idea of social action broadcasting goes back many years. Pease (1983) describes how BBC radio provided programmes – and wireless sets – for unemployment clubs in 1934 covering topics such as how to keep rabbits in the back garden. Even the Prince of Wales gave them a talk (but not on rabbits). Social action broadcasting has become increasingly common in Britain since 1974, partly stimulated by the early 'Werwinkel' project in Holland. Examples in Britain are Granada Television's 'Reports Action', Thames Television's 'Help!', and BBC television's 'Roadshow'. Other types of broadcasting that might be included, if the term is broadly defined, are phone-in or advice-giving programmes on radio, and charitable fund-raising appeals such as Thames Television's 'Telethon'.

Perhaps the most typical, or, from the voluntary organisations' point of view, the most notorious, is Granada's 'Reports Action'. Broadcast at 6.00 p.m. on a Sunday, each half-hour programme deals usually with three topics. After a short, sharp introduction of an organisation's work in the field, viewers are encouraged to ring or write for more information after or during the programme itself. Use is often made of specially manned switchboards or a central postal address. Switchboards are usually manned by volunteers. Information about the callers – usually their name and address and telephone number – is then collected and passed on to the relevant agency which then takes responsibility for follow-up action.

In a very perceptive article, McCron (1981) notes that social action broadcasting raises fundamental questions about the role and function of broadcasting in education. McCron uses an analogy less military than the Iranian's but equally apt. He likens broadcasting to the shop-window, and the support facility to the shop itself. He argues that such an analogy reflects a fundamental dilemma facing broadcasters. Social action broadcasting is capable of reaching much larger audiences and, even more importantly, reaching a much wider range of audience than conventional educational broadcasting. But while it can get attention, broadcasting is relatively poor at sustaining or capitalising on that initial interest. Consequently, broadcasting becomes dependent on other agencies for its full impact. This means though that broadcasters have to become much more involved in administration, publicity and publishing initiatives which, in the words of the 'On the Move' project leader:

> strain the traditional definitions of our role, and indeed the legal and constitutional frameworks democratically established to contain broadcasting. (Hargreaves, 1980)

The effectiveness of social action programming clearly depends very much on the planning and organisation of follow-up services. The experience gained from the Adult Literacy project in Britain, and difficulties caused to voluntary organisations by lack of prior consultation by producers of some of the other social action series, has led to the establishment of a permanent organisation, Broadcast Support Services. This provides liaison between broadcasters and voluntary organisations, although it is usually left to the individual voluntary organisations themselves to provide support for specific programmes. It is still the broadcasters who decide priorities, content and approach for social action broadcasts.

A very different form of social action programming is where groups seeking social action create their own programmes, independently of broadcasting organisations. The advent of Channel 4 in Britain offers access to a national transmission network by independent programme makers. As a result, several co-operatives of voluntary organisations have been formed to produce their own programmes deliberately designed to link in with the support services that these voluntary agencies can provide. Examples are the International Broadcasting Trust, which is concerned with promoting education about the plight and needs of developing countries, and Mediscreen, a group of voluntary organisations concerned with a range of disabilities. However, it is still the prerogative of Channel 4 to decide which programmes and agencies will be funded and which programmes will be transmitted.

To see the potential of fully independent production and distribution, one must look to Canada for what has become known as 'the Fogo Island Process'. Fogo Island is situated off the north coast of Newfoundland. With the decline of the local timber and fishing industries, the more remote coastal communities of Newfoundland suffer a good deal of poverty and hardship. In the 1960s, because of the difficulties of providing alternative local employment and essential health, education and social services, the federal government in Ottawa decided to resettle on the mainland a number of the communities located around the coast of Newfoundland and Labrador, including those living on Fogo Island. At about the same time, the National Film Board of Canada had been experimenting with the idea of providing 16 mm film-making equipment to remote communities or minority groups, training them how to use the equipment, then letting the communities themselves make their own programmes about their own communities. Fogo Island was one of the communities given film equipment.

The result was remarkable. The islanders did not want to be resettled on the mainland. They made a film about their way of life, what was needed for them to become economically self-sufficient and the services that were lacking and needed. The film played a major part in the islanders' successful campaign to reverse the government's decision. This 'process' is still operational in Newfoundland. The Extension Service of the Memorial University at St John's organises and finances field officers located in about a dozen of the more remote communities in Newfoundland and Labrador. Most of these communities have video equipment either provided by the University or bought by themselves, and access, where necessary, to production facilities provided by the University. Video is used by the local people for a wide variety of purposes, such as recording high school graduation ceremonies or local weddings. Occasionally, though, video is used to bring to the attention of provincial or federal government the needs of the local community. For instance, in Hawkes Bay an adult literacy course was to be closed down but the decision was reversed when the relevant Minister saw – through the locally produced programme – the effects this would have on the local community. Video tends to be used as the last resort when all the more conventional and constitutional channels have failed.

Community use of broadcasting for social action *could* grow rapidly. The technology is making it easier for non-professionals to communicate effectively and cheaply through broadcasting, particularly at a local level. Even a national broadcasting organisation such as the BBC has given access to groups to make their own programmes through its 'Open Door' series (although even then selection of groups, technical presentation and even editorial guidance is still primarily in the hands of the professional broadcasters). Channel 4 in Britain also in theory opens up access to more groups, although it remains to be seen whether pressure from the commercial television companies and the advertisers that finance Channel 4 will in practice restrict the number and range of programmes made by independent organisations. It is ominous that within six weeks of Channel 4 opening, there were calls from the major commercial television companies for a major change of policy, with greater use of repeats from the commercial companies' own programmes to increase Channel 4's ratings. Local radio broadcasting (and over the next few years, cable television) provide other opportunities, but once again commercialism and ratings seem to be the dominant factors (see Wright, 1980 and Booth, 1980, on the failure of local radio to develop community use fully).

There is no doubt that community use of broadcasting, particularly at a local level, has great potential for social action and the self-development of adults; where – as in Newfoundland – this potential has been allowed to develop, it has proved very effective. It must be said, however, that community use of broadcasting is extremely rare. Commercialism, government caution, and the control of all broadcasting by the major broadcasting organisations or commercial entertainment conglomerates seems more likely to prevent effective community use of broadcasting, even at a local level, in most countries.

RURAL PROGRAMMING

One of the most popular radio programmes in Kenya is 'Zaa Na Uwatunze', a soap opera about a mother with sixteen children, and her running battle with her hidebound, drunken, ignorant husband (Coldevin, 1980). Although presented in popular format, the programmes in fact skilfully present health and nutrition messages to a mass audience, as the English translation of the title ('Birth and Childcare') suggests. Radio and television have been used for rural programming not only in developing countries but frequently in developed countries as well.

With scattered rural populations, it becomes difficult or expensive to provide the same level of educational facilities that can be provided in large cities. Professional people are often reluctant to work in isolated, rural areas, which consequently often suffer from a great shortage of qualified teachers, doctors and community workers. There is a world-wide tendency for the more academically able or ambitious youngsters to leave rural areas for what they believe to be better educational and work opportunities in the big cities.

Because of low population densities and shortages of qualified people, those who stay suffer from a lack of convenient local further education opportunities. Yet, in many countries, the majority of people still live and work in rural areas because the economy depends on agriculture and mining as the main sources of wealth. It is not surprising therefore that rural programming has been one of the major educational uses for broadcasting, particularly radio. There are of course often major differences in the coverage of radio and television in rural areas, so it is necessary to treat them separately.

Radio

Jamison and McAnany (1978) identify two main ways of using radio for rural development: open broadcasting and regular listening groups.

Open broadcasting

Open broadcasting relies entirely on the broadcasts to carry the message. They are 'message-centred; typically reach people in their homes; (and) do not attempt to teach complicated behaviour, but rather to motivate and get across modest amounts of information . . .' (Jamison and McAnany, 1978). For instance, spot announcements, using the same format and techniques of radio advertising, have been used in Ecuador to get over simple health education messages, repeating the same short message ten to fifteen times a day over a period of a year in between popular entertainment programmes (Gunter and Theroux, 1977).

However, the most common technique is the use of drama (a single programme) or soap opera (a longer-running series) to implant education and development messages. Although 'Zaa Na Uwatunze' is an example from a developing country, British listeners will be familiar with one of the earliest programmes to use this technique: 'The Archers', a fifteen-minute daily programme about ordinary country folk, was originally created in 1953 not only to entertain but also to mould the attitudes of farmers and their families towards the major changes needed in post-war farming practice in Britain (Mason, 1954). This series is still running thirty years later, with the 'grandchildren' of the original characters now running their 'own' farms. The programme has a regular audience of 1½–2 million listeners and, while its educational purpose is now less deliberate and direct, the programme still raises major rural issues, such as the conflict between maximising profit and conservation, the morality of factory farming, and so on.

More overtly didactic than drama is the news magazine format which lends itself particularly to local news about development issues. In the Philippines a programme called 'Cotabato Ngayon' ('Cotabato Now') is a daily one-hour programme produced by the local radio station DXMS. This programme contains reports on relevant national and provincial issues, gives in-depth coverage to selected local news events, provides public service announcements, reflects through *vox populi* interviews local views on development issues, and promotes or assists local development activities. The vital element in this programme is the use of mobile programme production facilities to get out amongst the people (Bonzon, 1979). This use of mobile facilities and emphasis on using local people and events in the programme gives it an immediacy and a relevance to local people, a feature sometimes lacking in British local radio programming, according to detailed studies by Booth (1980) and Wright (1980).

A less common format for open broadcasting is the quiz show which through the questions and answers provides information on government policies and development projects. While questions about the 1977 grape harvest in Paghman may not sound like riveting listening, this kind of radio quiz show was transmitted regularly at one of the most popular times for listening in Afghanistan before the 1978 revolutions. (It is not true that this programme was one of the causes of the revolution.)

All these techniques of open broadcasting depend very heavily on the skills of the professional broadcaster. Gunter and Theroux (1977), however, reported on a project in Tabacundo, Ecuador, where unpaid 'auxiliares' were issued with forty cassette recorders and a large supply of tapes. The 'auxiliares' were asked to collect their own recordings from local farmers and peasants about local needs, problems and possible solutions as seen by the farmers themselves. This material was then edited and broadcast by the local radio station, Radio Mensaje. Although the early programmes were solemn and self-conscious, later programmes became more sophisticated, using music and more self-confident speakers. In developing countries in particular, the cultural gap between the sophisticated, highly-educated, urban-based radio producers and local farmers and peasants in isolated rural areas, can be very wide indeed. Greater participation of local people in development programming therefore would seem to be essential. Despite this, the Radio Mensaje project is an extremely rare example of truly participative radio programming by rural people.

The characteristic of open broadcasting is that it has to succeed on the strength of the programme material alone, without the help of support materials or follow-up activities. However, on balance, most rural development projects have tended to favour combining radio with group listening.

Regular listening groups
There are several common features of radio listening groups. A regular series of programmes would be produced in co-operation with other development agencies, such as departments in the Ministry of Health or Agriculture. The programmes would usually have supporting print materials. The key feature though is the organisation of local groups of listeners, usually within a village, with volunteer, unpaid leaders or monitors drawn from the membership of the groups.

Radio rural listening groups have a long history. Although Cassirer (1959) reports the use of radio by adults in locally organised groups in England as early as 1928, according to Rogers *et al.* (1977), the first *radio farm forums* were set up in Canada in 1941. India was one of the first developing countries in 1954 to adopt radio farm forums as a strategy for rural development, and by 1965 there were about 12,000 forums in India, with something like 250,000 participating villagers (Schramm *et al.*, 1967). The movement also spread widely throughout Africa and to a lesser extent to other Asian and one or two Latin American countries. A characteristic of radio farm forums is that the group decides what relevant action to take, as reflected in the Canadian farm forum motto: 'Listen, discuss, act'. Consequently, emphasis in the programmes is usually on practical aspects of rural life.

In Tanzania, there has evolved a unique form of radio, the *radio campaign*. Radio campaigns tend to be limited to one or two basic objectives and are concentrated into a relatively short period of time, backed by massive support from the government. The four campaigns below were reported by Hall and Dodds (1974).

Date	Campaign	No. of participants
1969	Publicising the government's five-year plan	1,000
1970	The electoral system, and political awareness	10,000
1971	History and achievements in Tanzania after ten years	20,000
1973	Health and hygiene	2,000,000

As the projects grew in size, so too did the complexity of

organisation and the extent of evaluation. The Health and Hygiene campaign 'Mtu Ni Afya' recruited very many people and led to the building of latrines, improved methods of purifying water, greater cleanliness around houses and substantial knowledge gains amongst those tested. It is interesting to note that these campaigns in Tanzania preceded the British Adult Literacy campaign, which shares several common features with the Tanzanian campaigns (although no latrines were built in Britain).

A rather different pattern of listening groups has developed in Latin America – what Jamison and McAnany (1978) describe as *radio schools*. These originate from the Acción Cultural Popular (ACPO), which in turn grew out of Radio Sutatenza. In 1947 two Jesuit priests set up a radio transmitter on a hill near the remote hamlet of Sutatenza in Colombia, to bring religious and educational programming to the poor farmers of this area, the 'campesinos'. Radio Sutatenza now has a national network of five radio stations which form the base for ACPO. The radio programmes are supported by specially prepared print materials and a whole network of 'radiophonic schools' – informal groups, led by a volunteer or 'auxiliary' (Bernal *et al.*, 1978). ACPO's activities have formed the basis of similar projects in over twenty other Latin American countries. Jamison and McAnany claim that the essential element that distinguishes radio schools from other kinds of listening groups is their continuing commitment to teaching literacy and school-equivalent forms of education, whereas other kinds of rural listening groups tend to be more action-oriented and functional in their approach. Another feature noted by McAnany (1976) is the role of the Catholic parish priest. They give support to the radio schools in rural areas where 'the power structure is generally oppressive to campesinos', and establish the radio schools' independence of the government and its policies in the eyes of the campesinos.

More similar to farm forums are the *radio animation groups*, found mainly in African countries such as Senegal and Niger, although the basic philosophy of 'animation' is French in origin. In theory, radio animation groups should be more participative than other forms of listening groups since they are supposed to define their own areas of interest (as with the Dutch Open School), with the group leader or animateur being non-directive. In Senegal this led to participative programming by the peasants, combined with a feedback system of letters circulated to government officials (Cassirer, 1977).

Finally, Jamison and McAnany include the use of *two-way telecommunications*, via satellite links, amongst their strategies for rural development. Direct satellite broadcast links to and from local ground stations have enabled local groups in rural communities to communicate with urban-based specialists in projects in Alaska, the Appalachians in the USA and North-East Ontario in Canada.

Radio listening groups appear to have several advantages as a means of assisting rural education and development. Rogers *et al* (1977) argue that radio listening groups combine the advantages of radio, with its ability to reach large numbers of people at comparatively little cost even in remote rural areas, with the advantages of group activities, which allow for inter-personal communication, self-help and community action. Certainly there is substantial evaluation evidence (e.g. Neurath, 1960; Schramm *et al.*, 1967; Abell, 1968; Yacoub *et al.*, 1976) that radio listening groups have been an effective means of education. Farm forums were found to be more effective than either transmissions to individual listeners or self-help group sessions without radio, both in terms of knowledge gains and action. The Tanzanian health campaign reached a mass audience and led to widespread activities which improved health and hygiene in villages.

Nevertheless, with one or two exceptions, this use of radio is still less widespread than one might expect. The use of radio farm forums has dwindled considerably since its peak in the 1960s, partly due to increased individual ownership of radios, even in developing countries, partly due to the spread of television to rural areas in developed countries, and partly due to changes in educational and broadcasting fashions. There are also some substantial difficulties with radio listening groups. Organising groups on a large scale presents formidable organisational and logistical problems. The costs of the necessary support print materials and the difficulties of organising the early preparation and distribution of printed materials to remote rural areas are further disadvantages. Animation groups, without skilled leadership, can easily deteriorate into actionless talking shops, and even when listening groups are willing and ready to act, the necessary resources, such as cash, seeds or fertilisers, may not be available. McAnany (1976) criticises the radio school movement in Latin America for their over-emphasis on literacy at the expense of more functional and practical approaches, their deliberate avoidance of direct action (or 'interference') in community affairs, their under-financing and poor management, and their lack of feedback into production. Above all, he fears that the radio schools are perhaps inadvertently merely keeping the campesinos satisfied with their underprivileged position in society, a fear also supported by White's study of radio schools in Honduras (1977). One of White's conslusions is that adult education on its own is inadequate to bring about the necessary improvements in economic productivity and the political effectiveness of the campesino movement; structural changes in the power base need to come first.

Gunter and Theroux (1977) argue that open broadcasting in fact has a number of advantages over listening groups. They argue that multi-media courses, while aiming to provide deep or lasting effects on those that participate, rarely reach truly mass audiences, whereas strategies that produce *less* learning on the part of *more* listeners might be a better allocation of resources in many circumstances. In particular, open broadcasting allows broadcasters to concentrate more on what they do best, that is, improving the quality of the broadcast message, rather than getting involved in organising or liaising with support services.

However, many of the structural and social arguments directed against radio schools apply even more forcefully to open broadcasting. Furthermore, the two methods are not necessarily in opposition. Open broadcasting methods can be used, as in social action programming, to recruit participants; listening groups can take participants further in their learning than open broadcasting can. The real criticism though of relying entirely on open broadcasting techniques is that education is more than just pumping messages into people, no matter how benevolent the messages may be. For instance, spot announcements make it even more difficult for people to differentiate between commercial and development announcements. Lastly, it should be noted that while structural and social changes are almost certainly needed in many of the societies where radio has been used for rural development, many of the difficulties of providing mass adult education in rural areas would still remain, even if structural changes were to take place. The balance of the evaluation evidence suggests that radio, combined with group activity, could still be a potent educational force for rural development.

Television

Television coverage is still less than radio in many rural areas. Television sets need a constant voltage supply which is best provided by mains electricity. Television is also more expensive and complex to produce than radio. Sets cost a great deal more, so in many countries fewer individuals own television sets than own radios, and those that do own television sets tend to live in the big cities. For these reasons, television has been used much less than radio for rural programming but there are still several rural education projects supported by television.

In Canada, the Québec provincial government set up a project in 1967 which came to be called Tevec. The project was aimed at the mainly rural, French-speaking communities living in the Gaspésie region of central Québec. Many of the people living in this area were poorer than the national average and nearly half the adult population (around 80,000) had less than the minimum nine years' education required to qualify for vocational training (Lallez, 1972). One aim therefore was to bring people up to a standard equivalent to nine years' schooling; a second, and perhaps even more import- ant aim in the context of French Canadian identity and politics, was to stimulate the adult population to take on a more participatory and decisive role in local affairs (Dodds, 1972). The project used daily television programmes, weekly tele-club broadcasts, and postal distribution of printed lessons, worksheets and questionnaires. Four full-time and twenty part-time field workers or 'animateurs' were employed, the latter concentrating on those with the least amount of previous formal education. Altogether, over the two year period of the project (1967 to 1969), 35,000 students were enrolled, and roughly a quarter worked through the courses to the examination at the end. More importantly, the course had an immediate impact on the actual living and working conditions of its students through the project-related activities. In some ways it was too successful since the political activities of the participants became very controversial, resulting in the follow-up project being delayed and considerably modified (Darveau *et al.*, 1971).

In France, the use of television for rural programming has a long history. As early as 1952, programmes were broadcast to link in with the provision of community television sets in small villages. Even today, France has a project, dating from 1966, using television and other media for rural development, called 'Télépromotion Rurale' (Girardin, 1982). By 1980 there were two regional centres for this project, one based at Grenoble, the other at Nancy. The project began in 1966 with group viewing of broadcast programmes on community sets, then changed to programmes broadcast to indi- viduals at home, as private ownership of TV sets became common- place in the rural areas. The project changed yet again in 1979 to group viewing of programmes distributed solely on video-cassette, through local agricultural trainers linked to an association of pro- fessional agricultural organisations.

As early as 1967 a pilot agricultural television project (Krishi Darshan) began in India in the Delhi area with eighty community sets distributed around the countryside, as a follow-up to the earlier radio farm forums. However, in 1975 India made a dramatic technological leap when, for a twelve-month period, television programmes were beamed down by satellite to 2,330 villages in six states scattered throughout India. This was the Indian Satellite Instructional Television Experiment (SITE). As well as schools and teacher-training programmes, there was a daily 2½-hour broadcast each evening aimed primarily at adults. This broadcast was comprised of three kinds of programmes: national news; instructional programmes on agriculture, animal husbandry, family planning, health and nutrition (termed 'hardcore' instructional programmes); and recreational programmes – fantasy and story-telling, musicals, dramas, songs – containing some social messages (termed 'softcore'). The programmes were broadcast in four languages (using different sound channels) to accommodate regional language variations. The programmes were viewed on community television sets, using specially designed, locally erected, low-cost dish-aerials and convertors. The programmes were usually viewed in the open air, with audiences settling down to around a hundred per set per evening, of whom about one third were children (Agrawal, 1981).

The project was extensively researched and evaluated. Almost a quarter of those who viewed the programmes had never heard radio, never seen films before, nor read a newspaper, although, in general, the average viewer tended to be younger and better educated. The evaluation studies show, according to Agrawal (1981), that the project helped to bridge the information gap between those who had access to development information and those who did not. He also argued that learning from the programmes seemed high and that the programmes helped trigger the process of change in agriculture, health, hygiene and nutrition. He also suggested that community viewing led to an easing of caste distinctions.

SITE was clearly a major achievement, technologically, organisationally and, to a lesser extent, educationally. It reached extremely large numbers of isolated and poor villagers, and had clear educational and social benefits. Many valuable lessons were learned from the experiment, not the least of which was that just as much attention has to be paid to the programming and teaching side as to the technology. Nevertheless, despite the large numbers of villagers covered by the satellite, they still represented only a tiny proportion of the Indian population. Given the tremendous efforts that went into the field organisation and programming, and the expectation the project raised in the participating villages, it is all the more a pity that the project was only a one-year experiment (the Americans wanted their satellite back). Financial and political considerations have so far prevented the implementation of a permanent Indian satellite system, although the government is committed to such a strategy.

It is in developing countries that effective rural programming is most needed. In these countries, the problems of social, economic and educational disadvantage are most acute in the rural areas. In general, radio has been more appropriate than television for rural programming in developing countries but there are already signs that the continuing spread of television and related technological developments of low-cost video and the blanket coverage promised by satellites will lead, even in developing countries, to a greater use of television. Nevertheless, rural programming is one area where, given the right conditions, radio has proved to be an effective and economical educational medium, and it would be most regrettable if the advantages of radio were to be ignored as television continues its remorseless expansion.

PROGRAMMING FOR DISADVANTAGED MINORITIES

Basic adult education, social action and rural programming are all aimed primarily at socially, educationally or economically disadvantaged groups. Such programming aims at a broad base of disadvantage. In other words, while the target audience may in fact be composed of a whole range of different minority sub-groups, the programmes cover problems presumably shared by all the different groups.

In contrast, there are programmes aimed at specific minority target groups which deal with problems in ways uniquely suited to each group. Programmes for instance for particular ethnic minorities usually aim at improving their use of the 'host' country's language, understanding better the culture and customs of the 'host' country and making full use of the rights and services available within that culture. The BBC television series 'Parosi', first broadcast in 1977, is a good example of this. 60 per cent of Asian women in Britain speak little or no English. Because of this language barrier, Asian immigrants in particular not only suffer from a sense of isolation and anxiety but also feel a sense of alienation even from their own children, who have absorbed the English language and some of the values of the English culture through their schooling. Because of their own cultural traditions, Asian women are very reluctant to join social activities without their husbands and consequently it can be very difficult to reach them through conventional adult education provision. One of the aims of 'Parosi' (which means 'neighbours') was to encourage Asian women to learn English, with the help of volunteer home tutors and local language teaching schemes. The television series used a drama format: the central characters were two Asian wives living in an inner-city area in Britain who were trying to learn English. The programmes placed particular emphasis on the move from home to class tuition. An important aspect of the series was its linking to local language schemes and voluntary support services. The BBC launched an appeal for volunteer home tutors and there was liaison with local education authorities and other providers of local language schemes for immigrants. A special book was designed, written in six different languages (Matthews, 1978).

As well as programmes with the specific aim of teaching languages to immigrants, several West European countries broadcast *general* programmes for ethnic minorities. In Britain there has been a regular Sunday morning television magazine programme for Asians living in Britain since 1965 ('Nai Zindagi Naya Jeevan'), watched regularly by two thirds of Asians in Britain. In Sweden local radio in particular has been used to broadcast news and magazine programmes to Yugoslav and Finnish immigrants in their own language, covering both Swedish events and events from 'home'.

Another disadvantaged minority group that has only recently been served by television or radio in Britain is the *physically and mentally handicapped* and their families. Reference has already been made to 'Let's Go . . .' (p. 52) in a school context but this series, first broadcast in 1976, was the world's first television series aimed also at mentally handicapped *adults*, either in residential centres or at home. The aim of these programmes is to help the moderately handicapped to develop basic social skills, such as shopping or travelling on a bus (Croton, 1980). At the time of writing (1983), 'Let's Go . . .' is still running and there are now series for the deaf (e.g. a series on lip-reading), for people with speech disorders and for professionals working with the handicapped. Croton and Pascoe (1981) provide a useful summary of BBC programming on mental and physical handicap.

A study by the Gulbenkian Foundation (1979), argued that there was not enough broadcasting aimed at the special needs of *young people* in the age range sixteen to twenty-four, and, in particular, young people did not get enough opportunity to put their own views over on broadcasts. Some broadcasters do not see this as a group with special needs; rather their needs are met, it is claimed, through the wide range of general programming. It is also argued that this group is perhaps the least interested, for social reasons, in sitting at home, perhaps with parents, watching television.

Nevertheless, there is some evidence that there is a need for programmes aimed at the unemployed young. 'Just the Job' (Westward TV) was a series of programmes aimed specifically at unemployed youngsters in the age range sixteen to nineteen living in South-West England. The programme used punk music and teenage presenters and language, essential features, according to Michael Rheinhold, the producer, since anyone over the age of twenty-five was considered by the youngsters in that area to be a 'boff' (a boring old fart). The series started in 1977 with six 20-minute programmes. As a result of close monitoring, the programmes by 1979 had been increased to twenty-five, but reduced in length to 6 minutes. Other changes made were to reduce the length of teenage interviews and to drop items encouraging the setting up of small businesses, as the youngsters were not really in a position to become self-employed. A most important part of the project was the role played by the National Extension College. With funding from the Manpower Services Commission (a government agency), NEC created 'Jobhunter' kits, which used plain language, cartoon strips and kept the number of points to be made to a minimum. These kits provided detailed information about jobs and services briefly referred to in the programmes. NEC also organised a voluntary counselling network which in 1977 attracted 1,000 youngsters – roughly 10 per cent of the target audience. Youngsters were put in contact through a telephone referral service, and the series were also supported by a half-hour weekly programme on local radio and centre page supplements in local papers (Rheinhold, 1980; Reeves, 1982).

A feature of all such minority programming is that it aims not only to provide a service directed at the minority group itself but also to raise the awareness of the general public to the needs and difficulties faced by the minority group. 'Just the Job' proved to be a particularly popular programme, receiving higher viewing figures in the South-West than the very popular 'Blue Peter', which was also transmitted at the same time on BBC. 'Parosi' was used to recruit volunteers (as was 'Just the Job') from the general public, and 'Parosi', 'Let's Go . . .' and 'Just the Job' were all able to suggest ways in which the general public could help. Thus, while such minority programming may not at first sight appear to be appropriate for mass audiences, 'Just the Job' in particular showed that minority programming can attract large audiences without compromising its aims. Lastly, 'Parosi', 'Just the Job', and to some extent 'Let's Go . . .' were all dependent on external agencies for their success.

The next chapter evaluates in detail the success of television and radio in non-formal basic education but already some important policy issues can be identified.

Firstly, the role of broadcasting in non-formal education is much broader than just the provision of programmes that extend academic subjects to those out of school. Many of the series described in this chapter were not in fact originated by educational broadcasting departments but by other general service departments, yet these programmes attempt to meet basic educational needs amongst the general public. Herein lies both the strength and the weakness of television and radio.

One strength lies in the ability to reach people who would run a mile at the thought of 'going back to school'. Given the serendipitous nature of much viewing and listening, broadcasting provides the opportunity to catch the viewer or listener unaware and then, through the development of the professional skills of the broadcasters, to hold, entertain and educate that viewer or listener.

There are also examples, such as 'Sesame Street' and the BBC Adult Literacy project, where broadcasters have taken the lead in initiating major movements in non-formal basic education, providing services which the formal education system had been unable to provide or had severely neglected. Often such initiatives went way beyond the creation of a series of programmes to the point of developing whole new teaching curricula where none had previously existed.

However, there have been few projects where broadcasting has been sufficient on its own. Most basic education projects using television or radio also depend very heavily on co-operation and follow-up services from other agencies. There seems to be doubt whether 'open broadcasting' unsupported by other activities can really provide the depth of impact necessary for major progress in basic education. Broadcasting has therefore rarely been an *alternative* to other forms of basic education but rather a valuable *supplementary* component. Consequently, television or even radio are unlikely to be cheap or simple alternatives to conventional non-formal provision because of the need for support and follow-up services. Associated group work, or at least the support of another individual, appears to have been an essential ingredient of most projects. The experience of the radio schools in particular also suggests that no matter how valuable the educational experience through broadcasting may be, it cannot be a substitute for major structural and political reforms, where these are needed.

The importance of support services and other agencies also raises the issue of broadcasters' accountability in initiating and implementing projects in the basic education area. Priority-setting for formal and non-formal educational services in most democratic countries is the responsibility of elected local or national representatives. Broadcasting organisations though are not subject to this control. While at least in Britain the broadcasting organisations have created a formal process of consultation for schools and further education broadcasting, no such formal arrangement covers the area of more basic education. Particularly with regard to social action broadcasting, it is the broadcast organisations that set the priorities. They may on occasion consult, but there is no obligation on them to do so. This would be questionable enough if the programmes were to stand alone. However, substantial resources and manpower are needed from other agencies to provide the follow-up and support that is essential if the programmes are to lead to effective action. It is pertinent then to ask whether some more formal consultative arrangements between broadcasters and other agencies are not necessary. The question of accountability and priority-setting in educational broadcasting is an issue of course that runs right through all programming but it is particularly acute in the sensitive area of basic education and social action programming.

Accountability will remain an important issue as long as the general public, educators and community workers are unable to access broadcasting directly. Social action and raising political awareness are obviously sensitive issues and it has proved extremely difficult for those who are not professional broadcasters to use broadcasting to run courses, express needs or stimulate action. When it has happened, it has usually been in the framework of programmes organised and run by the professional broadcasting organisations and subject to their editorial control. Yet the need to bridge the gap between the well-educated, urbanised, metropolitan professional broadcaster (or teacher) and the less-educated, poorer members of the community is just as great in industrialised as in developing countries. Currently, even in the area of basic education, the control of professional broadcasters over programming remains virtually absolute in most countries.

5

Getting it right:
helping the disadvantaged

When assessing the effectiveness of broadcasting in non-formal basic education, it has to be recognised that the educationally disadvantaged are a particularly difficult target group. By definition, the formal education system has failed them, and, to be frank, they get little joy from the adult education system either. It is optimistic then to expect broadcasting to succeed where others have failed. Also in this area more than any other, what constitutes success is very much open to argument. The aims and methods themselves are often controversial, irrespective of whether or not projects achieve what they set out to do. Lastly, as with the formal education system, it is usually the *conditions* surrounding the use of broadcasting which determine success or failure, rather than the use of broadcasting *per se*.

AUDIENCE CHARACTERISTICS AND EDUCATION
BY STEALTH

The psychological state of any individual viewer or listener will crucially influence whether or not a programme will be successful. This applies of course to all programming, but the attitudes and goals of the individual viewer are particularly important in non-formal basic education.

Learning is not a one-way process; it involves much more than merely a transfer of information from one person to another. The design of a programme must take into account what the majority of the target audience are likely to *want* from that programme, in terms of their learning needs. For instance, there is a major difference between Open University students, who have already made a firm commitment to follow a specific course of study, and those who, without any prior commitment, watch by chance an adult literacy programme like 'On the Move'. The two groups of viewers will have very different expectations of their respective programmes. Open University students are more likely to want a heavily didactic programme which will advance their understanding of the subject, clarify ideas and provide help with assignments. For them the programme is just one part of their course, a means to an end. Their approach to an Open University television programme therefore is likely to be strictly functional or instrumental. Viewers of 'On the Move', though, may start to watch the programme purely for entertainment purposes. A heavily didactic programme on developing reading skills is likely to have a negative effect, frightening them away from something which has always been an uncomfortable topic. They may desperately want to read but, at the beginning of viewing, the commitment to doing something about it has not been made; indeed, the programme is seeking to stimulate that commitment and must thus combine entertainment with practical help and encouragement.

Differences in the adult population regarding learning needs have been identified in a significant study carried out by Matsui (1981), for TV Ontario, which examined the relationship between media use, life interests and adult learning needs. A sample of the population was asked to state the level of interest and the importance that they attached to three types of learning: learning for formal qualifications; learning about society and the world; and learning for its own sake. Matsui identified six different groups of people, in terms of their interests in learning, but I shall simplify these to three, with respect to their expectations of programmes.

Firstly, there are those who really 'don't care a toss' about further education, described in Matsui's study as 'expressing below average interest in learning'. They tended to be younger, less educated and unskilled or blue collar workers. They were heavier users of television, but only for entertainment purposes not for information, culture or education. Many other studies have shown that the demand for further and continuing education comes primarily from those who already have a good general education. In particular, Trenaman (1957) identified just under *half the population* as being 'uninterested' in any form of further education, people he described as 'resistant to new ideas and higher values'. I shall call this group, by far the largest, 'not-interested' learners, i.e. not interested in pursuing activities which they see as being 'education' as they know it. 'Not-interested' covers two of Matsui's groups ('below average' and 'non-learners'). It is not-interested learners that form by and large – but not exclusively – the target group for basic adult education.

The second group Matsui labelled 'structured learners'. These constituted about 15 per cent of the population. This group was interested only in learning which led to formal qualifications and was not interested in learning about society and the world or learning for its own sake. They tended to be younger, in full-time employment, but with below-average incomes, and their dominant feature was a desire to get ahead. For this group, further education was clearly a means to the very precise ends of job advancement. Unlike others with an interest in learning, this group tended to use newspapers and broadcasting less, and did not look to television to provide information or learning opportunities.

Then there were three groups all interested in various ways in learning about society and the world, or learning for its own sake. Matsui labelled these three groups 'committed', 'unstructured' and 'above-average' learners, respectively. People in these three groups were on balance more likely to use television for information, cultural or educational purposes, and more likely to take advantage of further education opportunities. Together they constituted about a third of Matsui's sample. I will use the term 'open learners' for people in these three groups. (Note that Open University students are not necessarily 'open learners' in this sense – they are just as likely to be 'structured learners'.)

These three main groups are likely to react very differently to a particular programme series and their reaction would depend on their perceived needs. A programme which is seen as enrichment or ambivalent in its message may be considered a waste of time by a structured learner; the same programme, though, may be seen as stimulating and thought-provoking by an open learner; for a viewer who has not yet made any commitment to learning, an enrichment-type or entertainment-led educational programme may or may not be of interest, depending on the broader needs of that viewer, but a heavily didactic programme will almost certainly be unwelcome at this stage of the viewer's commitment to learning. This does not mean that viewers' attitudes to learning cannot be changed as a series progresses, but the *prevailing* state of viewers in the target group must be the starting point for the educational broadcaster who wants to win and keep the audience.

A major argument for using broadcasting in basic adult education then is that it is heavily used by those most in need of basic education, if only for entertainment purposes. While they may not be interested in conventional forms of education, an entertaining broadcast may gain their attention and change their commitment to learning. It is essentially education by stealth, by 'hooking' the viewer or listener through the interesting format of the programme and so awakening an interest in studying the topic or developing a skill. To assess the effectiveness of using broadcasting in this way, we need first of all to know how successful the broadcasters have been in reaching the educationally disadvantaged with their basic education programmes and to what level of commitment such an audience has been encouraged to study, bearing in mind that nearly half the population are not interested in further education.

LEVELS OF COMMITMENT

This brings us to the 'onion' phenomenon of educational broadcasting. (Robinson, 1982, describes it as 'the stone-in-the-pond', but stones sink without trace!) At the centre of the onion (or pond) is a small core of fully committed students who work through the whole course and, where available, take an end-of-course assessment or examination. Around the small core will be a rather larger layer of students who do not take any examination but do enrol with a local class or correspondence school. There may be an even larger layer of students who, as well as watching and listening, also buy the accompanying textbook, but who do not enrol on any courses. Then, by far the largest group, are those who just watch or listen to the programmes. Even within this last group there will be considerable variations, from those who watch or listen fairly regularly to those, again a much larger number, who watch or listen to just one programme.

This effect can be seen in two very different series, Swedish Radio's multi-media English course, 'START', and BBC/CE's radio series, 'What Right Have You Got?'. START was aimed primarily at Swedish adults with no previous knowledge of English and low educational qualifications, and 'What Right Have You Got?' was aimed at the educationally disadvantaged. Despite the differences in country, topic, mix of media and actual numbers attracted to the courses, the pattern of commitment is remarkably similar, as can be seen from Table 9.

In terms of total numbers, and numbers continuing to progress through the various courses, START is one of the world's most successful educational broadcast series. Just over 10 per cent of the adult population in Sweden in any one week would have watched the television programmes in the course's first year of presentation; book sales (800,000 in the first three years alone) were phenomenal, given a total adult population of five million; of those enrolling in study circles for the first course in year 1, 40 per cent eventually worked their way through to the sixth and last part of the course. (For more details of START, see Chapter 6.)

'What Right Have You Got?' on the other hand was frankly a disappointment. Not only were the numbers involved relatively small but the series did not really reach its primary target group, the

TABLE 9

LEVELS OF AUDIENCE COMMITMENT: TWO EXAMPLES

'START' (Sweden) (figures for 1971–74)		'What Right Have You Got?'	(BBC Radio) (1976)
No. of viewers each week	567,000	No. of listeners each week	50,000
No. of Part 1 books sold over 3 years	230,000	Book purchases Part 1	14,000
		Part 2	10,000
No. of books sold (all six parts) over 3 years	790,000		
No. enrolled in study circles 71/72	108,000	No. enrolled in local groups/classes	20,000
73/74	203,000		
No. of 1st enrolments entered for 6th course	43,000	Examination	10,000

Source: Horneij (1975).

Source: Salkeld (1979).

educationally disadvantaged. Nevertheless, the commitment pattern, in terms of the proportion of total viewers or listeners, was remarkably similar for both series. In both cases, the ratio of listeners or viewers to book purchasers was at least 5 to 1. The major difference is that for START, sales for books in any one year were slightly less than enrolments in study groups, whereas in most broadcast series, as with 'What Right Have You Got?', book sales are usually substantially higher than group enrolments. The START study group figures are more a reflection of the very strong tradition of study circles in Sweden. Otherwise, the pattern of commitment is similar and would be found in many other broadcast series.

These figures highlight some key issues in evaluating broadcasting in education. A sceptic may argue that the only ones who can be said to have learned effectively are the tiny minority that worked right through the course and successfully took the final assessment, and even their learning might have been due more to the other elements of the course than to the broadcasts. A counter-argument would be that broadcasting can be considered successful if it merely attracts viewers or listeners who might otherwise have shown no interest in the topic; it is the numbers exposed to the material that matter, since some learning is bound to take place and viewers or listeners once interested may take up the topic in a number of ways afterwards. In fact, if even relatively small numbers do go on to further study as a result of seeing or hearing the programme, then the programme could be considered worthwhile, since, while the numbers may be small in broadcasting terms, they will be large compared with those already engaged in non-formal basic education.

The key issue then is whether broadcasting *does* attract to education those who would not otherwise have been interested, or merely provides yet another educational opportunity for those who are already well educated and already willing participants in non-formal education.

GETTING IT WRONG

There is a good deal of evidence that it is still the better educated in Britain and Europe that make most use of non-formal educational broadcasting. For instance, Rybak (1980) summarised a series of research studies into BBC foreign language educational broadcasts, one of the major outputs of the BBC's education departments. The figures confirmed that the typical client of further education is someone who is already fairly well educated. Perhaps more significantly, she found that very few people started learning their *first* foreign language through television or radio, and a significant proportion of the audience, even for the beginners' series, were not true beginners, even for subjects not normally taught at school (e.g. 67 per cent had already previously studied Russian and 57 per cent Spanish before following 'Ochen Pryatno' and '¡Digame!' respectively).

However, BBC foreign language teaching is not aimed primarily at the educationally disadvantaged, so what of the programmes deliberately made for such an audience? Two BBC radio series, 'Living Decisions' and 'What Right Have You Got?' were made in response to the BBC's Further Education Advisory Council's request in 1970 that the BBC:

> should concentrate on providing . . . start support . . . for those adults, more significantly disadvantaged by their educational and life experiences, for whom 'O' level represented at worst, past failure and at best, a doubtful prospect (Stephens, 1976).

These two series were ambitious in that they attempted to introduce subject matter different from that found in the traditional school or further education college curriculum but appropriate to the needs of the target group. The two projects are well documented by the main producers (Stephens, 1976; Salkeld, 1979) and by an independent researcher (Sissons, 1974). Both courses did achieve considerable success with those students who were encouraged to enrol for supporting courses but unfortunately these were relatively few in number (4,000 and 2,000 respectively) and, above all, the courses failed to attract any significant numbers of educationally disadvantaged students. Two thirds of the participants (on both courses) had stayed on at school beyond the minimum leaving age, and between a quarter and a third had qualifications at 'Advance level' or above. For 'What Right Have You Got?' only 28 per cent were first-time adult education students. The largest group were housewives, and very few were unskilled or semi-skilled workers.

It would be wrong, however, to suggest that broadcasting cannot reach and teach the disadvantaged. It once again depends on the conditions. This can be seen by examining two projects where broadcasting has been relatively successful in reaching and teaching the disadvantaged. The two projects are 'Sesame Street' and the British Adult Literacy Campaign. I have chosen these two projects because they illustrate the problems in deciding what constitutes success, and they also illustrate some of the conditions required for successful use of broadcasting for the disadvantaged.

'Sesame Street' in its second year was reaching an estimated eight million children in the USA, approximately half of whom were from low income families. Within six years the programmes had spread to sixty-nine countries. Two independent summative evaluations carried out by Ball and Bogatz (1970 and 1972) found the following:

(1) over a six-month period, substantial learning gains were measured on the following learning objectives: naming geometric forms; functions of parts of the body; understanding the roles of community members; matching by form; naming letters; letter sounds; sight reading; recognising numbers; counting; relational terms; classification and sorting;
(2) those who viewed gained substantially more than those who did not view; the more children viewed, the greater the gains;
(3) significant learning gains were made by children from both low and middle income groups.

Despite this apparent success, there have been forceful criticisms of the effectiveness of 'Sesame Street'. These criticisms fall into three broad categories: the programmes did not *reduce* the learning gap between disadvantaged and advantaged children; the educational philosophy underlying the programmes is ideologically suspect; and the programmes considerably strengthened American cultural and commercial dominance abroad.

Cook (1975) criticised the methodological basis of the Ball and Bogatz evaluations. In particular, Cook and his colleagues pointed out that children counted as viewers were given strong *encouragement* to view by the researchers, through weekly visits and gifts of toys, books and games derived from the programmes. Thus, while Ball and Bogatz found that learning gains increased with viewing, this could be partly a function of the encouragement to view. Secondly, it was also found that advantaged viewers tended to watch more than disadvantaged viewers, thus leading to higher average gains for the advantaged. Surprisingly, Ball and Bogatz did not design their evaluation in such a way that direct comparisons could be made between advantaged and disadvantaged children under actual field conditions without variables such as encouragement to view confounding the issue. Consequently, it cannot be claimed that the programmes *alone* led to learning gains. Nor can it be claimed that the programmes reduced the gap between advantaged and disadvantaged children since advantaged children watched as much as the disadvantaged. What is undisputed though is that the programmes appealed to a wide range of children, including the disadvantaged, and *all* children, again including the disadvantaged, developed pre-specified learning skills in proportion to the amount of programmes that they watched. 'Sesame Street' was certainly an improvement on the alternative programmes available to children in the USA and, in that sense, it can certainly be considered a success.

The second criticism has already been discussed to some extent in Chapter 2 (pp. 13–32). Many educators have expressed concern about the didactic, direct teaching style, aiming at the development of certain pre-specified and tightly controlled learning skills, primarily based on recognition and rote-learning. For instance, Goldsen (1976), in a deeply critical paper, berates the programmes for using advertising techniques for teaching purposes, pointing out that teaching involves much more than the development, through practice, of narrow learning skills. She goes so far as to argue that 'Sesame Street' is not so much encouraging literacy in its broader sense but the skills needed to be a consumer in American society: how to 'read' advertisements; how to read labels on consumer products; how to read commercial television itself.

Defenders of 'Sesame Street' would argue that Goldsen's criticisms apply more to American television in general than to 'Sesame Street'. It was not 'Sesame Street' that introduced young minds to the techniques of commercial television. The first 'Sesame Street' viewers would have been bombarded by such techniques for at least 2½ years already. All that 'Sesame Street' did was to take techniques which clearly work with young children and apply them to an educational rather than a commercial purpose. These purposes were not set by advertisers but in fact were established through a series of seminars to which highly prestigious educators made major contributions. Indeed, it is unusual to find any educational television series with such clearly defined objectives. It may not have had the objectives that some educators would have liked, but it was not 'television' that set the objectives but educators themselves. It should also be remembered that the development of full literacy was never an aim of 'Sesame Street' but the development of *pre-reading skills*.

The fear of cultural dominance is well founded but again it could be argued that this is more a criticism of American values, culture and commercialism than of the programmes themselves. The programmes merely reflect the society to which they belong. 'Sesame Street' spread rapidly throughout the world for several reasons. The financial base of 'Sesame Street' has never been permanent. Income came from fixed-period charitable and federal grants and sales of ancillary materials. CTW therefore was forced to look overseas for continuing sources of revenue. At the same time, there was – and still is – a great shortage of high-quality, entertainment-based educational programmes in any country. Goldsen is absolutely right in pointing out that 'Sesame Street' has in fact turned out to be an agent by which the values and culture of America are being transmitted to millions of young non-Americans. But one has to look at the alternatives available. Indigenous programming is the only answer to cultural dominance from abroad but it is surely inconsistent for instance for the BBC to refuse to show 'Sesame Street' because it was culturally alien, while at the same time broadcasting 'Yogi Bear' and the 'Huckleberry Hound Show', neither of which is in the mainstream of British culture and traditions. Children's programming in particular seems to generate a lot of cant from broadcasters. 'Sesame Street' should be judged against the alternatives available, especially to disadvantaged children.

The last criticism is that 'Sesame Street' did not in practice reduce inequality. White kids watched as much as black kids and consequently gained just as much. It did not therefore reduce the gap between blacks and whites, but it did ease white guilt that 'something was being done' about racial equality. This again is similar to arguments already expressed about radio schools and using television for curriculum reform in developing countries. It is a delusion to think that broadcasting can ever, on its own, compensate for social, economic or racial inequalities. These can be solved only by radical political and economic activities.

'Sesame Street' however was successful in reaching large numbers of disadvantaged children, and while there is no evidence that it *reduced* differences between disadvantaged blacks and middle-class whites, there is also no evidence that it *widened* the gap. To use television to teach the disadvantaged at least *as well as* the advantaged is no mean achievement; to do so by means of programmes that have enchanted millions of children is to be successful with style.

The issue I have been primarily concerned with here is: *can* television reach the disadvantaged and teach them what it sets out to teach? I would argue that in the case of 'Sesame Street' it did, and in that sense it was successful.

TABLE 10

BBC ADULT LITERACY BROADCASTS

Target group	Title	Medium	Length (min.)	No. of programmes in series	Channel	Transmission times	Years transmitted	Average audience size	National Figures Seeing/hearing at least one programme	
									All	Socio-Economic Group D/E
General audience + adult illiterates	'On the Move'	TV	10	50	BBC1	18.05 Sundays 12.15 Thursdays 10.25 Saturdays	1975–78	1,500,000 70,000 525,000	67%	63%
Adult illiterates	'Your Move'	TV	25	20	BBC1 BBC2	12.05 Sundays 19.05 Thursdays	1976–78	500,000 250,000	12%	11%
Adult illiterates	'Next Move'	Radio	5	20	Radio 2	17.50 Sundays 18.45 Thursdays	1977	500,000 500,000	3%	3%

Adult illiterates	'Move On'	Radio	5	20	Radio 2	17.50 Sundays 17.15 Thursdays	1978	500,000 500,000	No information	No information
Tutors	'Teaching Adults to Read'	Radio	30	8	Radio 3	19.00 Tuesdays 19.00 Tuesdays 19.00 Tuesdays	1975 1976 1977	No information	8%	5%
Tutors	'Helping With Spelling'	Radio	30	4	Radio 3	19.00 Tuesdays 19.00 Mondays	1977 1978	No information	No information	No information

Sources: Hargreaves, 1980; Jones and Charnley, 1978.

THE BBC AND THE ADULT LITERACY CAMPAIGN

Similarly, while reservations could also be expressed about the role of broadcasting in the British Adult Literacy campaign between 1975 and 1978, by and large broadcasting was a crucial factor in the success of the project. The Adult Literacy Campaign was a complex operation. The BBC produced two television and four radio series, prepared an Adult Literacy Handbook for tutors and student workbooks, and initiated the establishment of a telephone referral service, later converted to a charitable trust. The government financed the Adult Literacy Resource Agency which provided additional funds for local authorities and voluntary agencies for tutor briefing and training, and helped organise the design and production of tutor handbooks and student workbooks. Volunteer tutors were recruited and were organised and trained by local authorities and voluntary organisations. There was extensive publicity given to the project by national and local radio channels, newspapers, commercial television, chain stores and libraries. Finally, a project evaluation, funded by the Department of Education and Science, was carried out by the National Institute of Adult Education. Table 10 summarises the broadcast provision and its impact.

From the evaluation reported by Jones and Charnley (1978), several critical conclusions regarding the broadcast components could be drawn:

(1) Tutors and students did not use the broadcasts as a learning resource in the tuition sessions. The main teaching then was not done by broadcasting but in interpersonal tutorial sessions. Few students watched large numbers of the programmes, although most saw a few. Tutors by and large did not listen to the radio programmes directed at them, nor did the students.

(2) Broadcasting did not appear to be the main source of recruitment to the campaign; only about one in three of the students coming forward appeared to have done so directly as a result of the broadcasts. Furthermore, the decision to enrol appears to have been the result of a complex process. While awareness may have been increased by seeing the programmes, local advertising and family pressure to enrol was also influential.

(3) The television programmes and student workbooks were considered by enrolled students and tutors to be at too basic a level. Many of the students who came forward did have

reading problems, but were not completely illiterate. Some tutors thought that the second television series encouraged poor spellers to come forward rather than poor readers. Consequently, training materials produced centrally by the BBC were not considered suitable at a local or individual level.

(4) The decision by the BBC to go ahead with programmes aimed at adult illiterates imposed burdens on local education authorities who had to provide the main field-work, resulting in changed priorities; particularly in some inner cities, local education authorities were not always able to cope with the demand.

(5) At the end of the campaign, only 5 per cent of the target group had come forward; there remain possibly millions still to be reached.

It is difficult to know what weight to give to such conclusions because of the way the evaluation was conducted. Quantitative postal surveys were considered inappropriate by the researchers given the nature of the target group, so the researchers decided to concentrate on personal interviews and qualitative analysis. The conclusions above stem from a *lack* of comments from students and tutors about the use of broadcasting, and from a lack of use of broadcast materials in the *tutorial* sessions. However, this is not altogether surprising since the researchers collected their evidence on learning aspects from group or tutorial sessions, where inevitably the emphasis of the teaching was on interpersonal activities. No measure was attempted by the researchers of the use of programmes by students individually in their homes, although equally there was no evidence either to suggest that this was a frequent or important activity.

The broadcasters had decided right from the beginning that the aim of the programmes should be to contact and mobilise potential students and volunteers, and that 'the most effective use of television would be in reducing anxiety and stigma, rather than in instruction' (Hargreaves, 1980). Hence the programmes were not designed primarily for use in tutorials. Although the second television series was more instructional in intent, the success of the broadcasting component should be judged primarily in terms of its ability to recruit the target audience, and there is a good deal of evidence to suggest that, despite the reservations of the NIAE evaluators, the broadcasts were highly successful in this respect.

In the first place, it is unlikely that there would ever have been an adult literacy campaign without the BBC initiative. While various voluntary organisations, such as the British Association of Settlements, had been battling away for years for improved facilities for adult literacy, it was only when the BBC decided in 1973 to run a series for adult illiterates that the campaign really began to roll. It should be noted too that the BBC commitment to this area preceded the establishment of the government-financed ALRA, which channelled funds to local education authorities and voluntary organisations for literacy work. Furthermore, it seems unlikely that local authorities would have moved as quickly as they did to provide the necessary organisation and training of tutors, nor pressed central government so effectively for the necessary funds during yet another period of financial austerity, had they not been concerned about the overwhelming demand likely to result from the BBC programmes.

Secondly, despite the NIAE researchers' reservations, there is no doubt that broadcasting did stimulate recruitment. Each broadcast was followed by a flood of telephone calls to the telephone referral service and the response continued right through the campaign. In all, over the length of the campaign, the telephone referral service received 45,712 calls from potential students, and 19,527 from potential volunteers. Table 11 gives figures for *all* students in tuition and active volunteers in 1976 and 1977, taken from ALRA's annual reports.

In 1973 there were only 5,000 adults receiving literacy tuition. By 1974, no doubt partly stimulated by the campaign's pre-publicity, this had increased to 17,000. Between 1974 and 1978 125,000 adults had received tuition and 75,000 volunteers been recruited.

Thus the campaign more than doubled the rate at which people were entering adult literacy tuition each year. While recruitment resulted from a very wide range of publicity sources, at least a third came forward as a direct result of the broadcasts. Furthermore, the

TABLE 11

NUMBERS OF TUTORS AND STUDENTS IN ADULT LITERACY
TUITION: 1976–77

	1976	1977
Students in tuition	49,522	65,647
Active tutors	41,618	44,494

Source: Jones and Charnley, 1978.

broadcasts reached a very large public. More than two thirds of the adult population saw at least one 'On the Move' programme, and some individual programmes had audiences of over three million. Nearly two thirds of those that saw the programmes were in the lower income categories (occupational groups D and E). There is no doubt that the broadcasts did bring the issue of adult literacy to the attention of the general public and provided a simple means to do something about it for those who wanted to.

Thirdly, when the adult literacy campaign was being planned, virtually no appropriate materials for teaching adult illiterates in Britain existed. There were no workbooks or reading books suitable for adults, no training manuals or guides for tutors, no visual aids or graphical materials and virtually no tutors trained in teaching adult literacy. First of all, the BBC produced the Adult Literacy Handbook for tutors, followed by workbooks for students to accompany the television programmes and a student reader to go with the two radio series for students. While the workbooks were later criticised as being too basic to meet many local or individual needs, they did provide models that could be adapted by tutors themselves for their own needs. Nearly 70,000 copies of the Handbook had been sold by 1980, and by 1978 over 53,000 of the 'On the Move' student workbooks had also been sold. Thus the BBC made a major contribution towards providing essential print and training materials, as well as producing the broadcasts themselves.

The broadcasters faced a particularly difficult task. Great skill and sensitivity are required to preserve the dignity of the adult illiterate, especially if watching the programmes in front of the family. At the same time, the programmes had to be interesting and entertaining so as to attract the adult illiterate in the first place. Furthermore, there was a need to get prime time slots for transmission if large numbers were to be recruited. Never before had peak viewing time on British television been allocated to a series with an explicit educational purpose. The slot eventually allotted was Sunday evening, immediately after the main news, when there is always a big family audience.

The Controller of BBC1, in allocating this time to 'On the Move', had insisted that the programmes be attractive and acceptable to such an audience. The programmes therefore had to appeal both to the general public *and* to the adult illiterates amongst that audience. Fortunately, this seemed to work out well, since the parent with reading difficulties was able to watch with the rest of the family, without being singled out as being rather special or 'odd'.

It is my view that the BBC programmes did successfully achieve their objectives. They attracted a large general audience, and from

that audience large numbers of students and volunteers were stimulated to come forward for formal tuition through the telephone
referral system. The programmes also stimulated a more general
awareness of the problem of adult literacy and probably indirectly
encouraged many more students and tutors to come forward, if not
directly through the telephone referral service.

COMMON FEATURES OF SUCCESS

Although 'Sesame Street' and 'On the Move' are very different, the
two projects have a surprising number of features in common which
suggest important conditions necessary for successfully reaching
and teaching the disadvantaged.

Neither of these two series would have succeeded unless the
programmes had been entertaining. 'Sesame Street' won the Japan
prize. 'On the Move' won the Royal Television Society's Original
Programme Award. Both series attracted a mass audience through
skilful use of popular television techniques but without compromising their educational objectives. Both series were fun to watch. This
alone does not guarantee success in educational terms but if the
programmes are to get through to the educationally disadvantaged,
they have to be at least as attractive as alternative and less socially
responsible programming.

Both series were expensive to mount. The BBC put £800,000 into
the production of the Adult Literacy Campaign programmes;
another £200,000 was raised from charitable sources, primarily the
Ford Foundation and the Cadbury Trust, for the telephone referral
service; central government put in £3 million for local tuition and
training resources, through ALRA; and local authorities provided
manpower and other resources from their own budgets, probably
equal to that received from ALRA. The total budget for the
three-year campaign was well over £7 million. Similarly, in its first
two years of operation (1968–70) Children's Television Workshop's
budget for 'Sesame Street' was just over $8 million. These levels of
funding are much greater than the sums normally available for
educational series. Money is no guarantee of quality but if the aim is
to attract large numbers of educationally disadvantaged people they
will expect to see top entertainers, and the programmes will need
writers and producers with proven popular appeal, putting the
programmes towards the more expensive end of broadcasting.
Television is not a cheap alternative to other forms of education for
the disadvantaged. It may be cheaper than establishing a comprehensive national system of nursery schools or providing regular

formal adult literacy tuition in every town; it may relieve the government of some of the costs; but it cannot be done on the cheap if it is to be successful. Adequate resources are essential.

Neither of the two projects went it alone. While both were essentially initiated by broadcasters, other agencies were extensively involved. In the end, collaboration was essential for success. This is more apparent with the Adult Literacy campaign than with 'Sesame Street'. Without the efforts of ALRA, the local authorities and the voluntary organisations, the programmes would have been pointless. Collaboration was established right from the beginning of the project. This was important, because a later adult numeracy project, 'Make it Count', failed to have an impact because the local education authorities were not involved early enough (see Stringer, 1979). One reason why collaboration worked so well was the appointment by the BBC of a full-time liaison officer. On the other hand, 'Sesame Street' does not appear at first to be a good example of collaboration between broadcasters and others. Polsky (1974) suggests that the project was successful because it was able to operate without being constrained by the educational community. While this may have been true regarding fund raising to initiate the project, it was not true regarding implementation. For instance, the detailed objectives for the programmes were defined as a result of a series of seminars attended by educators, child psychiatrists, television producers, children's book authors and artists, a children's music composer and a puppeteer. The seminars were organised by Dr Gerald Lesser, a Professor of Education at Harvard University. Also, full-time educational researchers were appointed to work alongside producers to test out ideas and evaluate the programmes before production. Nevertheless, if there had been more widespread and continuing involvement of the educational world, many of the cultural and philosophical objections to 'Sesame Street' might have been avoided.

Both series also developed what was in effect a new curriculum for the target group at which the programmes were aimed. In the case of the Adult Literacy campaign, there was no previously existing national curriculum, and above all no teaching materials suitable for adults. These all had to be specially created. With 'Sesame Street', a range of conflicting educational approaches had to be analysed and resolved. In fact, 'Sesame Street' narrowed down its objectives considerably as planning progressed due to constraints of time and money. Again, a wider range of objectives may have been possible if there had been additional materials prepared by other agencies. Nevertheless, in both cases the result was an approach specially developed for the specific target group at

which the programmes were aimed. Both projects, however, consequently needed longer planning times and larger budgets than for a
normal series of programmes.

One very significant feature common to both projects was the
important role of pre-testing and formative evaluation. Programme
ideas were tested and changed if necessary *before* transmission.
Formative evaluation was extensive and formalised in Children's
Television Workshop (see Palmer, 1972, for a full description). The
researchers identified existing abilities of the children in the target
group and programme characteristics that appealed to such children,
and tested out programme ideas prior to full production. Formative
evaluation was built into the production process and production
schedules were designed to allow for this. While pre-testing was less
rigorous and less extensive for 'On the Move', it virtually prevented
a disaster. The senior producer, David Hargreaves (1980), reported
that reactions from adult illiterates to the pilot material were 'often
violent and generally hostile . . . the predominant reaction was one
of bewilderment'. The initial comedy sequences went down badly,
while a science-fiction segment provoked rage. Hargreaves concluded that the plight of the non-reader was serious and had to be
treated seriously. Systematic pre-testing of programmes is still
strongly resisted by many producers and broadcasting managements; it adds to costs, slows up the rate of production, and requires
a different form of production scheduling. Above all, it challenges
the professional assumptions of producers. Nevertheless, early
programme plans for 'On the Move' had to be abandoned in the
light of the target group's reactions, despite the initial programmes
being made by some of the most successful television writers, actors
and producers. When producers are aiming at audiences with
special characteristics, as is always the case with programmes for
the disadvantaged, systematic formative evaluation seems to be
essential.

Another feature which emerges is the importance of the personal
touch. Viewing programmes in isolation appears to have been
inadequate for effective learning to take place on both projects. For
'On the Move', it was deliberate policy to encourage viewers to
contact a personal tutor. It was recognised that teaching adults
reading skills was best done on a person-to-person basis. 'Sesame
Street', though, seems at first sight to be an exception to this. It
looks initially as if 'Sesame Street' is a series which has used
television without extensive support or back-up from tutors.
However, careful examination of the studies by Bogatz and Ball
(1972) and by Cook (1975) reveal that what really affected learning
was encouragement to view. Consequently, Morris and Gregory

(1976), Beck (1979) and a number of other people have suggested that the presence of an 'encouraging' person, especially the mother, watching *with* the child during the programme, is what really counts if children are to learn from television. If personal support is therefore essential for the disadvantaged, the relative roles of the broadcasts and personal support need to be very carefully worked out. 'Listen with Mother' is absolutely right!

Broadcasts aimed at the disadvantaged need to be well marketed and publicised. CTW had its own Promotion and Utilisation Department which used all the tricks of the advertising trade to launch a promotional campaign before the first 'Sesame Street' programmes were transmitted. The Adult Literacy Campaign was promoted by disc jockeys on the popular Radio 1 and Radio 2 channels and on local radio, assisted by a pop record based on the music for 'On the Move'; items were carried on national television news and current affairs programmes; a short promotional film was made by the Central Office of Information and shown repeatedly during commercial breaks on ITV; 1·2 million leaflets and other promotional literature such as posters were distributed through national chain stores, such as Tescos and W. H. Smiths; and a special logo was designed, accompanied by local telephone referral numbers. These logoed posters and leaflets were displayed and distributed in public areas such as libraries, doctors' and dentists' waiting rooms, and in bookshops selling literacy materials. *Total* marketing seems to be necessary to reach disadvantaged groups in any large numbers.

Lastly, to get through to a mass audience, maximum exposure of the programme material on broadcasting services that are heavily used by the target group is necessary. This means lots of programmes, shown several times each year, for more than one year, at popular times. CTW made 130 one-hour programmes of 'Sesame Street' each season. The BBC made 50 'On the Move' and 50 'Your Move' programmes, broadcast twice a year for two or three years. Both series were given prime viewing slots, 'On the Move' on the more popular and less cultural of the two BBC television channels, and 'Sesame Street' on the PBS network.

THE IMPORTANCE OF NETWORK POLICIES

The importance of using popular networks at appropriate times to reach the disadvantaged cannot be too strongly emphasised. Not all educationally disadvantaged people will be found in working-class occupational groups, but many will, and there are major class differences in Britain in the use of different broadcast services.

On average, people in working-class occupations spend about two to five hours more a week watching television than people in middle-class occupations (the overall average for TV watching in Britain is between fifteen to twenty hours a week – BBC, 1979). Although BBC1 attracts quite heavy viewing from working-class people, they are more likely to watch ITV1 (the commercial channel). They spend about twice as much time watching ITV1 (ten to twelve hours a week) as the middle class (five to seven hours). Consequently, some of the tutors and organisers argued that the adult literacy programmes should have been shown on ITV – but then ITV didn't make the programmes!

There are even sharper differences on radio. The working class listen almost exclusively to BBC Radio 1, BBC Radio 2 and local radio stations. Hardly any (less than 1 per cent) listen to Radio 3 on a typical day (but then neither does the middle class – only 4 per cent). Middle-class people listen two or three times as much to Radio 4 as working-class people. Over a typical month, only 20 per cent of the working class will have listened *at all* to Radio 4, compared with over 90 per cent who will have listened to Radio 1.

The consequence of such sharp channel identities for educating the disadvantaged through broadcasting is profound. Programmes made by the educational radio department of the BBC are almost exclusively broadcast on Radio 3 and 4. Only about a third of the total population and a fifth of the working class will tune in at all to these channels in a typical month, never mind late at night when the majority of educational programmes are broadcast. It is not surprising then that programmes like 'Living Decisions' and 'What Right Have You Got?' failed to reach the educationally disadvantaged. They never had a chance.

Whenever the idea of a whole channel dedicated to education has been mooted in Britain, one of the main arguments raised against it is that it would lead to ghetto broadcasting; but we already have ghetto broadcasting. One of the major justifications for using broadcasting in education is its serendipitous effect: by chance someone may catch an educational programme who would otherwise not have bothered to look for it. Channel identity drastically reduces that likelihood. Unless there is a major change in overall policy, particularly regarding BBC radio, resulting in a greater mix of programmes on the same channel (which some may feel would be worthwhile for other than educational reasons), programmes for the educationally disadvantaged, to be effective, must be broadcast on the more popular channels of ITV1, BBC1, BBC Radio 1 and 2, and local radio stations. While this has been done to some extent, it cuts across the management lines for educational broadcasting, and the programming policies for popular channels. It seems therefore that popular channels could be used only *exceptionally* for educational programming for the disadvantaged, which inevitably limits the scope of broadcasting in this area.

SUMMING UP

Those in need of basic education tend to be heavy users of broadcasting but only for entertainment purposes. There is therefore an element of education by stealth in using broadcasting to attract people to basic education activities. This means starting where the viewer is, with respect to needs and expectancies. Using broadcasting successfully for basic education has in practice proved very difficult. Only a small proportion of those initially attracted by the programmes become 'serious' or heavily committed learners. The majority remain casual viewers or listeners, and those attracted to programmes for the disadvantaged have often tended to be the better educated.

Using 'Sesame Street' and 'On the Move' as examples, I have tried to identify the necessary conditions for successful programming in this area. Quality programming, programmes that entertain without diminishing their educational purpose, is essential. This means adequate production resources, at a level well above what is usually available for educational programming. Also essential is collaboration with other agencies. Television or radio alone are not enough for basic education and consequently the support of other agencies is necessary. In particular, some form of personal tuition or contact needs to be provided and encouraged. Special approaches and materials suitable for the target group need to be developed – it is unlikely that suitable existing materials will be found. Because of the special nature of the target groups, systematic formative evaluation becomes crucial if the programmes are to succeed. This has implications for programme budgets, production scheduling and the time-scale of projects. Broadcasting in this area is unlikely to be an adequate form of publicity in itself; total marketing through a variety of outlets will also be important. Lastly, and perhaps most important of all, the programmes have to be transmitted at popular times on popular channels, which suggests that broadcasting can only be used *exceptionally* for basic education.

Despite the potentially very large audiences for non-formal basic education, it is a difficult area for broadcasting. Even when all the necessary conditions are met, broadcasting is unlikely to *reduce* the gap between advantaged and disadvantaged sectors of society, although it could do more to prevent that gap from widening. For that to happen, though, major policy changes in general broadcasting would be necessary.

6

Continuing and distance higher education: strategic roles for broadcasting

THE USE OF GENERAL BROADCASTING IN CONTINUING EDUCATION

Some senior broadcasting executives in both the BBC and the commercial companies in Britain argue that *general* broadcasting is more educationally effective than the specialist and 'narrow' approach of educational broadcasting departments. 'Good television is good education'. Their argument is that much of the general output of broadcasting – especially news, current affairs, music and drama – is highly educative. Broadcasting improves people's knowledge of the world, raises cultural standards and provides educational stimulation. So, for example, children's television encourages the development of imagination through fantasy and story-telling, news bulletins keep the working population up to date with political and economic events, current affairs and documentary programmes help management and industry to keep abreast of financial and technological developments, and magazine-format programmes keep housewives informed of consumer matters. A British government inquiry into adult education, under the chairmanship of Sir Lionel Russell, was no doubt influenced by this kind of thinking when it commented that:

> the principal adult education force in Britain today may well be the *general* television output of the BBC and Independent Television (as *distinct* from their expressly educational work) (Great Britain: DES, 1973 – my emphases).

The view that general broadcasting has a strong educational role is also shared by the Public Broadcasting System in the USA: 'quality' general programming – including many programmes bought from the BBC and ITV companies – constitutes a large part of the output of this national educational network.

Sociologists would also argue that the mass media transmit and reinforce traditional cultural standards and ideals, and are in this sense a unifying force in society leading to consensus and conformity. Broadcasting reinforces stereotypes of what it is to be British, or a woman, or a married man, not just through drama and documentary, but also through comedy programmes, quiz shows and other entertainment programmes. This is not a role to which British broadcasters themselves would necessarily admit. Much of the transmission of cultural standards and ideals through broadcasting is unintentional or unconscious, both to broadcasters and the audience. Also, it is arguable whether the unquestioning transmission of stereotypes or traditional views is really educational. While not denying the importance of broadcasting as a means of transmitting and reinforcing traditional cultural values, I feel that this aspect of broadcasting cannot be considered educational in the perhaps narrow way I have chosen to define it (deliberate study organised by someone other than the learner). Those interested in the broader cultural role of mass media are referred to Tunstall (1970), MacQuail (1972), or Curran *et al.* (1977), for instance.

In any case, it is very much an open question whether general broadcasting does have a direct effect on learning. There is an astonishingly sparse amount of published research on what people actually learn from general television programmes. In one area where substantial research has been done, on what people remember from the main news programmes, the evidence from studies in Britain, Sweden, Israel and the USA is consistently unfavourable. Gunter, Berry and Clifford (1982) conclude in summarising this research: 'memory for the content of individual news programmes often appears very poor indeed only a short time after viewing'. Broadcasters' reactions to such research is usually very hostile – they refuse to believe it. Consequently, in one organisation, the management sprang a surprise factual test on the news production team as they arrived for work. They too were unable to answer many questions correctly – even though the test was based on the programme on which they had been working the previous day!

Findahl and Höijer (1978) claim that poor recall of the news is due to the way news programmes structure and package information in the form of short, unrelated items with inadequate background or interpretation. News programming is relatively popular with the general public, so there appears to be a conflict between entertainment and instructional values; news programmes are attracting viewers but not adequately informing them. It seems likely that general documentary programmes also may have questionable educational value because of the way they are structured and packaged. We will see in the next chapter that even with strongly motivated adult learners at a higher education level, learning from documentary-style programmes is difficult. There seems then to be considerable scope for more research into how general broadcasts affect what people learn, and how people think about issues covered by the programmes. Such research needs to look in particular at how learning and thinking are influenced by the way programmes are structured and packaged.

Some of the educational limitations of general broadcasts might be overcome by using them as a basis for adult education courses. Indeed, in America, many colleges run very successful courses around popular television series. However, in Britain the copyright restrictions and regulations regarding royalties negotiated as part of the programme contract are so severe and restrictive that it is a civil offence to record for use as part of an educational course any programme not formally designated as educational by the broad-casting organisations. Even if permission is requested, it is never formally given, because the contracts would have to be renego-tiated. Thus the situation for non-formal education is exactly the same as for formal education regarding the use of general program-ming. Such restrictions in practice mean that it is almost impossible in Britain to advertise courses built around popular television series.

Such courses though would have enormous potential. Some idea of this can be gleaned from a very modest project run in Yorkshire in 1978 based on the four programmes in the ATV series, 'Dizzy', about the life of Disraeli. A group of broadcasters and educators, called Northern Open Learning, put together a booklet with the intention of helping viewers to gain more knowledge of the back-ground to the programmes and the characters in them. In the booklet were suggestions for a whole range of follow-up activities, including visits to local museums and a list of relevant local courses (these courses though would be general history courses not based on the television series itself since they would not be allowed to show the programmes!). In the Yorkshire TV transmission area an announcement was made at the end of each programme inviting viewers to write in for the booklet, and more than 4,000 requests were received. It should be noted that this booklet differed con-siderably from the glossy coffee-table books often sold in connec-tion with popular television series. The booklet was much more modest in production and much more instructional in lay-out and design, yet the reaction of those who sent for it was very favourable (Elliott, 1979).

If then general broadcasters really do believe in the educational value of general broadcasting, they will need to make it much easier to use recordings of selected general broadcast series for adult educational purposes, and they will need to encourage more efforts along the lines of the Northern Open Learning group's project. Until they are prepared to do that, or until some evidence is available to show what people actually learn from general programming, their claim that good television is good education will continue to sound like special pleading.

CONTINUING EDUCATION PROGRAMMES:
THE BRITISH PERSPECTIVE

Last year Thames TV's 10-part series on evolution and ecology ('Botanic Man') broke new ground . . . In London the programmes figured in the 'Top 20' three times – on one occasion reaching number 1. If a university professor enthusing about green slime can do that (with a little help from his friends) what other possibilities – as yet unexplored – could exist? (IBA Audience Research Department, 1979).

Indeed. There is a truly astonishing quantity and variety of nationally networked adult education programming in Britain. Categorising broadcasts is an arid and thankless task, but to give an adequate picture of non-formal broadcasting in the UK it is necessary to analyse and summarise the output formally designated as 'continuing education' by British broadcasting agencies. Continuing education programming in Britain in fact has a very specific definition. For instance, the programming discussed in Chapter 5 – programmes for the disadvantaged, minority groups, the handicapped and some social action programming – constitutes a relatively small proportion of what is formally designated 'continuing education broadcasting'. Other programming – such as children's television, rural programming and a lot of social action broadcasting – is not part at all of the output of continuing education departments of British broadcasting organisations. Table 12 lists the total number of series and programmes designated as continuing education broadcast over a twelve-month period during 1980–81, excluding ITV repeats. This is equivalent to roughly 500 hours of television and 200 hours of radio per year.

In 1981 the BBC alone used twenty-one categories to describe their 90 TV and 45 radio series – not always consistently, as the same series sometimes occurred under different categories in different publications. Nevertheless, these twenty-one BBC categories can be collapsed without too much force into eleven basic headings, and

TABLE 12

TOTAL CONTINUING EDUCATION PROGRAMMING, 1981

	Television		Radio	
	Series	Programmes	Series	Programmes
BBC CE – new	32	246	} 45	} 345
BBC CE – repeats	58	458		
ITV – new only	29	207	–	–
OU CE – new	2	11	} 13	} 106
OU CE – repeats	16	120		
Total	137	1,042	58	451

the other agencies' output can be sorted into these eleven headings. This results in the crude categorisation system used in Table 13.

Unfortunately, at the time of this study, Channel 4 had not begun transmission. Since 15 per cent of its output is supposed to be educational programming, nearly all of a continuing education nature and much of it aimed at minority groups, there is a substantial amount of additional educational programming now available in the United Kingdom but not included in these figures.

The eleven categories in Table 13 can be further grouped into three rather different types of programming, differentiated not only by the content of programmes but also by major differences in the nature of the target audiences. Table 13 gives details. The three main groups of programmes can be identified as follows:

Programmes for the disadvantaged

These are programmes aimed at significant minorities and/or disadvantaged groups. These would be series concerned with basic coping skills (literacy, basic numeracy), women's studies, or series aimed at physically or mentally handicapped adults, ethnic minorities and the elderly. These target audiences are likely to have either low income *or* low educational levels, as measured by formal qualifications, *or* some form of physical or mental handicap. Such programming has already been discussed in previous chapters.

General interest programmes

These are programmes likely to appeal to a wide range of people, irrespective of occupation, educational level or income. As with

TABLE 13

NEW ADULT EDUCATION NATIONALLY NETWORKED TELEVISION PROGRAMMES PRODUCED IN UK, 1981

	BBC CE (Jan.-Dec., 1981)			ITV (Apr. '80-March '81)			OU CE (Jan.-Dec., 1981)		
	Series	Pro-grammes	%	Series	Pro-grammes	%	Series	Pro-grammes	%
Disadvantaged									
Basic and coping skills	1	10	4	0	0	0	0	0	0
Physically and mentally handicapped	4	37	15	1	7	3	0	0	0
Women's studies/young adults/elderly/ethnic minorities	3	25	10	6	45	22	0	0	0
Sub-total	8	72	29	7	52	24	0	0	0
General interest									
Family, community and health education	3	33	13	7	50	24	1	4	36
Crafts, leisure and household skills	3	20	8	7	54	26	0	0	0
Environment/nature	3	19	8	0	0	0	0	0	0
Sub-total	9	72	29	14	104	50	1	4	36

'Up-market'									
Work, training, industry, management	4	25	10	0	0	0	0	0	0
Literature, arts, history	2	16	7	1	13	6	0	0	0
Public affairs, political education, media studies	4	18	7	4	25	12	0	0	0
Education	3	23	9	2	7	3	1	7	64
Modern languages	2	20	8	1	6	3	0	0	0
Sub-total	15	102	41	8	51	25	1	7	64
Grand total	32	246	100	29	207	100	2	11	100

programmes for the disadvantaged, these programmes assume no previous knowledge. General interest programmes, however, *are* concerned with the non-vocational, non-academic, everyday interests of adults. They are not aimed primarily at the less educated nor the disadvantaged, nor is it assumed that those with good formal educational qualifications will form the bulk of the audience.

General interest programmes could be further divided into two main sub-groups: home and leisure programmes; and community education programmes. Typical of *leisure* programmes would be series such as 'Better Badminton', 'Training Dogs', 'Delia Smith's Cookery', 'Mr Smith's Fruit Garden' (all BBC), 'As Good as New' (Yorkshire) and 'Camera' (Granada). 'Leisure' programmes tend to be self-contained, in that each programme is complete in itself, although many leisure series are accompanied by glossy books on sale through local bookshops.

Community education programmes, however, tend to deal with more serious issues of everyday life. The Open University's Continuing Education Division runs a series of community education short courses which, it says, are:

> designed to help people, often leading busy lives, to make a comprehensive review of a particular aspect of their lives, whether as a parent, consumer, employee, or as a concerned citizen . . . These short courses help you, through a well-planned educational approach, to take stock of your changing experience and play a fuller role in your family and community life (Open University, 1982).

These programmes are likely to include series such as 'Energy in the Home', 'The First Years of Life', 'Consumer Decisions' (Open University); 'Wainright's Law', 'Play it Safe', 'Principles of Counselling' (BBC); 'Moneywise' (on family budgeting – Scottish TV); and 'Village Action' (Westward).

In Open University community education courses, television and radio programmes are usually just two components of a multi-media package with simply written, highly illustrated books or booklets. These courses may also be supported by locally arranged group meetings, either organised through the Open University's own regional system or through sponsors or co-operating agencies such as the Pre-School Playgroups' Association. The BBC and ITV series in this area tend to be more broadcast-led, though there is often support material available in the form of group discussion notes, leaflets or a telephone contact for further information.

'*Up-market*' *programmes*

These are programmes likely to appeal to a more serious, committed audience, with above average work responsibilities, incomes or formal educational qualifications. These may be considered truly 'continuing' education programmes in that they continue on from where people left off at school, or may help people to continue to develop vocationally or professionally. As can be seen in Table 13, I have divided these programmes into five broad groups.

The first group contains vocationally-oriented series, such as 'Supervisors', 'Trades Union Studies', 'Your Own Business' (BBC); 'Industrial Relations' and 'The Effective Manager' (Open University). Also in this group – although growing at such a rate that it will soon need its own heading – are series on technology and microelectronics. Particularly significant here is the BBC initiative on computer literacy. In 1981 the BBC negotiated with a British computer manufacturer to produce a low-cost microcomputer to the BBC's specification which could be used in conjunction with its TV series 'The Computer Programme' aimed both at adults and schools. This resulted in over 80,000 orders for the microcomputer over a period of about a year. Almost immediately after its launch in 1982, this particular microcomputer became one of the models on which the Department of Education and Science encouraged schools to standardise by offering to pay half the cost of one of these micros if the school would find the other half.

Perhaps the most significant sub-group of programmes in this group, because of the large number actually transmitted each year, are the modern language series broadcast almost exclusively by the BBC (although the Open University is also beginning to get involved in advanced language courses). In 1981 the BBC broadcast twenty-three series, in French, Spanish, German, Welsh, Italian, Russian and Gaelic. The BBC began modern language radio programming as early as 1930, and in 1981 these programmes constituted 14 per cent of the BBC CE's total TV output and over a third (38 per cent) of BBC CE's radio output. Programmes can range from short five-programme series for people with no previous knowledge of a language (for holidays, etc. – e.g. 'Get By in Spanish') to third-level advanced language series of twenty-five programmes.

Also in this up-market group are programmes covering the arts, literature, history, public affairs, politics, media studies and educational issues for teachers and parents. Examples would be 'Artists in Print', 'Shakespeare Perspectives', 'The Past at Work' (BBC); 'Public Office' (Granada); 'The Television Programme' (Westward); and 'Maths across the Curriculum' (Open University).

TABLE 14

TOTAL OUTPUT, BBC CE AND OU CE, 1981 (ITV FIGURES NOT AVAILABLE IN THIS FORM)

	Television						Radio					
	BBC CE			OU CE			BBC CE			OU CE		
	Series	Pro-grammes	%	Series	Pro-grammes	%	Series	Pro-grammes	%	Series	Pro-grammes	%
Disadvantaged												
Basic and coping skills	5	50	7	0	0	0	1	8	2	0	0	0
Physically and mentally handicapped	8	57	8	1	11	8	1	4	1	1	11	10
Women's studies/ young adults/elderly/ ethnic minorities	3	23	3	1	8	6	2	17	5	1	16	15
Sub-total	16	130	18	2	19	14	4	29	8	2	27	25

General interest												
Family, community and health education	8	65	9	8	36	27	10	61	18	6	21	20
Crafts, leisure and household skills	21	166	24	0	0	0	3	18	5	0	0	0
Environment/nature	3	22	3	0	0	0	1	5	1	0	0	0
Sub-total	32	253	36	8	36	27	14	84	24	6	21	20
'Up-market'												
Work, training, industry, management	7	48	7	3	31	24	2	13	4	3	39	37
Literature, arts, history	7	51	7	0	0	0	7	54	16	0	0	0
Public affairs, political education, media studies	13	85	12	0	0	0	1	12	3	0	0	0
Education	5	37	5	5	45	34	4	22	6	2	19	18
Modern languages	10	100	14	0	0	0	13	131	38	0	0	0
Sub-total	42	321	45	8	76	58	27	232	67	5	58	58
Grand Total	90	704	100	18	131	100	45	345	100	13	106	100

Since programmes in this general up-market group are likely to attract the more serious and committed learner, the broadcasts are much more likely to be components of multi-media courses, although with the BBC and ITV series the programmes tend to play a more leading role than with Open University Continuing Education courses where the printed materials are more significant. To give an indication of the multi-media approaches adopted, '¡Digame!' (a BBC beginners' Spanish course) has twenty-five TV programmes, twenty radio programmes, a students' book, tutors' notes, two audio-cassettes or LP records, with a third cassette or LP record containing exercises from the programme. Local adult education classes based on the series may also be available.

The BBC's 'The Computer Programme' has an accompanying BBC book and viewers following the series are recommended to get the associated BBC computer and some specially commissioned computer programmes. There is also an associated correspondence course on programming run by the National Extension College, and the BBC series encourages the establishment of local computer clubs. Again, local adult education classes may be run based on the programmes and materials. For a good description of programme series in the continuing education area, and indeed for a comprehensive history of such programmes, see Robinson (1982).

Table 14 provides total output figures in 1981 for BBC and Open University CE programming (figures for ITV were not available in this form). Combining all the information from Tables 13 and 14, the overall pattern of provision can be identified.

Around 20–25 per cent of both television and radio programmes from all the agencies are directed at *disadvantaged* groups, ITV being particularly strong in 1981 on programmes for young adults, and BBC on programmes for the physically handicapped. With only fifteen new series a year directed at disadvantaged or minority groups, and even allowing for programmes directed at these groups by other broadcasting departments, plenty of scope remains for Channel 4 in minority programming. BBC CE radio had very few programmes for the disadvantaged, Open University CE radio having a higher proportion (29 per cent) and almost as many in total from a smaller output.

In the *general interest* area, ITV has the largest proportion (50 per cent) and the largest number of programmes, while between a fifth and a third of both BBC and Open University CE programmes are in this area, both for television and radio.

As one might expect, a higher proportion of Open University CE television programmes are aimed *up-market* (64 per cent), with BBC CE TV next (41 per cent). ITV has 25 per cent of its CE programming in this area. Over two thirds of BBC CE radio output was aimed at this up-market audience (language programmes particularly dominating).

Britain then is uniquely fortunate in the range of programming available in the continuing education field. However, the very variety of provision creates a problem for users. It is in fact extremely difficult for the general public or even colleges to get a coherent picture of what is available. In a field where there is a good deal of co-operation between the four main agencies to avoid duplication and competition, it is a pity that there is no single publication covering the offerings of all the agencies. Without such a single source of information available well in advance of transmissions, it is difficult to see how adult education institutions can plan sensibly to provide courses linked with broadcasts. It is even more difficult for the individual viewer or listener to find out what is available and so plan *in advance* to use broadcasts.

CONTINUING EDUCATION:
AN INTERNATIONAL PERSPECTIVE

The diversity of continuing education broadcasting in Britain is matched by the variety of arrangements and provision in other countries. While the major national broadcasting organisations provide and control the use of television and radio for non-graduate continuing education in Britain, this is not the only pattern, and a brief look at some other systems will identify some interesting differences.

USA

Nowhere is the diversity of organisational arrangements greater than in the USA. A major provider is the Public Broadcasting System, funded partly by the federal government and partly by charitable foundations, such as Carnegie and Ford. The Public Broadcasting System operates through a network of educational television stations across the nation, many operating on cable, and linked to PBS via satellite. These educational television stations can take programmes from the PBS network or they may produce their own. Programmes offered through PBS may be specially commissioned or funded by the Corporation for Public Broadcasting, or may be bought in by CPB from other production agencies such as the BBC or ITV companies. Since each individual station decides which programmes to take, the offerings vary completely from station to station. A good deal of the PBS output would be considered general broadcasting in Britain, but colleges in the USA have proved much more willing than British educational institutions to build adult education courses around general broadcast series like 'The Ascent of Man' and 'The Long Search'.

Some ETV stations are funded by the State, such as the Nebraska Educational Communications Authority and Kentucky Educational Television. These both produce and transmit general cultural and adult education programming, as well as school and college programmes.

The Chicago TV College is an extension of the City Colleges of Chicago, and in its twenty-five-year existence has enrolled upward of 150,000 students in its TV courses. Until recently, the Chicago TV College produced low-cost, 'talking-head' programmes that were little more than simulated classroom lectures, but more recently, like many American community colleges, it has been participating in consortia of colleges to produce joint courses, enabling more expensive productions to be mounted.

One of the oldest networked adult education series is seen mainly by insomniacs, jet-lagged tourists in hotel-rooms, shiftworkers and early risers. This is New York University's 'Sunrise Semester', broadcast by many stations across the USA between 6.00 and 6.30 a.m. These too are low-budget studio programmes given mainly by professors from New York University and their invited guests. However, unlike the Chicago TV College, 'Sunrise Semester' programmes are not part of any course offering since each programme is complete in itself and has no supporting materials.

Thus in the USA one finds a wide range of organisations for adult education programming, from independent, self-standing programmes to integrated college TV courses, from the cheapest type of production to the most glossy and expensive (see Lewis, 1983, for an excellent overview of the use of broadcasting in post-secondary education in the USA).

Canada

Here too there is a diverse system of continuing education broadcasting. Like the American networks, the Canadian Broadcasting Corporation carries general cultural programming, and again some of these series may be used by local colleges as a basis for adult education courses. However, the main source of adult education programming in Canada comes from the several large educational television and radio stations financed by some of the provinces, such as TV Ontario; Radio Québec; and ACCESS, Alberta.

TV Ontario's budget for 1982 was C$35 million (£18 million), which compares with the £16 million devoted to BBC Schools and Continuing Education television programmes in the same year. TV Ontario covers both schools and adult education programming, producing its own and buying in series from elsewhere. TV Ontario's transmissions can be received in 90 per cent of the homes in the province using a mix of broadcast transmitters, cable systems and direct broadcasting by satellite. In Toronto and several other areas, TV Ontario has its own cable channel, competing at times with up to twenty-seven other cable channels. All three of these Canadian provincial stations are increasingly involved in co-production and networking agreements, not only with each other but also with other agencies such as Children's Television Workshop in New York. Somewhat surprisingly, though, TV Ontario does not have its own production facilities, instead using some of the other production agencies in the province.

Like Radio Québec and ACCESS, TV Ontario is a broadcasting organisation and not an educational institution *per se*; it does not offer any credit courses on its own behalf. However, recently it has come very close to this through its TV Academy. The basic component of TV Academy is a series of television programmes covering a well-defined body of knowledge, supported by a printed handbook which includes a learner's guide and specially written essays to accompany each programme, and a set of computer-marked multiple-choice questions which, when sent in to TV Ontario, result in a set of 'individualised' comments from the computer, dependent on the background of the respondent and the answers provided (see Waniewicz, 1981, for further details).

Sweden

In comparison with North America, Sweden has had a unified system of adult education broadcasting since 1978 when the Educational Broadcasting Department of Sveriges Radio merged with TRU (a council set up by the government to study the role of television and radio in education) to form Utbildningsradion (the Swedish Educational Broadcasting Company). A characteristic of Swedish adult education is the establishment of local study circles in practically every town or large village in Sweden and most of the continuing education broadcast series make full use of this dynamic and independent infrastructure. A large part of the success of

START, referred to in the previous chapter, is due to the close support for the series given by the study circles. START is a typical example of the way Swedish broadcasting co-operates with other agencies in the field of adult education.

START was designed by a project team headed by a producer from Sveriges Radio, and included authors of the print material, an editor from Sveriges Radio's publishing department, an editor from a correspondence school, a publicity officer and several radio and television producers. A major adult voluntary organisation arranged courses for group leaders, and several other study associations also set up study circles for the course. Ultimately START consisted of six course books (one per term, each term of 13 weeks); two radio programmes per week, each programme broadcast three times; several TV programmes per week in year 1 (fewer in later years), each broadcast three times; an audio tape and recorded versions of the course book; questions to be answered and corrected by a correspondence school; revision books; picture cards and film-strips for group work; manuals for study-circle leaders; and study circles organised by the voluntary study associations.

The course was designed so that students could manage if necessary with just the course book, which contained all the subject matter, although weekly radio programmes were also considered essential for the oral aspect. In practice, most students studied through a *combination* of broadcasts, individual work and study circles. The course was also used in Norway, Finland and Denmark, with minor adaptations, and was eventually replaced in 1982 by a new beginners' series, 'Take It Easy'.

France

Adult education programmes are produced by a state institution financed by the Ministry of National Education. Since the early 1970s there have been many changes of policy, organisation and names for the institution, programmes at one time or another being under the imprimatur of IPN, OFRATEME, RTS/Promotion, CNDP and, if changes proposed in 1983 are approved, the Institut National de Communications Éducatives (INCÉ). Although the names keep changing, programming has been mainly the responsibility of the Centre National de Documentation Pédagogique (CNDP) which has its own staff and production facilities. Transmission time, however, has to be bought from FR 3, one of the national broadcasting channels. During the same period, the output of adult education programming in France has declined steadily, from 5½ hours a week in 1974 to 1½ hours a week in 1983. In 1982 CNDP was broadcasting a total of nine television series, or ninety-five programmes in all. The series titles ('Electronics in the Home', 'Know Your Rights', 'Computing in Everyday Life', etc.) would not have looked out of place in the BBC/CE schedules, although production styles are rather different. CNDP also produced and distributed accompanying printed material and a monthly magazine about its programmes, called 'Téléformation', distributed free of charge to subscribers. As well as broadcasts, 16 mm film, video-cassettes, individual booklets and sometimes kits were made and distributed by CNDP to adult education organisations and even Francophone agencies overseas. In 1983, however, adult education broadcasting went through yet another change of policy. The multi-media concept was dropped and the programming became more like 'pure' broadcasting: 'éducation au sens large du terme' – education in the broadest sense. This resulted in a 1½-hour magazine programme on Saturday afternoons with a variety of single items and discussion. Production and transmission costs remain high, each Saturday afternoon costing Fr.800,000 (or £80,000). So in 1983 there were virtually no links between the broadcasts and the rest of the French adult education system, and no support materials. Ironically, though, the programmes have still failed to attract a large audience. Despite the reasonably good transmission time, the audience in 1983 was only about 20,000–25,000, or 0·065 per cent of the adult population.

ROLES IN CONTINUING EDUCATION: SOME CONCLUSIONS

Television and radio are used for continuing education in many other countries, for example by TELEAC and NOS in Holland, Funkkolleg in West Germany, NRK and Norsk Fjernundervisning in Norway, and NHK in Japan. There are large differences between each country in the range of provision, the extent to which other media are used, and the links between broadcast organisations and other institutions. Even so, there are some conclusions that can be drawn from an international comparison.

Because of the quantity of output and the resources devoted to it, the use of broadcasting in continuing education does warrant more analysis than is often given to it in educational circles. For instance, is the balance right between the different kinds of adult education broadcasting? In Britain, as in many other countries, the majority of adult education programming is still 'up-market' despite more programming in recent years for minority and disadvantaged groups. The small amount of broadcasting devoted to vocational training below management level is particularly noticeable, and it will be interesting to see whether the creation of Channel 4 and the Open Tech will change this.

Nevertheless, Britain is exceptionally fortunate. No single institution in the world compares with the BBC in terms of the quantity and range of output of continuing education broadcasting and, although no individual ITV company produces a wide range of programmes at this level, their co-ordinated network system also results in a range of programming almost as wide as the BBC's. In addition, Channel 4, the Open Tech and the expansion of the Open University's non-graduate programme suggest that over the next ten years the amount of broadcasting in this area will if anything grow rather than decrease.

With one or two exceptions, again it is broadcasters who determine policy regarding the use of television and radio in this as in other areas. Broadcasters lead, and other organisations join in, if they wish. Consequently, and again there are exceptions, programmes at this level are often not tightly integrated with other forms of adult education or training. It is, for instance, unusual to find programmes built in to courses leading to formal educational qualifications. Thus, in Britain, there are now no programmes linked to the Ordinary or Advanced Level General Certificate of Education, nor to professional or vocational qualifications, yet such courses form the bulk of adult education in Britain. In this sense, television and radio are an *alternative* to conventional adult education. This raises similar questions of accountability to those discussed in Chapter 4.

Despite the lack of strong formal links with other educational institutions, continuing education broadcasts have become increasingly part of a multi-media offering over the last decade; in some cases 'secondary' sales of support materials or cassettes have become almost as significant as the broadcasts themselves.

Radio has become overshadowed by television at this level in most developed countries. It has almost disappeared as a form of adult education in North America and France; even for the BBC, continuing education radio output is half that of television and is heavily biased towards 'up-market' audiences. Indeed, over the last few years educational radio for adults has been in deep decline in Britain, being relegated to unsocial hours (late at night), available only to those with VHF (FM) reception (still by no means universally available in Britain) and broadcast on minority channels. While some local radio stations are relatively active in community and social action broadcasting, very few provide any form of continuing education programmes outside the general cultural and informational areas.

In general, continuing education programmes are inadequately publicised. Glikman and Corduant (1977) claimed that 90 per cent of French viewers were unaware of the existence of CNDP's programmes, and that most of those that did know about them found out by chance. In a cable environment such as Toronto's, chance is not a good marketing strategy since with twenty-eight channels there is only a 1 in 28 chance of randomly finding TV Ontario's programmes! In Britain, there is no one central source of information regarding continuing education programmes, either for teachers or for the interested adult learner, making advance planning of learning based on broadcasts almost impossible. It seems that the broadcasting organisations rely too much on seren-dipitous viewing and listening, suggesting that it is the making of the programmes that matters most rather than their sensible utilisation.

Lastly, much seems to depend on the nature of the broadcasting organisation and its relation with government and adult education agencies, as to the range, quality and effectiveness of the pro-gramming. In comparing the British and the French situations, Glikman and Corduant (1977) concluded that the lack of inte-gration of CNDP with the French television system essentially limited the volume of production and the hours of transmission; these in turn influenced the content and style of the programmes and the potential audience that is actually reached. On the other hand, if the broadcasting organisation is responsible for educational broadcasting but is totally independent or isolated from other adult education agencies, the programmes are broadcast in a vacuum and their teaching effectiveness then becomes highly suspect. When broadcasters and other agencies work together co-operatively, as with the 'Start' series, broadcasting can play a very powerful role in continuing education; getting such an act together, though, appears to be the exception rather than the rule.

TELEVISION AND RADIO IN DISTANCE HIGHER EDUCATION

The concept of the Open University evolved from the conver-gence of three major post-war educational trends. The first of these concerns developments in the provision for adult edu-cation, the second the growth of educational broadcasting, and the third the political objective of promoting the spread of egalitarianism in education (Lord Perry, 1976).

When the creation of an Open University was being considered in the mid 1960s, it was impossible for most adults in Britain to study part-time for a university degree. Even today, a highly selective higher education system operates in Britain, where many with valid entry qualifications cannot find a place at a university. In the late 1960s, as today, conventional universities were hard pressed to meet the demand from school leavers and so there was little likelihood of adult students being allowed to study *part-time* for degrees at conventional universities.

Secondly, in the 1960s, there was world-wide interest in the potential of broadcasting for education, both as a means of educational expansion and as an effective teaching medium in its own right. During this period, the British government had lifted restrictions on the hours of broadcasting and the BBC needed to fill this extra programme time during one of those regular periods when the level of its licence fee was being held down by the government. A source of educational programming directly financed by the government, but over which the BBC would retain production control, was therefore an attractive proposition for filling this extra time.

The main factor, though, was the attempt by the Labour Party in the mid 1960s to find ways of providing more equal educational opportunities during one of Britain's recurring financial crises. The Robbins Committee on Higher Education (1963) had reported that of those entering university in 1961, 45 per cent came from families where the father was in a higher professional occupation and only 4 per cent from families where the father was a manual worker. On reaching power in 1964, the Prime Minister, Harold Wilson, believed that by creating an 'open' university, a second chance of higher education would be made available to those who had not had the opportunity to go to university when young.

For reasons which will be discussed more fully later, there is a tendency today to play down the importance of broadcasting in the Open University, but it needs emphasising that, without the early involvement of the BBC, it is almost certain that the Open University would not have been created. It was the potential of broadcasting which first led Harold Wilson to consider the establishment of the Open University, the initial concept of which was significantly called the 'University of the Air'. Furthermore, the relationship with the BBC gave credibility and respectability to a project which many at the time considered to be a political gimmick. Perhaps most important of all, the link with the BBC provided the publicity and access to the public which led to over 50,000 applicants in the first and subsequent years of operation. Without broadcasting, it is very doubtful that the Open University would have survived or prospered.

An American ambassador to Britain said that the two most significant contributions Britain had made to the world since the Second World War were Concorde and the Open University. Some may feel that this was a subtle way of putting Britain down, but the influence of the Open University throughout the world has undoubtedly been widespread. Nevertheless, the Open University is neither the first nor the only higher education institution to use broadcasting. Furthermore, it is important to be aware that broadcasting has always been only one, relatively minor, component of the Open University's teaching system. The relationship between broadcasting and distance higher education therefore needs to be looked at as a special aspect of non-formal education, and in a much broader context than just the Open University.

Distance teaching institutions have distinct features from both formal education systems and broadcasting organisations. Keegan (1980) has attempted to define the essential features of distance education which he claims is characterised by physical separation of teacher and learner; the use of technical media, usually print, to carry the contents; a central integrated organisation for the design, delivery, and monitoring of the teaching process; provision of some form of two-way communication between the learner and the system; the possibility of occasional meetings between students; and the use of industrialised methods to produce and deliver materials. In this definition, broadcasting is *not* an essential feature of distance education. Television and radio are of course technical media but Keegan is right in asserting that print is usually the dominant medium in distance education. Nevertheless, a number of distance higher education institutions have used broadcasting.

Kaye and Rumble (1982) have classified distance teaching at a higher education level into five models. I will take these five models and identify the extent to which broadcasting has been used in each model. The first is *correspondence tuition provided by an independent, perhaps commercial, organisation for external degrees awarded by a public university*. For instance, correspondence colleges, such as Wolsey Hall, have provided tuition for London University external degrees. This model is now comparatively rare and I know of no instances where broadcasting has been used.

The second is *centralised State provision for correspondence education at university level*. The two main countries where this model is found are France and the Soviet Union. The Centre National de Télé-Enseignement (CNTE) uses neither television nor radio. However, in the Soviet Union, television programmes have been broadcast regularly in twenty-three cities since 1964/5 to support correspondence students enrolled in the all-union correspondence institutions. For instance, television has been used in connection with courses run by the Moscow Polytechnical Correspondence Institute, the North-West (Leningrad) Polytechnical Correspondence Institute, and the Urals Polytechnical Institute (Kuznetsov, 1975).

The third model is based on analogies or variations of the Open University: *autonomous, multi-media, credit-giving higher education institutions established solely for distance learners*. In 1983 there were fourteen operational institutions in this model, another one (FUI in Iran) had been closed down, and there are plans for three more (in Holland, Japan and the Middle East). Table 15 summarises the use of broadcasting and related audio-visual media in these institutions.

The first point to note is that with few exceptions broadcasting is not much used by these institutions. Five of the open universities do not use television at all and the rest use less than five hours transmission per week, except for Téléuniversité and Athabasca in Canada, CCTU in China and the Open University in Britain. All Athabasca University's programmes are transmitted on cable, as are most of Téléuniversité's.

In terms of the quantity of broadcasting the Chinese CCTU and the British Open University are clearly exceptional. The British Open University transmits nationally thirty-five hours a week television over a thirty-two-week academic year, to over 85,000 students. In any one year there will be a stock of 1,500 programmes to transmit. BBC/OUP (the department responsible for Open University broadcasting) produces 240 new television programmes a year, with a staff of around sixty producers (who are also responsible for audio production), plus full technical and administrative support, using one of the most modern and sophisticated purpose-built studio complexes in the world.

The Chinese CCTU produces and transmits over thirty hours of *new* programming each week to 300,000 students using a total of ten producers. In stark contrast to the Open University, programmes are mainly pre-recorded lectures, written out on a blackboard in the style of lectures at a conventional university with little use being made of pre-prepared material. The programmes have to cover the whole syllabus. McCormick (1982) reports that a typical lecture lasts fifty minutes, followed by a short break, with often the same lecture then continuing after the break. Staff are aware of the technical shortcomings of the programmes but more elaborate programme production is prevented by inadequate technical facilities, the quantity of production required each week and above all by lack of staff and resources. However, strenuous efforts are currently being made to improve both the training of production staff and technical facilities.

For the other institutions in this model, television is a marginal activity, the icing on the cake. Most are dependent for both transmission and production facilities on separate broadcasting organisations. Several of the smaller institutions, such as Athabasca and Everyman's University, buy in television material from other sources as well as commissioning their own productions. In most of the open universities, many courses have no television support at all.

A similar situation exists regarding radio although it is used slightly more than television. Of the fourteen operational institutions, twelve use radio to some extent. The two exceptions are Fernuniversität, West Germany, and the University of South Africa, neither of which uses broadcasting at all. The largest planned user is Sukhothaithammathirat, the Thai Open University, which aims to use fifty hours a week on a new, national educational radio channel due to open in 1984. Whether or not the Thai Open University will sustain such a heavy radio output once operational remains to be seen. The British Open University was a heavy user of radio up to 1980, with twenty-eight hours a week of transmission time. Spain's Open University, with fifteen hours a week, is also a relatively heavy user.

There has been a significant development in the use of radio at the British Open University. There, between 1980 and 1983, radio transmissions were reduced from twenty-eight hours to twelve hours a week. This is a consequence of perhaps the most important teaching development in the short history of the British Open University – a massive increase in the use of audio-cassettes. In 1977 hardly any audio-cassettes were being distributed to students, yet by 1983 250,000 a year were being mailed to students' homes. This trend away from radio to audio-cassettes has taken several forms. Firstly, the University set up a scheme whereby students could borrow, free of charge, on returnable audio-cassettes, copies of broadcast radio programmes. Then, on courses with lower student numbers, programmes made originally for radio transmission were transferred to audio-cassettes mailed to students with their course materials and no longer broadcast. Lastly, from 1977, more and more course teams stopped making programmes for radio transmission, but instead designed audio material from the start so as to exploit the special characteristics of cassette use. This has resulted

TABLE 15

USE OF AUDIO-VISUAL MEDIA IN AUTONOMOUS DISTANCE TEACHING UNIVERSITIES
Situation in 1980/81

Country	Institution	Date	No. of students	Broadcast TV Hrs per week	Video cassettes	Radio Hrs per week	Audio cassettes	Main medium
Canada	Athabasca University	1975	3,500	12	At centres	·1	0	Print
Canada	Téléuniversité, Québec	1972	30,000	9	0	2	0	Print
China	Central Broadcasting and Television University	1978	300,000	33	0	2½	0	TV
Costa Rica	UNED	1977	7,000	4	At centres	1½	Planned	Print
Holland	Open University	1983	?	3 (planned)	Probably	0	Possibly	Print
Iran	Free University of Iran	1973*	1,400	1½	Planned	1½	0	Print
Israel	Everyman's University	1974	10,000	3	At centres	5	0	Print

Pakistan	Allam Iqbal Open University	1974	31,000	1½	0	5	0	Print
Poland	National University of Radio and Television	1974	70,000	3	At centres	2	0	TV
South Africa	University of South Africa	1951	56,000	0	Some	0	Some	Print
Spain	UNED	1972	51,000	0	30	15	3,000	Print
Sri Lanka	Open University	1981	5,000	0	0	Planned	Some	Print
Thailand	Sukhothaithammathirat	1978	150,000	0	0	50 (planned)	?	Print
United Kingdom	Open University	1969	85,000	35	Planned	28	50,000	Print
Venezuela	UNA	1977	13,000	<2	At centres	<1	0	Print
West Germany	Fernuniversität	1974	36,000	0	1% of courses	0	3% of courses	Print

* Dissolved in 1977, following the revolution, after only one semester of enrolled students.

Sources: Bates, 1980; Rumble and Harry, 1983; Mackenzie, Postgate and Scupham, 1975; and private sources.

in a rapid reduction in the level of both transmission and production of radio programmes. Production dropped from over 300 new programmes in 1977 to less than 100 in 1984. This reduction in radio production, however, has been more than compensated for by the increase in audio-cassette production, with over 300 'radio prog-ramme equivalents' (i.e. units of twenty minutes) being produced on cassette in 1984, mainly by BBC/OUP, although the OU itself produces about a third of the cassettes.

There were several factors behind this trend. The radio transmis-sion times offered by the BBC to the Open University deteriorated in quality from 1977. Students by and large preferred programmes, even those made as broadcasts, on cassette. It proved to be cheaper to distribute material on cassettes rather than to broadcast for courses with less than 1,000 students. Lastly, and most significantly, course teams have increasingly exploited the unique educational features of cassette technology. These factors are so important that they will be discussed more fully in the next chapter and Chapter 9. For the moment, it suffices to note that other open universities, except for the Spanish Open University, have *not* used audio cassettes to any extent.

Surprisingly, given the difference in costs, video-cassettes are more widely used than audio-cassettes, in terms of the number of open universities involved. However, where video cassettes have been made available to students this has been done much more cautiously than the British Open University's confident plunge into home-delivered audio-cassettes. Five institutions provided video-cassette replay facilities in local centres, as well as broadcasts, and Fernuniversität and the University of South Africa, while not using broadcasting, do provide a small number of programmes on video-cassette for use at local centres. The planned Dutch Open Univer-sity is also likely to make use of video-cassettes.

In 1982 the British Open University introduced an experimental national video-cassette loan scheme for its students. Recordings of broadcasts could be borrowed from the University for use by students either on their own machines or on machines at local study centres provided by the Open University or other co-operative institutions. Another significant development is the University's decision to allow a number of future courses to design programmes from the outset for use on video cassette, rather than as broadcasts. Although to date the use of video-cassettes is far less than that of audio-cassettes at the British Open University, it is such an im-portant development that it too will be discussed more fully in Chapter 9.

In summary, then, the use of broadcasting in open universities is either marginal or non-existent, with a few notable exceptions. In nearly all of these institutions, print is the main teaching medium, even when broadcasting is extensively used. Lastly, there is a significant move in the British Open University towards increased use of non-broadcast audio-visual media, a move not yet followed to any extent by other open universities.

Kaye and Rumble's fourth model is the *extension services of conventional universities* which use distance education methods for off-campus teaching but give similar accreditation to that given to on-campus students. This in fact is the most common form of distance teaching at a higher education level. Keegan and Rumble (1982) claim that there are over 100 such institutions in the Soviet Union, 64 in the USA, 30 in East Germany, 23 in India, 20 in Canada, 5 in Australia and others in New Zealand, Fiji, Zambia and Jamaica. Sweden is another country where this is the model for distance higher education.

Despite the many institutions covered by this model, two main strategies predominate. The first is for central staff from the main campus to travel out to local centres to give face-to-face lectures or tutorials at evenings or weekends. (Sometimes approved local tutors are employed instead.) The other strategy is to mail to students campus lecture notes – or sometimes audio tapes of lectures, with telephone tutorials as a support.

Either way, it is very rare for broadcasting to be used by extension services, although as always there are important exceptions. For instance, the University of Wisconsin has a long history of using television and radio to support its extension courses. Memorial University, St John's, Newfoundland, distributes video-taped lectures to remote local centres. In France, Centres de Télé-Enseignement Universitaire (CTUs) have been set up in sixteen French universities, using regional broadcasting for off-campus teaching.

In general, though, G. K. Chesterton's comment about virtue would equally apply to the use of broadcasting by most conventional universities in this model: 'It's not so much that it's been tried and found wanting; it's never really been tried.' There are several reasons for this. Extension programmes are often an extra work-load on campus-based staff. Extension teaching tends to interfere with research and there is often inadequate financial reward for it. To have to produce television and radio programmes would be yet another burden and would also increase the cost of extension services which are often run on the cheap. Secondly, campus-based academic staff have no experience or familiarity in teaching through television and radio and are therefore largely unaware of its potential. Perhaps the most important reason though is that many such institutions do not have easy access to production and transmission facilities. Related to this, the extension departments are not staffed or structured so as to facilitate the integration of television and radio into extension courses, which are often based on straight replication of on-campus lectures. This is the great advantage that institutions such as the Open University have over extension services. In the former the course design process is structured so as to allow broadcasting to be integrated in the course from the beginning. Extension services in many universities are just that: an extension of conventional teaching to off-campus students, and it would be difficult to integrate broadcasting or other audio-visual media in any meaningful way (for a more optimistic view, see Fortosky, 1982).

Lastly, Kaye and Rumble's fifth model covers *co-operative systems in which several independent institutions collaborate to offer different elements of a single course.* This arrangement is not limited to higher education, as the 'Start' project in Sweden has shown, but there are several interesting examples at a higher education level. The significance of co-operative models is that they bring together existing institutions with their own area of specialism, thus avoiding the need to create new, large and expensive autonomous state institutions, such as the Open University, which sometimes duplicate services already offered in isolation by existing agencies. A co-operative model also allows conventional universities to use media which would otherwise not be available to them and in which they have no expertise.

One of the earliest and most interesting co-operative ventures is the West German Funkkolleg, or Radio College. Established originally in 1966 by Hessischer Rundfunk, a radio station in the state ('Land') of Hesse, and directed by Professor Gerd Kadelbach, Funkkolleg has gradually grown to involve six radio stations, in different parts of Germany and Switzerland; the Deutsches Institut für Fernstudien (DIFF); the Ministry of Education in each of six states ('Länder'); six universities (roughly one per Land); a private publisher; and adult education institutes in the six states.

For each series, a team is recruited from this consortium of interests responsible for the production of radio programmes and support print materials, for the organisation of local optional meetings and seminars, and for setting homework assignments and examinations. The cost of running courses is shared between the various partners, supplemented by modest student fees.

Funkkolleg offers courses to meet a variety of needs. In the early days the courses concentrated on upgrading teachers' qualifications but today some Funkkolleg courses can count towards qualification for entrance to some universities, while others can be used by students already at university as a substitute for part of their course (a form of credit transfer). General interest in the subject though appears to be the main reason for enrolment, according to Kanocz (1975).

One new course is offered each year (courses are not generally repeated), and the responsibility for radio production alternates between the six radio stations. The main continuity is provided by DIFF, which is a federally funded organisation based at Tübingen. DIFF helps draft course syllabuses, recruits academic teams, pays their fees and expenses, and helps the team compile the accompanying print material, which is published and distributed by an independent publisher. Each course has over thirty radio programmes which are broadcast by all six participating radio stations. The University and Ministry of Education representatives set the computer-marked examinations.

Up to 1982, 350,000 students had enrolled in Funkkolleg courses, course size varying between 20,000 to 40,000, depending on the subject matter. About a quarter of the students have gone on to take the examinations, most of them passing. The cost to public funds is very modest. In 1974/5 the cost per student per year was £30. In the context of higher education in West Germany, which is extremely conservative and traditional in its teaching methods, Funkkolleg is an interesting achievement. It was not developed as a result of government initiatives, yet in terms of student numbers it enrols about the same each year as the State-created Fernuniversität, even though the latter is in the position of being able to offer full degree qualifications, which Funkkolleg cannot do.

In France a rather different kind of co-operative arrangement exists between seven universities in the east of France, officially known as 'Fédération Interuniversitaire des Centres de Télé-Enseignement de l'Est', but more graphically and colloquially as 'L'Entente de l'Est'. This system is based on the distance teaching units (CTU's) created in a number of French universities in the 1960s. The main disadvantage of the CTU's, according to Manuelian (1980), is the very wide range of courses that have to be broadcast even within the Arts disciplines to which the scheme is limited. Universities found that none of these courses could be comprehensively taught by broadcasts, even when substantially supported by duplicated texts of lectures, given the limited air-time available and the competition between universities to use it. Consequently, two university teachers (Clement Bouillon in Nancy and Guy Lecomte in Dijon) brought together those involved in running CTU courses in eastern France to rationalise their efforts. Instead of every CTU attempting to cover all its courses, each of the seven centres was to concentrate on one or two. Each course would then be offered, via television, radio and post, to all the part-time students in the whole area covered by the seven universities. The nearest university would be responsible for the administration of each student and would award the degree, even though the courses taken may have been designed and produced by one of the other universities. Thus while the University of Nancy would be responsible for the course on English, a student living in Strasbourg would enrol at Strasbourg University II and follow the television and radio programmes emanating from Nancy. As well as broadcast television and radio programmes (mainly of on-campus lectures), frequent and voluminous printed materials are sent to students by the university responsible for the administration of students in their area. Each centre has a library of cassette recordings of programmes. The student will sit the examination (in the case of English, set and marked by staff at Nancy) at his or her local university. About 2,000 students a year are thus able to follow university courses off-campus in eastern France through the co-operation of the seven universities (Besançon, Dijon, Metz, Mulhouse, Nancy II, Reims and Strasbourg II).

Lastly, a very significant co-operative venture is developing in British Columbia, Canada, based around the Knowledge Network. Several institutions there are engaged in distance education. Simon Fraser University, the British Columbia Institute of Technology, the University of British Columbia and the University of Victoria, are all conventional campus-based institutions with some off-campus or distance teaching. However, the Open Learning Institute, with 13,500 course enrolments and no on-campus students, has the largest number engaged in distance education. About half of OLI's 120 or so courses are of equivalent credit value to on-campus University credit, while the rest are career, vocational or secondary school courses. The Knowledge Network itself is a provincial educational communications authority which, according to its constitution, is meant to act primarily as an agent for the various educational organisations in the province. It is thus available to any of the regional community colleges, schools, universities, institutes and other public agencies in the province that wish to make and distribute television programmes. In this sense, it is very different from the other Canadian provincial educational communications authorities, such as TV Ontario, Radio Québec, and ACCESS, Alberta, which are semi-autonomous and decide their own programming.

A key feature of Knowledge Network is its distribution system based on three different methods. Knowledge Network has the only educational channel on British Columbian cable systems and can in this way access over 80 per cent of the provincial population. In addition to the narrowband cable channel, Knowledge Network also operates its own broadband cable network, which links up three universities, five teaching hospitals, the British Columbia Institute of Technology and the Law Courts. This two-way broadband cable system enables material generated in any of the studios on each campus to be communicated directly to any other part of the broadband network. Material generated at any of these points can also be switched over to the public cable system if so desired. Lastly, Knowledge Network has access to one channel on the Anik-C satellite and is negotiating for a second satellite channel. Satellite is used to reach the 20 per cent of the population living outside the heavily populated south-west corner of the province. Satellite transmissions are either fed into local cable systems or re-broadcast via low-powered local broadcast transmitters.

Any institution wishing to use the Knowledge Network is responsible for producing and directing its own programmes after consultation with a Knowledge Network adviser. Knowledge Network provides the technical facilities and staff but does not try to impose editorial or production control, other than ensuring that the users have thought out what they want to do and that the programmes meet minimal technical standards.

There are two distinct types of programmes broadcast by Knowledge Network. The first are public-broadcast programmes which have general educational value but are not part of a learning system. These are mostly bought in, and do not differ from the public broadcasts of many North American TV stations. The other type are programmes which are part of a fully developed distance teaching package, run by one of the educational institutions. The amount of time available as a result of a whole channel being devoted to education, and the comparatively low production budget, leads to a unique production style. For instance, a programme may be two hours in length, and consist of several segments. A university lecturer may talk directly to camera for ten minutes or so and then introduce all or part of a bought-in programme. This may be followed by a studio discussion between two or three invited experts. There may then be a break while students do a short piece of work, followed by a session in which students can phone in questions and have them answered on screen.

Knowledge Network is very new, having been established in 1980, and is still finding its feet. It remains to be seen to what extent the other institutions will make use of this unique arrangement. For instance, in 1982 OLI had only seven courses out of ninety-eight with a television component. Also, some form of rationalisation of distance education in British Columbia seems inevitable. Nevertheless, Knowledge Network is a serious attempt to provide educational institutions with a centralised production and distribution system covering a whole province, to use in the way they see as best. Knowledge Network also provides some pointers to the opportunities and difficulties likely to be faced by educational institutions in other countries as a result of the introduction of cable and satellite systems.

ROLES IN DISTANCE HIGHER EDUCATION: SOME CONCLUSIONS

There is a very wide range of organisations and provision for distance higher education, yet, in general, broadcasting has not been heavily used at this level. The Open University, only one of many distance education institutions, uses broadcasting exceptionally. Even at the Open University, though, television and radio are not the main teaching media.

The next chapter provides a more detailed evaluation but, even at this stage, it is clear why broadcasting has not been more heavily used for distance higher education. Firstly, an enormous quantity of broadcasting is required to cover the *whole* of a university curriculum, as both the French CTU's and the Chinese CCTU have discovered. Therefore broadcasting ends up by being just one component of a multi-media teaching system. Secondly, broadcasting organisations and universities are not the easiest of companions: they both want the middle of the bed. Neither producers nor academics like to feel that they are taking orders from someone outside their profession; universities and broadcasting organisations jealously guard their autonomy and independence. Thirdly, audiences for distance higher education programmes will inevitably be tiny, even by minority programming standards, and broadcast managements have to consider the needs of their wider audiences. Fourthly, many academics have no training, background or interest in using media for teaching. Their lives and careers have been almost exclusively bound up with books, lectures and personal contacts with students or colleagues. Consequently, few academics are aware of the teaching potential of television or radio, other than in the vaguest terms; many are downright suspicious, believing mass media by their nature to be unintellectual. Many academics not prejudiced against media are still reluctant to put in the considerable effort and time needed to master the new skills required for television and radio to be used well. Lastly, broadcasting is a high cost to educational institutions if they have to pay for the service. Given these factors, the wonder is that broadcasting has been used at all in distance higher education.

Consequently, the Open University and co-operative models are particularly significant. In both cases, the organisational structure encourages, even forces, academics and producers to work together as equal partners. In the Open University, courses are designed from the start with the assumption that television and radio (or audio) will be used. Co-operative models promise the advantage of allowing each specialist organisation to make its own unique contribution, concentrating on what it knows and does best, but with all the organisations together providing a comprehensive and integrated service to students. Co-operative models furthermore avoid the construction of new, large, centralised institutions which inevitably partly duplicate or compete with existing provision. However, there are very few examples of co-operative models at a higher education level. The ideal may be fine, but the practice is much more difficult. Institutional autonomy appears to be a formidable barrier to co-operation, and those institutions that have been willing to share their beds deserve credit for their flexibility.

7

Getting it right:
continuing and higher education

Broadcasting can be used effectively for learning purposes in continuing and higher education but not without overcoming many obstacles. At this level too, many things have to be right for it to work: course planning and support services, transmission arrangements, the relationship between broadcasting and other media, financial arrangements and programme design, to mention but a few.

COURSE PLANNING AND SUPPORT SERVICES

Viewing and listening rates are affected by decisions about the length of a series of programmes and the provision of courses at different levels. In particular, it is very difficult to keep the same students watching or listening to educational programmes over a long period of time by broadcasting alone. The longer the series progresses, the greater the loss of the regular audience; there are further losses of students between one level and another, and the more diverse and varied the courses, the more fragmented and tiny becomes the audience for each series.

Rybak (1980) found that on average about half the students dropped out from beginners' foreign language courses, and about a third from the more advanced series. Audience figures, in terms of total numbers, may appear to be steady throughout a series, but this is due to earlier viewers being replaced by new viewers who themselves see only one or two programmes. At the Open University, the key factor influencing listening rate is the time elapsed from the beginning of the course (Bates *et al.*, 1982a). Using multiple regression analysis, we found this factor to be more influential than student workload, the time of transmission, the perceived value of the programmes, or even the total number of programmes on a course. For instance, other things being equal, the last programme of sixteen, transmitted late in the year, would have fewer listeners than the twenty-fourth programme of thirty-two transmitted two thirds of the way through the year. Listening figures tend to drop by an average of 1 per cent per week across all courses, whether or not many or few students listen initially. Thus the average listening rate was about 60 per cent early in the course, and around 25 per cent at the end of the 32-week academic year, as can be seen from Fig. 1.

An additional loss of viewers from lower to higher level courses can be seen in Fig. 2, which illustrates data obtained by Rybak (1980) from sales of course books associated with BBC foreign language series.

For the first-level French and German courses ('Ensemble' and 'Kontakte') there was a substantial drop in book sales between the first and second parts. By the more advanced series ('Sur-le-Vif' and 'Wegweiser'), sales have dropped considerably. At this level, radio is used but television is not. The dropping of television, however, does not account for the loss of students because television was used for the second parts of 'Ensemble' and 'Kontakte' and substantial reductions are also found at this change-over.

Cumulative loss of audiences over a series of courses is a particular problem for distance teaching institutions such as the Open University, offering degrees made up from a series of credits or courses. While some Open University programmes transmitted at

Fig. 1   Listening rates by transmission week at the Open University (1979 and 1980).

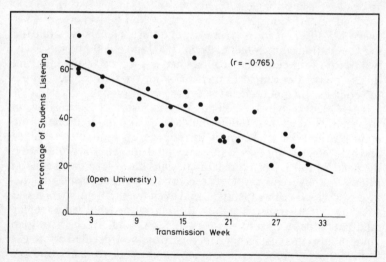

Note: Each dot represents the listening figure for each of twenty-nine different programmes.

Fig. 2   Audiences for BBC foreign language courses.

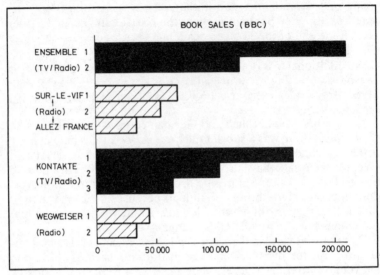

weekend mornings are watched by a general audience ranging from
200,000 to 800,000 (BARB, 1982), the primary target audience –
students enrolled for the courses with which the programmes are
associated – may be less than 200. In 1981 there were 60,000
enrolled undergraduate students at the Open University split between 125 different courses across four different levels. So while the
five foundation courses had between 3,000 and 6,000 students each,
two thirds of the remaining courses had less than 500 students, and
thirty-one (25 per cent) less than 200 students. Only eight of these
125 courses had no broadcast television programmes.

   The Open University defends its past use of broadcasting on
courses with such low student numbers by arguing that one of the
main purposes of television is to transmit experiments, evidence
and data which home-based students could not get in any other way;
the need for this is just as great on specialist third-level courses as on
foundation-level courses. Until recently, most students did not have
access to video replay facilities, and even for small numbers it was
still cheaper to transmit nationally than to provide video replay
equipment for every student on a course. As student access to video
equipment is increasing, the University has now decided not to use
broadcasting on future courses with less than 300 students, an issue
discussed more fully in Chapter 9.

   Whether or not one accepts the Open University's argument for broadcasting on courses with low student numbers, the need to offer a wide range of courses is a problem for all distance teaching institutions wishing to use broadcasting as a major component. Broadcasters are naturally reluctant to allocate national transmission facilities to such tiny, specialist audiences, except at the margin of their other services, yet the provision of a wide range of courses to meet individual requirements is considered essential by most distance teaching institutions.

Educational audiences can fragment and disappear very quickly. While there may be substantial numbers of casual viewers, those who use the broadcasts as part of more intensive study will be much smaller. There will be a substantial drop in regular viewers as a series progresses, and of those that complete a series many will not continue to higher levels. The greater the choice of course available, the more fragmented the audience will become.

These facts are disheartening for those (like myself) who believe that learning is more likely to be effective when programmes are broadcast in a series leading to a coherent progression of teaching. It seems difficult to maintain motivation over a long period for part-time study through broadcasting alone. The BBC have tried to solve this problem by running short language series ('Get By In . . .'). While this keeps up the viewing figures, it does not solve the problem of sustaining interest and progressing learners beyond the basic stage. What needs to be done is to discover ways to keep viewers and listeners interested over a long series of programmes.

A study carried out by Rybak (1983) therefore is particularly important. She managed to cut by half the drop-out rate on a BBC language series through the provision of support services. Almost single-handedly, she organised a variety of support schemes for people following the BBC series 'Ensemble'. She had very little direct help from the BBC, who even initially refused a request for broadcast publicity for the support services. Rybak edited and distributed a regular magazine/newspaper ('La Vue d'Ensemble') for subscribers, organised self-help study groups, a telephone request service and, in conjunction with the National Extension College, a Home Tuition Pack. The newspaper was the most successful scheme, and the self-help groups were also moderately successful, particularly when they were led by an animateur who spoke French reasonably well. Better broadcast publicity in advance of the programmes would have made a lot of difference to the success of the support schemes, particularly the self-help groups, in that the larger numbers attracted would have enabled more local groups to have been set up. Rybak, though, was able to show that even the relatively thin support schemes she was able to organise on her own reduced drop-out by over a half, compared with previous BBC language courses.

At the Open University, the reduction in viewing and listening as a course progresses is far greater than the actual drop-out from the course. The relatively low course drop-out rates at the Open University are due to the *combination* of media and support services available to students. Support services therefore will greatly increase the effectiveness of broadcast series at both continuing and higher education levels, and they should be an essential part of any long series of continuing education programmes.

TRANSMISSION ARRANGEMENTS

Although the subject is tediously complex, nothing influences the effectiveness of broadcasting in continuing and distance education more than transmission arrangements. For continuing education series it is essential that the programmes *reach* the target group. For distance education systems, course designers must know whether or not the students can watch or listen. If too many students, say more than a third, are unable regularly to view or listen, broadcasts cannot be made a vital part of the course. If adult part-time students notice though that the broadcasts are not essential, they will not bother to use them. The whole rationale of using broadcasting then becomes questionable. No matter how valuable the programmes might appear to be in themselves, repeats and good quality transmission times are essential for high viewing figures. While the problem is not quite so severe for continuing education series in Britain, their transmission arrangements too are far from satisfactory.

The potential coverage is not usually the problem since in many countries the reception of television and radio in the home is almost universal. 98·5 per cent of Open University students can get the TV broadcasts, and 94 per cent the VHF (FM) radio broadcasts. The problems usually arise from the unsuitable times at which programmes are broadcast.

The Open University has clear evidence of the effect of poor quality transmission times on students' use of broadcasting, since viewing on transmission declined from an average of 65 per cent in 1976 to 52 per cent in 1982 (Grundin, 1983). An average viewing rate of 65 per cent can be interpreted to mean that either 65 per cent of the students on a course would watch each programme on average, or that over a whole course an average student would watch 65 per cent of the programmes on that course. (All viewing and listening rates refer to finally registered students who completed the course.) A transmission viewing rate of 52 per cent means that Open University programmes reach barely half the students on a course on transmission, a delivery rate that would be totally unacceptable for the correspondence texts. Up to 1976, average viewing figures were acceptably high. It has already been demonstrated that listening figures decline during the year, and the same situation exists for television, particularly from mid-summer when students are away at summer school or on holiday. (The Open University academic year runs from February to October.) Viewing figures drop even further just before examinations due to concentration on revision. With a viewing rate of 65 per cent for the whole year, viewing figures for the first half-year were averaging between 75 per cent and 80 per cent, and for some courses, particularly science, they were over 90 per cent, comparing very favourably with attendance rates at most conventional university lectures. Listening figures for radio have always been lower and less volatile over the years, averaging around 50 per cent. Thus up to 1976 most students watched most television programmes and heard about half the radio programmes (Bates, 1975; Gallagher, 1977a).

The decline in viewing on transmission has been due primarily to a deterioration in the *quality* of transmission times, although other factors have also played a part. The most popular slots available to the University have been from 6.00 p.m. to 7.30 p.m. on weekday evenings, the later the better (Grundin, 1981). By 1983 these had all been withdrawn, not only from the Open University but also from BBC Continuing Education, because the Controller of BBC2 wanted to start popular programming earlier to compete with the newly created Channel 4. Although the Open University still retains the extremely valuable Saturday and Sunday day-time slots on BBC2, many of its broadcasts are now transmitted in the early morning, between 5.55 a.m. and 8.00 a.m. Radio transmission times by 1983 were even worse. There were no transmissions after 7.00 a.m. or before 11.15 p.m. during the week, and no transmissions after 8.00 a.m. at weekends.

The drop in viewing figures on transmission is not due solely to the deterioration in transmission times but it is a major cause. Even in 1982, programmes fortunate enough to have good transmission times and repeats achieved high viewing figures but the proportion of programmes with poor quality transmission times had increased. Programmes broadcast before 7.00 a.m. or between 9.00 a.m. and 5.00 p.m. during the week never reach more than 20 per cent of the students on a course (Grundin, 1981). Claims by BBC management that students would watch at inconvenient times if the programmes were important enough to them are not supported by the evidence: programmes with good viewing figures one year have poorer viewing figures the following when moved to poorer times. So far, figures have referred to viewing on *transmission*. Fortunately, the increased use of domestic video-cassette machines came just in time for the Open University. In 1979 the *overall* viewing figure (transmissions plus recordings) had dropped to 55 per cent; by 1983 the *overall* rate had increased to 60 per cent, due to 8 per cent of all viewing being on recordings only (Grundin, 1983).

The *amount* of time required for transmissions by the Open University is another factor which has affected viewing figures. Any distance education university which wishes to use broadcasting as a major component on many courses will need a great deal of transmission time. In the Open University's case, the situation has been exacerbated by administrative and financial decisions whose repercussions on broadcasting were not allowed for at the time. Originally, courses at the Open University were planned to run for four years; thus the amount of transmission time needed was four times the amount of new programmes produced each year since programmes made in previous years also had to be transmitted. If each programme also needs to be broadcast twice (repeated) at different times in a week, then the annual number of transmission slots will be *eight* times the number of new programmes produced each year. Thus if 300 programmes a year are produced, then 2,400 slots are needed annually for courses with a four-year life. Over a 32-week academic year, roughly seventy-five slots a week would be needed. At twenty-five minutes per programme, that works out at just over thirty hours a week, which is what the BBC offered the University when it was established.

In distance teaching a large part of the cost of a course is incurred in its initial design and production; once produced it pays to run the course for as long as possible. Consequently, from 1974 the Open University, partly on cost grounds, and partly as a way of increasing the number of courses available, began increasing the life of courses from four to eight years. Many academics were unhappy about this on educational grounds, but because the process happened gradually, as the life of each individual course was extended, few appreciated that this policy was in effect doubling the number of programmes that would eventually have to be fitted into the transmission schedule. The consequence was that ultimately the University had to choose between doubling its transmission time, dropping repeats, or halving broadcast production. Despite appeals to the Annan Committee for over fifty hours a week on a new Open Channel, and to the Home Office for a new educational channel, the best the University was able to achieve was an extension to just over thirty-five hours a week from the BBC, mainly by an increase in very early morning transmissions. Others argued for a major reduction in production, and to some extent this has happened, from 300 to 230 programmes a year. Any further reductions would have meant substantially fewer programmes per course, under-utilisation of expensive capital equipment, a large increase in the unit cost per programme and almost certainly a reduction in BBC/OUP staffing levels. It became far less painful therefore to drop repeats gradually.

However, repeats are very important in a distance teaching context. Less than two thirds of the students on any course will watch a single transmission, no matter how good the transmission time. About 20 per cent of the students will be unable *ever* to watch at that time because of work commitments (shift work or travelling). Another 15 per cent will miss the programme, either for unavoidable, one-off reasons (e.g. had to work late) or for possibly avoidable reasons (e.g. forgot). A combination of two transmissions at different times of day will enable 90 per cent of students on any course to watch, provided that *one* of the transmissions is at a good quality time (Bates, 1975). Even repeats though are not sufficient to ensure high viewing rates if *both* transmissions are at poor times (Grundin, 1980). Thus both repeats *and* good quality times are necessary for high viewing levels, that is, to reach more than two thirds of students on a course.

The Open University experience shows the critical and complex relationship between course life, production levels, repeats and the quality and quantity of transmission times. These factors must be in balance to ensure high viewing levels, if there are large numbers of programmes to be transmitted. Furthermore, that balance must be maintained over a number of years, or adjusted as any one factor varies. This places a tiresome obligation on broadcasting organisations to maintain the initial quality and quantity of times for the agreed life-span of courses. There is an even greater obligation on the distance teaching institution to husband its broadcasting resources carefully, ensuring that levels of production and the life-span of courses are consistent with the amount and quality of transmission time available. Given these very demanding conditions, it says a lot for the BBC/Open University relationship that it has lasted so long and so well, and even more so for the University's students, who have had to put up with extremely inconvenient times for their broadcasts.

MULTI-MEDIA FACTORS

Earlier chapters indicated a trend towards multi-media teaching. There is a fundamental shift of philosophy, though, once broadcasting is used in *conjunction* with other media, rather than using it alone. If broadcasting is the only medium through which the teaching material is presented, the programmes themselves need to be self-contained and understandable by most of the target audience on one showing. Each programme has to be a complete learning experience in itself. That is its teaching function, and the producer is then free to concentrate on the programme and how it can best achieve that function.

When broadcasts are used with other media, however, questions arise about the relative teaching roles of each medium. Are the programmes to be made so that they exploit the *unique* characteristics of television or radio, or are they to *duplicate* teaching functions also carried out by other media? What *are* the unique teaching functions, if any, of broadcasting in a multi-media context? What can television or radio do *better* than other media? Furthermore, the role of different media will vary according to organisational factors. Where, as in most continuing education programming, the broadcasting organisation is the originating institution, print and support services will be very much subsidiary to the broadcasts. Other media are there to support the broadcasts. In a distance education institution, though, the role of broadcasting is likely to be reversed, in that it will support other media, particularly the texts. In that situation, it becomes more important to identify the specific and unique teaching functions of broadcasting – what it can do *better* than other media. Students will not use the programmes unless they contribute uniquely and relevantly to their studies, because broadcasts have major disadvantages over other media for intensive study purposes. For instance, a book can be used whenever it suits a student; it can be referred to as often as necessary; it can be searched easily for relevant sections; and parts can be skipped or left out, as necessary. A tutor can diagnose difficulties and explain in different ways until understanding is reached. These are all features of the learning process that are impossible via broadcasting. Thus any programme in a multi-media course must provide something that cannot be so easily achieved through other available media.

What then are the unique teaching features of broadcasting? Unfortunately, there is no adequate existing theory of media selection (see Heidt, 1978). The appropriateness of a given medium can be judged only in the specific context in which that medium will be used. There is not space in this book to elaborate a theory of media selection in which the role of broadcasting could be placed. (See Bates, 1981b and 1983 for a more detailed discussion of this issue.) Nevertheless, it is possible to show that television and radio *can* have unique teaching functions in a multi-media distance education context by using the Open University as an example.

Course teams at the Open University must submit a written bid for programmes which contains a justification for their use of broadcasting, before programmes are allocated by the University's Broadcast and Audio-Visual Sub-Committee. This Committee attempts to apply two main criteria when allocating resources: balancing allocations to match annual production resources (i.e. ensuring maximum utilisation of production capacity); and then giving priority allocations to courses which identify functions for television or radio which could not be achieved as effectively or economically in any other way. (Such functions must also be important to the teaching of that subject.) By analysing past bids, it has been possible to identify five general functions for television or radio at the Open University (i.e. functions which would apply to all Open University courses), eighteen functions for the use of television on specific courses, six functions appropriate to radio, three to audio-cassettes and another seven functions suitable for either radio or audio-cassettes. These are all listed in full in the Appendix.

Several points emerge from this list of functions. First of all, when television and radio are available on the scale of the Open University, they not only provide unique resources that would be difficult or impossible to provide in any other way for home-based adult students; they also provide resources sometimes not available even to conventional campus-based universities. Thus unusual, rare or dangerous experiments can be shown via television for science students. Field sites in remote and distant locations can be observed and analysed by Earth Science students. Cameras can look down powerful microscopes, and teachers can be sure that students are observing the correct phenomena. Complex mathematical relationships can be modelled through animation or specially constructed physical models. Controlled and carefully selected classroom interaction and social behaviour can be observed and analysed by Educational Studies and Social Science students. Specially staged drama presentations and analysis of historical archive film can be provided for Literature and History students. Technology students can observe industrial applications of engineering principles and analyse complex industrial systems in operation. Many more examples could be given, so broadcast television and radio clearly have many unique educational functions in the Open University.

Secondly, these functions are context-specific. They would not necessarily apply to another institution. Television would not be necessary, for example, for demonstrating more or less standard laboratory and experimental techniques at institutions with appropriate local facilities. At the Open University, however, students are studying primarily at home and receive no more than one week at a summer school for any course, and it is difficult to see how science and technology could be taught to a suitable standard to these students without using television.

Thirdly, the necessity to use television or radio for these functions is as much an academic as a production decision. It is only subject experts who can really decide how important it is to use broadcasting in a particular way for a particular subject, and to some extent such a decision has to be subjective. Nevertheless, once television and radio are available, they provide opportunities to teach in ways that would not have been considered had broadcasting not been available.

Fourthly, the list of functions is derived from an analysis of intentions – there is no guarantee that all programmes will concentrate solely on these functions, nor that students will necessarily benefit from such uses of television or radio. It is in practice not easy to convert these particular intentions into actual programmes. Individual producers and academics have to be aware of such principles, agree with them, and know how and when to apply them to specific programmes. Producers in particular tend to be sceptical of any theoretical attempts to match appropriate media to specific teaching functions or learning activities, as illustrated by the following comments of a senior BBC/OUP producer:

One might also ask, were a course designed in which the media were perfectly matched to objectives, would it necessarily be an interesting, attractive course to those who have to study it? Teaching is an art as well as a science and technology. The more we know of the latter two, the better, but meanwhile many teachers do very well because of their skill at the art, and that art will include, in our case, a 'feel' for the choice of media (Taylor, 1979).

The difficulty course designers have had in distance learning institutions in making rational decisions about the use of television and radio is well expressed by Beardsley (1975) reporting on the now defunct Free University of Iran:

At the beginning of the strategic planning phase, it was hoped – a rather naive expectation in retrospect – to find a set of practical procedures, based upon sound psychological and pedagogical foundations, which would allow the planners to define overall objectives for different media used by the University, and which would serve as guidelines for the selection of media between and within individual programmes and courses. In the event, there was considerable high-level discussion of abstractions, and no significant criteria were elucidated. A series of difficult analyses were often found to end in some commonsense decisions. In the last resort, the selection of media in the Free University was guided by several non-pedagogical factors: ignorance, logistics, and external politics.

In the Open University, because allocations are made by a committee made up of individual broadcasters and academics (including myself), similar 'non-pedagogical' factors often intrude. The decision-making is really 'bottom-up', with course teams constructing arguments about how they want to use television, often before the course has even a decent outline; to some extent, an allocation is then made on trust, knowing that the course may develop in such a way that original programme plans cannot be met.

Nevertheless, despite the very real difficulties in constructing a theory of media selection, and despite the scepticism regarding its potential value, any institution contemplating the use of broadcasting needs to be very clear about what teaching functions it considers to be uniquely appropriate for television or radio. New developments in technology are rapidly expanding the choice of media open to educators, and some of these new media appear to be much more powerful than broadcasting for teaching purposes, as will become apparent in Chapter 9. It is too complacent to assume that broadcasting is automatically beneficial for even a distance teaching institution, given the expense and the alternatives available. It is essential, therefore, to know more precisely what broadcasting does best in a given situation and to make sure it is used in that way.

Even though the advent of other media such as video-cassettes and video-discs is making the list in the Appendix rapidly obsolete, there are clearly unique contributions that broadcasting or video can make. The actual listing of appropriate functions is in fact less important than *thinking* in those terms when making programmes. And there's the rub. Producers and even academics are much happier discussing a programme's content, style, location and scheduling than discussing its teaching function in relation to other media. What learning skills is it trying to develop? What are acceptable ways for students to respond to this programme? What unique contribution is the programme making to the students' learning experience? How could students use the programme material in assessment or examination questions? What is in the programme that is not more easily available in the texts – and is this important or relevant? The asking of such questions before and during production is essential if the programme is to make a unique and valuable contribution to students' learning. It is even more difficult to *design* programmes to meet adequately such demands; the sheer mechanics of production often get in the way.

Related to the question of teaching function is the *relevance* of programmes in multi-media teaching. Lack of relevance is one of the main reasons given by Open University students for not watching or listening or for rating programmes lowly (Grundin, 1978).

Relevance may seem to be a curious issue. One might think that anything put into a course by a course team – including the programmes – would be relevant by definition. And who are students in any case to question the relevance of academic material? Relevance is not indeed a major issue for continuing education programmes, provided programmes appeal in very broad terms to the target group. Trenaman (1967) found that most people can sensitively predict the kinds of programmes that will interest them from very brief programme details. In other words, they just don't watch programmes that don't interest them.

But in multi-media courses, programme relevance is more complex. To understand this, it is necessary to consider the context of distance learners. They are likely to be in full-time employment and having to find over twelve hours a week in their own time for their studies. Many will be trying to acquire the best qualifications with the least effort, not through laziness, but merely to preserve their family life and other interests, not to mention their sanity. On top of this, they may have to make the effort to get up at 5.30 a.m. in order to watch the programme. They therefore start with the attitude: 'This damned programme had better be good'! And 'good' means substantially and self-evidently helping them in their studies. So, in respect of broadcasts, they are likely to be highly structured learners with strong views on what they want from the programmes.

There are several factors which influence the perceived relevance of programmes, in a multi-media context. First of all, some programmes are indeed irrelevant; with the best will in the world, it would be difficult even for the producer or the course team to make valid links between the television programmes and the rest of the course. But this does not happen so frequently. More puzzling is when students find programme material irrelevant which the course team believe to be important. For instance, in an evaluation of an Open University Technology foundation course (T101), Brown (1981) found that many students failed to see the relevance of the programmes, despite actually learning from the programmes what the course team wanted them to learn. Students' failure to see the programmes' relevance might not have mattered had it not affected their viewing behaviour. However, after a good start, viewing figures on T101 were lower by the end of the year than on all other foundation courses.

Perceived relevance is very much related to the way multi-media courses are assessed. At the Open University, students obtain credits through a combination of supervised, end-of-course examinations and continuous assessment based on regular tutor-marked or computer-marked assignments during the course. For many Open University students, with time a precious commodity, their main criterion in deciding whether or not to watch or listen is: Can I get good marks on assignment and examination questions without watching or listening to the programmes? The answer to that question often appears to be: yes.

Programmes rarely contain content or topics not already covered in the texts, or *new* content on which they will be assessed. Because of the difficulties many students now have in seeing the programmes, course teams are prevented from setting tutor-marked assignment questions which can be answered only if students have seen or heard the programmes, unless an alternative question is also available. Where this has been done, students generally avoid the broadcast-based question, and those that do choose it tend to do worse than students answering the other question (Gallagher, 1977b). There is also evidence that deliberately setting questions on computer-marked assignments which can be answered only through watching the programmes does increase viewing figures and students' ratings of relevance, but at the price of increased student resentment, trivial questions, or questions that do not really test the visual components of the programmes (Kern, 1976).

Artificially assessing broadcast material may increase perceived relevance, but it not only unnecessarily disadvantages many students who cannot see the programmes, it is also an ill-conceived policy, being based on a misconception about the role of media in teaching. Different media can present the *same* knowledge in different ways, and media differ in their facility to develop student *skills* in *acquiring* or *using* knowledge (see Olsen and Bruner, 1974;

Salomon, 1979). Thus in a multi-media situation, the function of a medium like television is not to present *new* knowledge but to help students acquire a better understanding through alternative means of presentation and to help students develop skills in the use or application of that knowledge. Thus it does not make sense to assess broadcasts separately since their content will be the *same* as that in other media.

The danger, of course, is that students thus see the broadcasts as redundant. However, they are only redundant with regard to *acquiring* knowledge if students obtain *full* understanding through other sources; and the broadcasts will not be redundant at all if they uniquely develop important skills which will be assessed. It is, however, essential to explain clearly to students those skills which broadcasting in particular will seek to develop, skills such as analysis, generalisation, classification and evaluation. It is also vital that students know examiners will be looking for evidence of these skills in assessment questions. Indeed, an appropriate assessment policy would be a request to students to analyse a short segment of video-tape under examination conditions (e.g. 'Explain the situation portrayed in the programme segment in terms of the main principles outlined in the correspondence texts'). Students who had not seen the programmes might still be able to answer this question adequately but those who had seen the programmes would probably be at an advantage. However, for such a policy of work, course teams would need to be clear about what skills they intend the broadcasts to develop, and these intentions must be successfully communicated to the students.

Also, the timing of broadcasts affects their relevance. On most courses, students are usually studying at least two or three weeks behind schedule. Students then often watch or listen to broadcasts *before* they have studied the texts to which the programmes are related. An advantage claimed for broadcasting is that the fixed dates of transmissions help to keep students on schedule. Broadcasting, though, has a weak pacing effect. It is the deadlines for tutor-marked assignments which govern student study schedules, with students 'bunching' work in the week or so before the deadline (Ahrens *et al.*, 1975). Students often then fail to synchronise the broadcasts with their study of the text material to which the programmes relate, with an obvious adverse effect on their perceived relevance.

A number of strategies have been tried by course teams to overcome this problem, such as making the programmes introductory to the block of work, or showing repeats three weeks after first transmission. Rather than accept these compromises, though, a new Mathematics foundation course team (M101) took the bull by the horns and imposed a Prussian discipline on students' work patterns. The television and radio programmes, the audio-cassettes and the correspondence texts were so tightly integrated that students had to work to schedule on all components to survive the course. Students had to carry out work based on the broadcasts immediately following the programmes and before they could progress to the next section. The strategy was highly successful. The viewing rate for M101 was 78 per cent, compared with 63 per cent for the course it replaced (M100), and the helpfulness ratings for the television programmes were also considerably higher. Over 75 per cent of the students kept on schedule with their study of the other components, and of the 25 per cent that dropped behind schedule, half were studying the relevant texts less than one week after the broadcasts. Close integration of texts and broadcasts clearly increased the relevance of programmes on this course.

The M101 experience though is still exceptional. Many courses do not have explicit links between the programmes and the correspondence texts. Reference is not often made in the programmes to the texts; it is even rarer to find any form of analysis or discussion of the broadcasts within the texts themselves, although on some courses audio-cassettes are used to analyse television material. Usually, the bridge between text and broadcast is made through late-printed broadcast notes which can sometimes run to more than twenty pages of analysis and supplementary materials for a single programme. Consequently, on many courses students rate the broadcast notes more highly than the programmes themselves! ('If you read the notes you don't have to watch the programmes.') Even with a great deal of help from broadcast notes, students still find it very difficult to relate the programmes to the texts in ways which they see as relevant and helpful (Gallagher, 1977b).

Lack of integration is primarily due to the separate scheduling of print and television production. To achieve the level of integration of M101, programme scripting, editing and commentary must take account of draft texts, and final versions of the text must take account of programme material. In practice, however, the close synchronisation of production schedules needed to work in this way is very difficult to achieve between two large and complex organisations such as the BBC and the Open University. The will is usually there but producers with specialist knowledge in the subject may not be available or are assigned to other course teams, or key academics may not be available when programmes have to be scripted or edited. The consequence is a set of programmes and texts which from the students' perspective stand relatively independent of each other.

For students therefore in a multi-media system, it is essential that the programmes are integrated with other media so that the role and function of the programmes, their relationship with other media and their relevance to fundamental course objectives, are all blindingly clear. Otherwise students will invest little effort in watching or listening.

FINANCIAL ARRANGEMENTS

Financial arrangements between organisations very much affect the extent to which broadcasting will be used in multi-media distance education systems. A study of twelve distance teaching institutions (Bates, 1980) identified a variety of ways in which broadcasting was costed. Financial arrangements between broadcasting organisations and distance teaching institutions were in several cases a clear disincentive against extended use of broadcasting, nor was there any apparent logic in differences in arrangements between different institutions. Furthermore, in comparison with other media such as printed texts, broadcast programmes are very expensive in terms of cost per student per study hour.

The study of the twelve institutions identified four different principles of costing broadcast services for distance teaching institutions. The most expensive arrangement is to charge market costs – what the market would bear in commercial terms for use of transmission and production facilities, such as the rates advertisers are willing to pay per minute for air-time. This was the basis for radio programmes for the unfortunate Allama Iqbal Open University in Pakistan (but curiously not for television, which meant that their radio costs were higher than their television costs!).

The second principle is to charge the full cost of providing the service but with no 'profit' for the broadcasting organisation. Full cost (perhaps on a pro-rata basis) would include salaries of production and administrative staff engaged in activities for the distance education institution, programme costs, a charge for use of studios and other facilities, capital depreciation and building costs. Indirect costs – such as overheads – will therefore be included as well as direct programme costs. The Open University pays full costs to the BBC for its production services, since the BBC manages a separate studio facility and has a separate self-contained production department devoted solely to Open University productions. The overheads also include costs for the wide range of services available from other parts of the BBC, such as copyright, legal services and film and video archives. Eight of the twelve institutions paid full costs for production.

The third principle is to charge marginal costs. In this case, it is only the actual, *additional* expenditure directly incurred by extending an already existing service which is charged. Thus if a fully operational broadcasting organisation with spare capacity made one extra programme for a distance teaching institution, on a marginal cost basis, it would charge only for the extra materials, fees, film stock, travel, etc., directly incurred by the making of that programme. The Open University pays marginal costs for transmission – just the extra manpower and technical costs incurred in extending transmissions a little longer. Three of the twelve institutions paid marginal costs for production.

Lastly, there is the Father Christmas principle, by which the broadcasting organisation makes no charge to the distance teaching institution. Apparently, Father Christmas still exists in Canada, since Athabasca gets free production facilities from ACCESS, Alberta, but it should be noted that ACCESS itself is a provincial educational communication authority, so it is merely a convenient arrangement between two provincial government departments. Five of the other twelve institutions also received free transmission time, mostly for radio.

Not knowing what constituted a fair price or principle for the service they were getting was a major concern of most of the twelve distance teaching institutions. For instance, few received detailed information indicating how broadcasting charges were arrived at. Some institutions queried whether it was 'fair' to be charged full costs (including overheads) when their broadcasting organisation was clearly making marginal use of existing studios and staff. In practice, distance teaching institutions are like customers in a shop – they either pay the price demanded, or go without the service. Particularly where there are monopoly or State-controlled broadcasting arrangements, distance teaching institutions are dependent on the good will of broadcasting organisations, and that clearly varied from one place to another.

The way broadcasting is costed also limits a distance education institution's freedom to reallocate money spent on broadcasting to other purposes. On a full-cost price system, a very large amount of the bill is tied up in overheads. For instance, the BBC set up a department and recruited extra staff specially to provide an agreed service to the Open University. The BBC claims that if staff costs are included, 80 per cent of the Open University costs are fixed and must be paid, irrespective of the number of programmes made or transmitted. Cutting the number of programmes made each year then does not lead to an equivalent saving in expenditure, and in fact increases the average unit cost per programme. All the Open University can do when it is under severe financial pressure is to ask (not demand) that BBC/OUP works within an agreed cash and programme production limit.

For many distance education institutions, broadcasting costs are much higher proportionately than the cost of other media. Deciding what a programme actually costs is not a simple matter. The crudest method is to divide the total cost of broadcasting by the number of programmes made in a year, after allowing for transmission costs. On this basis, each Open University television programme in 1983 cost about £34,000, or £82,000 per programme hour. (This does not include the cost of academic time involved in production but does include 15 per cent Value Added Tax, as do all subsequent cost figures for broadcasting at the Open University.) However, given the overheads and existing staff and assuming spare capacity, the average cost of making an additional programme (the actual programme budget) is about £8,000 – which is what would be saved per programme if programme production was reduced without firing staff. The average cost per 25-minute transmission slot in 1983 was about £400, or £950 an hour.

The cost per viewer will of course vary enormously depending on the size of course, course life and the proportion of students that view. For instance, on the Arts foundation course, the average cost per user per programme is about £1. For all *post*-foundation courses, the average cost per user per programme is about £10, and per *study hour* about £25 (taking an eight-year course life). Grundin (1983), who has calculated these costs, estimates that if other components or services were to cost the same as television per student hour at post-foundation level, the University's overall budget would need to be increased seven-fold! However, the only way that substantial savings could be made on broadcasting at the Open University would be to abandon it altogether because of the high proportion of fixed costs.

The hard reality for distance education institutions is that they just have to accept the financial arrangements offered by the broadcasting organisations or keep out of broadcasting altogether. The distance education institution (or its Ministry) may pay the bill, and the bill may be high, but it cannot dictate the play since its only financial sanction – to withdraw from broadcasting altogether – is too blunt to influence day-to-day programming decisions. In this way, individual programme decisions inevitably remain firmly within the control of the producer, in this area of broadcasting as in others.

It will be frustrating for producers, for whom the programme has to be the main focus of attention, to find so many factors outside the programme itself influencing its effectiveness. Nevertheless, what goes into a programme and how viewers or listeners respond to specific elements of that programme are obviously also extremely important.

Salomon (1981) points out that there should be two prime considerations for a producer of educational programmes: what the *programme* does *to* the viewer or listener; and what the *viewer* or *listener* does *with* the programme. Salomon argues that television has several unique teaching characteristics not found in other media which need to be exploited. For instance, programmes can provide particular *illustrations* or examples of generic principles or concepts; programmes can provide *uncertainty*, which causes viewers to work mentally to resolve the uncertainty (what Salomon calls the amount of invested mental effort – AIME); programmes can *dramatise* complex processes, by eliminating less important factors and highlighting essential features; and, above all, programmes can be used to *supplant* appropriate mental images of processes which viewers would be incapable of generating by themselves. However, these characteristics of television must, Salomon argues, be developed in appropriate ways – used inappropriately, they can actually hinder learning. Secondly, Salomon and a number of other commentators (e.g. Blumler and Katz, 1974; Heidt, 1978) have drawn attention to the fact that the audience is made up of individuals who actively respond to broadcasts in terms of their individual needs and interests. Different people will obtain different information from and react differently to the same programme. It will be seen that these are important factors influencing the effectiveness of programmes in continuing and distance education.

Brown (1980) for instance found that students' use of general radio *prior* to entry to the Open University markedly influenced the way they used radio for study purposes on Open university courses. Students planning to follow the Arts foundation course were much more likely to listen to documentaries, dramas and talks on Radio 3 or 4, than students planning to follow other foundation courses. Mathematics and Technology students in particular tended to listen primarily to pop music on Radios 1 and 2. Brown also found that at the end of their foundation course, Arts students had listened far more to Open University radio programmes than students in other faculties, and Arts students were far more willing to see the value of radio for broadening the course and providing new perspectives on subject matter. Students on other foundation courses, however, wanted the radio programmes to be more didactic and directly helpful in explaining and supporting the correspondence texts. Brown also found that half the students questioned *never* listened to radio without doing something else, like ironing or driving. He concluded that for most Open University students, their use of general radio was a poor preparation for their Open University studies.

Arts students therefore were more 'open' learners, better prepared and more willing to see Open University radio programmes as a way of broadening the subject. Mathematics, Science or Technology students, though, appeared to be more 'structured' learners, less likely to see radio as having any value as an instructional medium. This latter point relates to a finding by Salomon (1981). He found that people were less willing to invest mental effort in television than in text – their approach to television was more 'mindless'. It appears from Brown's study that Arts students did generally invest mental effort in radio prior to becoming Open University students, and therefore continued to do so with Open University programmes. Other students, though, invested little mental effort in general radio, using it as 'wallpaper', and consequently carried over this attitude to Open University radio. If radio is to be used, it must be given a teaching role whose importance is obvious to such students, and they may need some help in developing the skills required to learn from radio. This could be done by building into the programmes themselves didactic summaries, questions and listening activities. In other words, non-Arts students will need a different programme style from that found on Radio 3 and 4, at least initially. Something needs to be done because over a quarter of Open University mathematics students never listen to any programmes on their foundation course.

Trenaman (1967) carried out a major study using seventy programmes and over 1,600 people on what factors influenced adults' comprehension of BBC programmes with a general educational purpose. Firstly, he found differences in comprehension to be at least six times greater between programmes in the *same* medium than between similar topics dealt with by different media. In other words, variation in comprehension between different television programmes was far greater than comprehension of the same topics through radio, television or print. He did not find any one medium generally superior to the others. This suggests that *general* factors influence comprehension and these factors operate across *all* media. It is dangerous then to think that broadcasting is 'special', that principles governing comprehension generally do not also apply to television or radio.

Secondly, Trenaman found that of all the programme and human variables that he analysed, occupation and educational level were the most important in terms of differences in comprehension, although the main points in nearly half the programmes were 'adequately understood' by 75 per cent of a (representative) sample audience. Research has repeatedly shown the difficulty less educated people have in fully comprehending informational or educational programmes on radio and television. As early as 1950, the distinguished British psychologist, Philip Vernon, said of radio talks broadcast to the British Armed Forces: 'little of the average broadcast gets across, except to listeners who have had some secondary education, or are of superior intelligence'. In a similar study, Belson (1952) found that the average listener could answer correctly only about a quarter of the questions set on a series of radio talks. More importantly, Belson was able to identify the main faults which impaired comprehension. Although this research is now over thirty years old, and was based on radio programmes, his main findings would apply equally well to many radio and television programmes today: broadcasters tended to overestimate listeners' background knowledge of the topic; listeners had great difficulty in comprehension when left to sort out the principal points for themselves; and broadcasters too often used words which their listeners simply did not understand.

Trenaman (1967) also found that with regard to television, programmes which were 'concrete' were much more comprehensible than programmes which were 'abstract'. He defined 'concrete' as 'things directly perceived' and 'abstract' as 'general concepts unrelated to perceived objects'. He also found that a high degree of personification and dramatisation considerably improved the intelligibility of programmes, particularly for those of low occupational and educational status. High personification he defined as 'the subject of a programme is the personal lives of individuals'. He provided evidence that even abstract ideas can be communicated to wide levels of the population through some element of personification and dramatisation.

The extent to which television can teach abstract ideas is crucial for assessing its effectiveness in further and higher education. Trenaman argued that language was essential for the development of abstract thought; television's power was that it was able to combine concrete visual images with language. It is interesting to note then that Jacquinot (1977), in a study of French educational television programmes, found that the sound-track carried the main educational message and strongly controlled the viewer's interpretation of the visual message; the sound, she claimed, dominated the visuals. Porter (1982) has already shown that there are often incongruities between sound and visuals in programmes for handicapped children. The relationship between sound and visuals therefore becomes crucial. Television's particular strength appears to be that it can act as a bridge between the concrete, empirical world and the conceptual world of abstraction and generalisation captured through language. However, television will serve this function only if conscious and explicit attempts are made within the programme itself to identify the abstract concepts embedded in the concrete visuals, illustrations and dramatisations. Visuals which are not directly and explicitly related to abstractions will merely serve to confuse in education. Salomon (1983) for instance points out the dangers of illustration on television. Because televised illustrations of general principles can be so involving – or familiar – to the viewer, there is a grave risk that without explicit linking of example and principle, viewers will focus on the example and fail to comprehend the principle, particularly if they are accustomed to investing little mental effort in watching television.

There is considerable support for this view from our studies of Open University documentary-style programmes (e.g. Bates and Gallagher, 1977). Such programmes tend to present concrete examples of behaviour or technological processes operating in 'real life'. Documentary programmes thus are anchored in the real world, reflecting and synthesizing its complexity and the inter-relatedness of people, processes and events. The correspondence texts on the other hand tend to be more abstract and analytic, presented in a sequential or linear structure, breaking down the subject into 'chunks' and drawing from it general principles. There are various pedagogical dimensions to Open University programmes, and one programme can differ considerably on each dimension. Programmes can vary in their teaching explicitness; the extent to which they overtly encourage specific student activity or responses; the complexity of their structure; their explicit integration with other media; and their 'stance' – i.e. whether they are polemical or neutral. Documentary programmes, which are used extensively in Social Science, Educational Studies and Technology courses, and can also be found in all the other faculty areas, tend to be open to interpretation (i.e. not didactic); do not give explicit indications of the kind of response expected from students; are complex in structure (i.e. non-linear); are not explicitly integrated with other media; and tend to be neutral in stance, at least on the surface. In other words, they look like 'Horizon' programmes. Indeed, a number of such Open University programmes have been shown on the 'Horizon' slot at peak times on BBC2. These structural aspects have major implications for teaching and learning.

My colleagues and I in the Audio-Visual Media Research Group collected student information on a relatively large number of Open University documentary-style programmes. Firstly, we found that such programmes were meant to perform a valuable function in the Open University context. The skills required of students and the treatment of content in the programmes were quite different from those found in the correspondence texts. Students were expected to *analyse* the programmes themselves, using the theoretical or analytic constructs provided in the texts (or broadcast notes); to *apply* what they had learned in the texts to the 'real-world' situations presented in the programmes; to *generalise* or draw conclusions from the specific instances in the programmes; and to test, *evaluate* or compare the validity of general principles contained in the texts with respect to the real-world instances shown in the programmes. In several instances, the programmes provided the only opportunity in the course to practise such skills, outside examination or assessment questions.

That then was the intention. The reality was different. Roughly one third of students watching such programmes completely misunderstood the purpose of documentaries. They were looking for new information or explanation of difficulties in the text. When they realised that the programmes did not do this, they dismissed them as irrelevant and a waste of time. Other students – again about a third of viewers – understood the purpose of the programmes but were *unable* to respond in the way intended. Lastly, roughly one third – sometimes as little as one sixth – of the students both understood the purpose of the programme and were able to use the programme material in the way intended. You will not be surprised to learn that this group tended to get high grades in the final examination.

One might have predicted from Trenaman's findings that Open University documentary-style programmes would have been *more* comprehensible than didactic programmes since, by definition, documentary programmes tend to present concrete, real-life situations. Trenaman's studies, however, were concerned *only* with comprehension and the programme was the only source of information on which comprehension was tested. For Open University students though, it is the correspondence text that carries the bulk of the content. The aim of documentaries is not to add important extra information or reinforce the text by re-explanation but, at least implicitly, to exercise different – and higher order – learning skills than comprehension; they are there to allow students to *use* or *test* out the knowledge that they should have already 'comprehended', but in an abstract form.

Adult students, with their rich life experiences, can find it particularly difficult to move from concrete, often personal or emotive, 'instances' to more general or abstract principles. Open-ended documentaries by definition give little direct help in moving students from the concrete to the abstract. With such programmes the students have to do this for themselves. This is only good for them if (a) they *know* they are supposed to do this and (b) they know *how* to do this. It is not really surprising that two thirds of the students said they needed help since there was no direct guidance *within* the programme on how to go about analysis. Analysis, interpretation, application of abstract principles to real problems, restructuring and re-ordering of facts are all difficult high-level skills to develop without explicit guidance.

There is also the Warm Bath theory of realism. Thompson (1977) argues that 'realism' in documentaries makes it difficult for students to adopt an analytical approach. Like a warm bath, realism 'engenders an unconscious relaxation because it is familiar . . . and encourages an accepting type of response . . . Such programmes transform nothing but simply reinforce existing experiential notions of what life is really like'. This is a particular problem for Open University students studying in isolation since they do not have the stimulus of a tutor or group discussion session to break through the apparent seamlessness of such programmes in order to interrogate their meaning. Salomon (1981) argues that learning will not take place unless mental effort is invested. Such programmes have strong connotations with relaxed, 'mindless' viewing of television for entertainment purposes.

It is important to distinguish between *involvement* in and *attention* to a programme, and *learning*. Involvement and attention are necessary but not sufficient prerequisites for learning. Producers have developed sophisticated techniques for arousing and maintaining interest and attention during documentary programmes. For instance, the complex structure often found in documentary programmes, the juxtaposition of shots out of temporal or logical sequence, abrupt changes in theme, are all used to create uncertainty – to get the viewer to make sense of what is being presented, to work at achieving meaning. But this technique, while suitable for involving a general audience, needs to be used very carefully with Open University students. The uncertainty created must be resolved by *valid* applications of thought relevant to the main teaching objectives of the programme or unit of study. Students whose mental effort is invested primarily in making sense of the internal logic of a programme or working out how one part of a programme relates to another, may be deflected from understanding the relationship between what they are seeing and the more abstract concepts they are studying in the texts.

At a higher-education level, it is also essential for students to be aware of the unique formal properties of television, particularly where it is used to present evidence or arguments. Students and tutors are often *unable* to read documentary television programmes as critically as they have learned to read books. Television has its own unique ways of supporting or attacking arguments or viewpoints, of choosing and presenting evidence, of manipulating the feelings and emotions of viewers. They are no more or less valid than the techniques used in writing but it is vital that higher education students in all subject areas appreciate how television constructs an argument through the use of visuals, editing and selection, and how it presents and uses evidence. For instance, interviewers' questions are often edited out, the response to the question then appearing in the programme as a spontaneous comment. Visuals are often added later to a commentary (or vice versa) to reinforce an argument, although there may have been no previous relationship between the film and the sound before they came together in the editing or dubbing suite. Often the same film could be used to reinforce totally different arguments. Nevertheless, the juxtaposition of film and sound gives the effect of the picture 'validating' the argument. These 'production' decisions therefore have profound effects on the meaning of a programme.

There is thus a responsibility to provide explicit help and guidance for students, to enable them to analyse documentary material in ways that are relevant to the educational objectives of their course. It is too much to expect most students to develop such skills unaided. The Open University has in recent years tried to help students in several ways. On many of the courses developed in the mid 1970s (e.g. 'Urban Development' and 'Mass Communication in Society'), broadcast notes or even glossy media booklets were designed to draw out the main teaching points from the documentaries. In later years, audio-cassettes have served a similar function. Substantial support material, however, increases the cost of the course and students still find it difficult to analyse the television programmes because the analysis in the support materials is separated both physically and in time from the programmes.

A more successful approach has been to use one programme to

analyse another. Students were shown in a following programme how to analyse the first fifty-minute documentary programme on their course. It was found that the second programme increased by one third the students who were able to analyse the first programme in the way intended, and nearly all students wanted more analytic programmes of this kind (Gallagher, 1977c). It is, however, an expensive way of making programmes effective. The Open University also developed a training package for new students and tutors called 'Learning from Television', giving examples of different ways in which television is used in the Open University and suggesting how best to approach the programmes. Again, though, this is a separate activity from using television on a specific course and we do not know how well such general skills will transfer to specific instances.

However, these various approaches are necessary at all only because programmes avoid guidance on analysis within the programmes themselves. The development of the skills required for analysis ought to be built into the programmes, using a deliberate, progressive teaching strategy over a whole course. At the beginning, programmes should be heavily didactic, simply structured and require active responses and activities from the student during and after the programme. Gradually, more and more film and video material should be introduced, with cues on what students should look for, how the material could be analysed and interpreted and how it links to concepts dealt with in the text. Students should be encouraged to make their own interpretations, and feedback on suitable responses should be provided within the programmes. Material should be repeated for reviewing and analysis, and examples should be given of how the television evidence could have been alternatively presented. By the end of the series, programmes can become much more open-ended and complexly structured, resembling traditional documentary formats. Such an ambitious teaching strategy has been attempted on the new Social Sciences Foundation Course (D102), and early evaluations show that these programmes have been much better received by students than on the previous Social Sciences foundation courses (D100 and D101).

Documentary-style programmes thus can play a valuable role in distance higher education, getting the students to think for themselves. They can play a key role in moving students from low-level skills of comprehension and surface processing to broader conceptions of learning, involving high-level skills and deep processing. Careful and progressive development, though, is needed to reach this point, suggesting that 'open-ended' documentary or dramatised programmes should be used more sparingly or carefully than they have been at the Open University. A good documentary or drama in general television terms may be fun to make and a valuable addition to a producer's professional portfolio but it may not be what is most needed at a particular point in a student's course. The decision to use the documentary or drama format thus should be based on the carefully defined intended teaching function of the programme and the skills students are likely to possess in analysing such material at that point of a course, and not on the blind application of popular broadcasting formats.

GETTING IT RIGHT IN CONTINUING AND DISTANCE HIGHER EDUCATION: CONCLUSIONS

Once again there are formidable difficulties in using broadcasting effectively. In continuing and distance higher education, audiences differ markedly in their learning needs even within the same target group. Diversity of courses and drop-out can lead to very small audiences. Transmission times have to be reasonably convenient and hence conflict with the needs of the general audience, and a great deal of transmission time is needed if broadcasting is to play a significant role in distance education. Unique and relevant teaching functions have to be identified, selected and used on multi-media courses, and programmes must also be clearly relevant within the students' broader learning context, with implications for how students are assessed. Close integration with other media puts demanding requirements on production scheduling. To increase the comprehension of continuing education programmes, they need to be concrete, and for lower occupational and educational levels, dramatised or personified. Documentary-style programmes can be valuable for developing higher-level learning skills in distance education but students need a coherent teaching strategy to develop skills of analysis and interpretation of such programmes, preferably within the programmes themselves. Television imposes its own meaning on learning materials, and higher education students using broadcasting need to know how this occurs. Lastly, financial arrangements can seriously discourage the use of broadcasting in distance higher education, and broadcast television is likely to cost far more than other media in terms of student contact time.

Given these difficulties, it is surprising that broadcasting is used at all in distance higher education. However, broadcasting even at this level can attract a large general audience, and when used well it brings unique benefits to students, providing variety, motivation and the opportunity to develop skills which are a crucial part of higher education; the price both financially and in terms of student inconvenience though can be very high.

8

Broadcasters, professionalism and educational effectiveness

Time and again, in each education sector and in many countries, certain fundamental questions about the role of broadcasting keep recurring. *Why* do broadcasting organisations with an obvious commitment to education consult too little and too late with other educational agencies? *Why* is so little done to discover the specific learning needs of target audiences and the effects of educational programmes? *Why* are certain formats, like documentaries, so popular with educational broadcasters, compared with more overtly instructional formats? For instance, Hall (1980), a project organiser for local courses associated with the BBC series 'Your Own Business', commented:

> It is possible to discover in advance the intention of broadcasters to produce programmes . . . but it is not easy . . . This process rarely takes place early enough for an organisation to arrange for substantial resources of people and money to provide for adequate follow up . . . The approach is paternalistic and often condescending . . .

Few attempts are made, even with slow-learning children or other particularly difficult target groups, to identify what the audience is capable of, what approaches the programme should take, what special needs must be met. Once programmes are made, little is done by the broadcasters themselves to find out in a systematic way what students have learned from them. The Annan Committee on the Future of Broadcasting in the United Kingdom was particularly critical of the broadcasting organisations' attitudes to research:

> It was indeed extraordinarily difficult to get any objective evidence on the reality, as distinct from the aspirations, of educational broadcasting. The broadcasters and leading educational bodies told us they were convinced of its effectiveness. But there was little research material to substantiate this act of faith . . . in

fact, the broadcasters were suspicious of such research. They preferred to rely on the subjective appraisal of those involved (Great Britain: Home Office, 1977).

We have seen evidence that certain popular programme formats need to be used very carefully and selectively for educational purposes. We have seen that general rules of good teaching are likely to apply just as much to television and radio for effective learning to take place. We have seen that the kinds of programmes likely to appeal to committed learners will be very different from programmes likely to appeal to a general audience. Why then do educational programmes still look similar in style and format to general programmes? Why do educational programmes so often flaunt basic principles of teaching?

There are always exceptions of course; there is no denying the strong commitment to education of many broadcasting organisations; at a formal level, there is also a commitment (at least from the BBC and IBA) to closer partnership and collaboration with other educational agencies. But in practice, the main stream of educational broadcasting operates independently of the education sectors regarding programme planning, design and production, and formal links with other agencies. Basically, broadcasters do what they want to do, in education as in other sectors.

This attitude can best be understood by examining the professional ideology of broadcasting, that is, the main value-systems which guide the way people work in broadcasting organisations. When under the control of a general broadcasting organisation, educational broadcasters are bound to be influenced by the values and principles of the organisation as a whole. Educational broadcasting constitutes less than 3 per cent of the BBC budget, so producers in educational broadcasting departments are small fish in a big pool. They may have been initially recruited from educational institutions but they attend the same internal training courses – which concentrate on drama, current affairs and variety – as producers from other departments. Many naturally see educational broadcasting as a stepping stone to other, perhaps more prestigious programming, with bigger budgets, better viewing times and much larger audiences. As one BBC/Open University producer put it:

What one is after is . . . building up prestige or kudos and becoming known as a 'good producer' within the organisation. Now of course this affects the way one makes programmes. For instance, you make more documentaries than straight teaching programmes, or at least it's those programmes you put a lot of effort into and regard as your selling point when it comes to Appointment Boards . . . What you want is to go along to the Current Affairs Unit and say 'I'm the guy who makes programmes about urban problems in Liverpool' and show them what you've done (from Gallagher, 1977d).

What then are the value-systems which most influence broadcasting?

QUALITY IN PROGRAMMING

There is, for a start, a fundamental difference in terminology between broadcasters and educators. As Wilbur Schramm (1972) noted: 'Most educational broadcasters tend to talk of a 'good' programme in terms of *quality*; most scholars, in terms of *effectiveness*.' Schramm tended to play down the difference, but there is a significance far greater than the superior choice of words by broadcasters. The words represent two quite different philosophies.

The basic premise underlying 'quality' is that programmes should be judged by certain *professional standards* developed by broadcasters themselves from long experience. 'Quality' lies in the programme itself – it can be *seen* by the trained eye. By contrast, the basic premise underlying 'effectiveness' is that programmes should be judged by their *observed impact on learners* in terms of criteria educators believe to be important. 'Effectiveness' is 'out there' – it depends on how learners respond to the programme. Quality and effectiveness are not mutually exclusive – quality in a programme may be necessary for it to be effective – but the starting point for judgement is different between broadcasters and educators. Professional standards, at least at the BBC, require producers to balance three pressures: the need for excitement, the need for integrity and the need for reliability. This requires programmes which have audience appeal, which enhance the quality of national life and which are competently managed. The balance between these components will vary between broadcasting organisations, or within the same institution over time, but they will usually be found to some extent or other in any broadcasting organisation.

In a competitive situation, no broadcasting organisation – not even the BBC – can afford to ignore *audience appeal*. For instance, soon after the establishment of commercial television in Britain in 1955, it became clear that once the BBC's share of the audience dropped too far, it would be difficult to persuade the public, and hence Parliament, of the need for increased revenue, with a consequent downward spiralling effect on its ability to keep good staff, to maintain high quality programming and so on. For the last thirty years, the BBC has had to take seriously the need to attract and keep audiences and has more than held its own in developing techniques and standards which ensure audience appeal. The use of techniques which attract and hold the audience is probably the most highly valued of producers' skills within the profession itself. These techniques are not constant, varying according to fashion, the type of programme and the newest technology.

In the field of documentaries, current affairs and dramas – programmes most similar in style to those found in educational broadcasting – various strategies are used to enhance audience appeal. A basic requirement is clear, unambiguous presentation: sharp sound and picture and good lighting; the basic grammar of television and radio – correct camera angles, cutting and mixing – to give smooth, unobtrusive links between shots and scenes. Conventions, even clichés, are used to establish quickly the kind of programme being presented and the roles or functions of people in the programme. Vaughan (1976) illustrates how firmly the conventions and 'language' of television have become established:

> If we switch on our sets and see someone addressing us directly, we know he is a narrator or presenter. If his gaze is directed slightly off-camera, we know he is an interviewee, a talking head. If he is turned away from us by an angle of more than 15°, he is part of an action sequence.

For the radio and television producer, the use of basic conventions is an essential platform on which creative programming can be built. The aim then at this level is naturalism: smoothness and clarity, 'hiding' technique so that the viewer or listener is unaware of the way in which the programme has been composed and assembled.

While necessary to give a programme a 'professional' look, clear, unambiguous presentation on its own would be boring and have little audience appeal. Other strategies then are used to switch, regain or focus the audience's attention. The aim is to jolt the audience but without the audience being aware of how the effect was achieved. For instance, deliberately breaking continuity between adjacent scenes is a common 'arousal' technique. Thus one scene ends and another begins in a different place or at a different time or with different characters. The two adjacent scenes do not immediately have any apparent relationship although the confusion is usually quickly resolved. Other examples would be deliberately contrasting or intercutting scenes (from a dinner for international bankers to starving black children in a village in Africa); laying the sound track from the end of one scene over the start of a completely different scene; use of unusual camera angles (e.g. shooting upwards from ground level); the use of filters to distort light and angles; and the use of sounds or music to denote a sudden shift of mood.

Many more examples could be given. They serve to increase the audience's curiosity and uncertainty by setting up a disparity, then resolving it. Used carefully, such techniques can be extremely valuable for educational purposes where the audience is encouraged to construct for themselves the meaning or relationship between various, apparently disconnected events. When such techniques, however, are unrelated to the main educational purposes of the programme and are used merely to jazz it up, they will distract learners from the primary learning task. Furthermore, presentational techniques are not free of meaning. Their use can subtly change the audience's perception of content, of what is important and what is not. For instance, the choice of location, props, furniture, clothes, actors, what fills the screen when action or commentary takes place, all add meaning to the programme. If included to increase audience appeal, they will again distract learners unless the programme ingredients are directly relevant to the primary learning tasks, particularly if learners have only one opportunity in real time to view or listen.

Arousal techniques complemented by smooth, natural presentation, though, are only means to an end. The aim is to create a rhythm, a flow, a shape within a programme, and this requires the programme to be structured in ways which are interesting for the audience. There is a need for 'peaks' and 'troughs' of attention within the programme and a need for the programme to keep moving. Advertising techniques, which have to hook the audience and get a message over very quickly and efficiently, have been particularly influential on the structure of television programmes. The result is constant change: of shots, scenes, themes, locations, of sharp or 'hip' dialogue, concise language and minimal commentary. The average length of shot on television is between three and twelve seconds; the average length of an item on an American current affairs programme is sixty seconds; in one hour, the American viewer is likely to receive 1,200 different images, according to Postman (1983). It is rare on British television for any single programme participant to be allowed to speak for more than sixty seconds on any topic without some form of interruption, either from the professional 'link-man' or from one of the other participants who, having worked out the arithmetic, knows that his own chance of a contribution is quickly running out.

Postman (1983) has drawn attention to the consequences of such programming structures on logical or linear thinking and on our sensibilities:

> First, it makes it difficult to think about an event, and second, it makes it difficult to feel about an event . . . All events on TV come completely devoid of historical continuity or any other context, and in such fragmented and rapid succession that they wash over our minds in an undifferentiated stream. This is television as narcosis, dulling to both sense and sensibility.

The magazine format, a mixture of short items often unrelated or at best loosely connected, is a particularly popular way of packaging programmes. Postman reports Vidal Sassoon ending a segment of one of his shows with the classic: 'Don't go away. We'll be back with a marvellous new diet and then, a quick look at incest.' Although the American experience may be more crass and extreme, it would be a delusion to believe that the same processes were not at work on British television. MacLeod (1981), a participant in one of York-shire TV's medical series 'Where There's Life . . .', criticised the use of this format for dealing with complex issues. Anorexia was one of five different topics covered in the same programme. In the space of six minutes, Sheila MacLeod and two other participants found themselves with the task of unravelling a tangle of misapprehension about anorexia on the part of the public (and the presenter). The result was inevitably 'a set of assertions rather than argument'. Presenting a series of short, unrelated items means that explanations are never adequately given or discussed and therefore there is no chance of understanding what the issues are really about. Maybe most of the twelve million audience that started watching 'Where There's Life . . .' didn't care a damn about anorexia (in which case six minutes was too long), but those that did were surely entitled to more than two minutes from each expert.

This does not mean that even in education there is no value in magazine formats (for instance, for up-dating people already well informed, or suggesting new sources of information). The assumption, though, that the attention span of the general public is about five minutes maximum, is peculiar to broadcasting and has no scientific basis, other than research done primarily on advertising techniques. Attention span can be increased or decreased over a very wide range, dependent on the relevance of the subject matter, the skilled use of language, the density of information, the needs of the learner and so on. Given the amount of exposure most people have to broadcasting and the prevalence of the one-minute comment on almost any topic, in news as well as educational programming, the long-term effect on people's thought-processes, intellectual development and political decision-making is frightening.

Thus great care is needed to ensure that structures and techniques which enhance attention and audience appeal in general television do not run counter to the educational aims of a programme which may occasionally require students to stop and think. The restless and fragmented nature of popular television formats is the greatest obstacle to learning directly from broadcasting. To slow down the pace and to hold shots, giving learners time to observe, to think, to make their own connections; to provide repetition, summaries and feedback within a programme; to provide a simple and clear structure, all require courage and a willingness to be unorthodox, so entrenched is the idea that complex structures and short, sharp sequences are the essence of 'good' television.

Another idea associated with audience appeal is ambition. Large budgets, exotic location, famous people, expensive sets and costumes, are all ingredients associated with quality programming in general television. Ambition in a production, provided it is well handled, is highly respected within the broadcasting profession. Producers in an organisation like the BBC have tremendous resources at their disposal. Enormous care is taken to provide authentic sets and costumes in drama, access is available to the highest in the land, cameras can be made available to cover major political, economic or social events. Great efforts are made to achieve authenticity and first-hand reporting – straight from the horse's mouth. From an educational point of view, ambition can enable material to be brought to learners which would be otherwise impossible to provide. The opportunity to observe the Grand Canyon, to hear leading statesmen speak of their experiences, to see professional actors interpret classic drama, are all immensely valuable educationally. But ambition can also be a deadly sin. In an educational context, it needs to be handled very carefully. The temptation to go overseas to collect material which could just as easily be found at home can be wasteful both financially and in terms of academic time. Ambition can lead to the inclusion of material which is not always relevant to learners' needs. Having gone to enormous lengths to collect material, it must be shown. Making programmes is fun – and should be fun – but it is easy to get carried away by the sheer glamour of the process. In terms of approval within the profession it is easier to see how well the ambition has been converted into exciting programme material than to decide whether the material is what learners need most at that time in their course.

The development of character and the portrayal of inter-personal relations has enormous popular appeal, especially everyday relationships between ordinary people in ordinary circumstances. This aspect of content can be found not only in soap operas or more 'serious' drama but also in a wide range of programmes, from crime series to documentaries. These programmes provide the viewer with an opportunity to experience a wide range of emotions, particularly through identification with the characters.

Controversy also gives a programme audience appeal. The topic itself, such as immigration or law and order, may be the cause of controversy. However, public broadcasting organisations have to be careful in the way they handle controversial issues. Controversy must be dealt with in a balanced way, avoiding at all cost the appearance of supporting one side or another. A common strategy then is to invite or obtain contributions from spokesmen or participants of 'both sides', with an employee of the broadcasting organisation, such as Sir Robin Day, as a neutral chairman, thus clearly distancing the broadcasting organisation from the views expressed. Similarly, the inclusion of fashionable topics or people currently in the news or in the forefront of the public's attention is considered to increase programme appeal. This process can of course be self-perpetuating, with the media creating interest and then feeding off it.

Thus to increase interest and audience appeal, even in educational programmes, one will frequently find entertainment characters such as Basil Brush, a famous footballer or a pop star presenting or participating in the programme, controversial events being used to illustrate educational material, little dramas within a programme, or educational topics being dealt with in the form of debates between participants associated with a particular point of view.

Again, though, in an educational context, such techniques must be used carefully. They can easily distract learners from the learning tasks and introduce irrelevant material. The antics of Basil Brush *during* the presentation of important information may be humorous but self-defeating in educational terms. What will be remembered is Basil Brush being naughty and not the information. We have already seen that illustrations or examples can be too effective, causing concentration on the example itself rather than on the *principle* being illustrated. There is a particular danger in using controversial issues to illustrate certain principles because viewers get angered or aroused by the example and miss the broader point being made.

Many producers are aware of these dangers, but the way controversial issues are handled in general programming can have a more subtle influence on educational programming. Techniques such as the use of equal time for different views, a neutral chairman or a panel discussion after a controversial documentary, weaken the treatment and the force of ideas, according to Hood (1972). There are not always just two alternative viewpoints, but many; some ideas need lengthy treatment, a whole programme, to appreciate the range and depth of the argument; it is easier to comprehend and remember a single, coherent set of arguments than to take in simultaneously two contradictory arguments. In educational terms, therefore, a programme could justifiably be polemical – just as university lectures often are. This does not mean that teaching should be biased, or that alternative ideas should not be presented at some stage during a course, but, particularly in a multi-media context, there should be scope for a single view or argument to be strongly stated in a programme. Each programme therefore should not have to be 'balanced' in itself, but in practice, it is extremely difficult with certain controversial issues to make a strong, polemical argument using public broadcasting, even in an educational context.

Many more examples could be given of the enormous variety of ways in which producers can give programmes audience appeal. This is not to deny that, individually, these techniques are subservient to creating a whole experience from the programme as an entity, and that what really counts for most producers are the universals of entertainment: good writers; good topics; good performers. But television in particular depends very much on material being 'wrapped' and presented attractively and interestingly. The sheer quantity of programme material required to fill four television channels every day of the year inevitably forces producers to pay great attention to presentational aspects, to use routine production methods which are known to appeal to an audience. The pace of production is such that many of these presentational techniques have become almost instinctive and unquestioned.

What then gives a television programme quality, in the eyes of fellow broadcasting professionals, is the skill of the production team in exploiting and harnessing the presentational features of television or radio, in such a way that the content or material in the programme – the topic under discussion, the script, the location being observed – is developed to the full. Although subsidiary to the content, presentational features are essential for this development and many are unique to the medium.

Audience appeal, however, is only one side of the coin of quality programming. The other side is the ideal of *public service*. British broadcasting has since its establishment been expected to be a public service, with a moral responsibility to enhance the quality of national life. This ideal has been most clearly and forcibly expressed by its originator, Lord Reith:

> There was to hand a mighty instrument to instruct and fashion public opinion; to banish ignorance and misery; to contribute richly and in many ways to the sum total of human well-being. The present concern of those to whom the stewardship had, by accident, been committed was that those basic ideals should be sealed and safeguarded, so that broadcasting might play its destined part . . . So the responsibility at the outset conceived, and despite all discouragement pursued, was to carry into the greatest number of homes the best in every department of human knowledge, endeavour and achievement; and to avoid whatever was and might be hurtful. In the earliest years accused of setting out to give the public not what it wanted but what it needed, the answer was that few knew what they wanted, fewer what they needed (Reith, 1949).

Times of course have changed. Such sentiments today – or at least their manner of expression – are unacceptably arrogant and elitist for many people, including broadcasters. By 1963 Burns (1969) had identified a section of opinion within the BBC which rejected altogether such a 'normative' approach to public broadcasting. Nevertheless, while some of the more missionary aspects of Reith's philosophy have gone, the tradition of public service still exerts a powerful influence on not only the BBC but also the independent television companies. Public service is *expected* of British broadcasting by the people and Parliament; it is part of the collective cultural ideology of the British.

Cultural and intellectual enrichment is an important facet of public service broadcasting in Britain. This can mean providing programmes which are likely to appeal exclusively to an intellectual or cultural elite, but more often it means offering programmes with a broad popular appeal but which embody high cultural and intellectual standards in their production. Opera or Shakespeare may be scheduled at peak viewing times in the hope that a wider public may be attracted, perhaps for the first time, to classical works of art. The aim is not only to provide the cultural elite with programmes which they will enjoy but also to raise gradually and even unconsciously the cultural and intellectual standards of the public as a whole. Such a philosophy accepts that programmes will not always appeal to the majority of viewers. On the other hand, the balance is crucial: too many programmes with too little appeal will result in permanent loss of audiences.

Enhancing the cultural and intellectual standards means recruiting production staff who share and can skilfully promote those standards within relatively popular programming. The BBC in particular tends to recruit graduates straight from university, particularly from Oxford and Cambridge, with little or no technical knowledge of television production, but with a good general education, and then trains them in-house.

For years BBC television has been first choice of a quite disproportionate number of the nation's best qualified graduates. The number and quality of the BBC's unsolicited applications still astonishes recruitment officers from other corporations (Jay, 1972).

Although the independent television companies appear more willing to recruit producers from film and television departments in polytechnics, they also often employ experienced producers from the BBC. There is no doubt that broadcasting in Britain is seen as a high-status career. It is not surprising then to find a great deal of self-belief amongst producers in British broadcasting organisations which inevitably influences their reaction to external appraisal.

Another aspect of public service broadcasting is responsibility. This means that the broadcaster's duty is to ensure as far as possible that the audience is not misled or its baser emotions exploited, but that the topic or subject being dealt with is treated as openly and as fairly as possible. Responsibility is one area where guidelines are clearly spelt out and codified by management, partly because of legal requirements and partly to avoid unnecessary conflicts with major power groups in British society, particularly the political parties. Thus the following is an extract from a BBC set of guidelines on the making of documentaries:

The BBC is formally required to refrain from expressing its own opinion on current affairs or matters of public policy. Also, its own code of practice developed over the years – in recognition of the powerful position it occupies – demands that its programmes should be fair and without bias, and that those who produce programmes should never abuse their position for purposes of propaganda or the expression of personal commitment (Cawston *et al.*, 1972).

However, although guidelines can be clearly stated, in practice their interpretation is much more difficult. Also, the idea that programmes in the news and current affairs areas are neutral and objective has come under increasing question in recent years. It is clear that what appears on our sets – what is thought to be news and worth discussion – is the result of a highly selective process. These processes of selection, and the way the topics are treated, are not 'neutral', it is argued, but are influenced partly by the limitations or demands of the technological processes of broadcasting and partly by the ideology of the broadcasters themselves (see, for instance, Glasgow University Media Group, 1976 and 1980).

Whether or not these criticisms are accepted, most broadcasters *believe* that responsibility, objectivity and fairness are important standards to apply to news, current affairs and documentary programmes, and most broadcasters believe that their training, experience and the companies' procedures do result in such standards being incorporated into programme production, even if it means occasionally coming into conflict with government and other powerful groups in society. Public service and independence, therefore, are mutually dependent ideas.

Educational broadcasting is one aspect of public service broadcasting – it is another means by which cultural, intellectual and responsible programming can be provided. Educational broadcasts are subject to the same professional criteria of judgement as other programmes with cultural or intellectual qualities. A programme in the end is always a compromise between the ideas and ambition of the production team and the pressures of limited time and resources, a balance between a number of conflicting standards: of audience appeal against integrity, of responsibility against sensationalism. When broadcasters assess the quality of a programme, they will be looking at how the production team have resolved these conflicts and how the programme as a whole holds together.

PROFESSIONALISM IN BROADCASTING

These standards are not acquired accidentally or haphazardly. They result from a whole set of occupational pressures brought about by the technical nature of broadcasting and the institutional and political environment in which broadcasters work.

Burns (1969) found that the use of the term 'professional' was widespread in the BBC, particularly in the sense of meaning 'expert'. As a BBC/Open University Productions senior producer put it:

The BBC is characterized by different levels of professionalism in different areas: for example, design here is super-professional, engineering is super-professional, the whole programme-making process is super-professional (from Gallagher, 1977d).

There is a striving for *perfection* in specialist departments which at least in part stems from the way the BBC interprets its duty as a public service. The basic non-commercial nature of the BBC enables it to focus on one clear, overall objective: the production and transmission of programmes. That is the business of the BBC. While its financial base is important, money is a means to an end. This end can be very simply stated as to provide the public with the 'best' broadcasting service that money can buy. Consequently, the goal of each of the various subdivisions within the BBC concerned with programme production is to meet the highest standards possible in its own area of expertise. A producer must try within the limitations of his budget to get the best writers, the best actors or performers, the best equipment, the best services.

However, 'best' is defined in terms of professional standards which do not always reflect audience needs. Picture quality for instance is measured in terms of absolute technical standards. Further improvements in the quality of pictures go largely unnoticed by the public; the quality of transmitted sound is far beyond the reproduction capability of loudspeakers on domestic television sets. Professional standards can get in the way of more important educational objectives. An obvious example is the recording of actual classroom situations. Without a great deal of intrusion, it is extremely difficult to get sound and picture recordings to a standard which would satisfy broadcast engineers, although the pedagogic value of a recording may justify the risk of loss of clarity on reception. Specialists have their own careers, and their names are likely to appear on the credits. Most producers are unwilling to override a specialist if the argument is about acceptable standards within the specialist's profession.

Nevertheless, perfectionism has without doubt set standards which the public has come to expect from British television and radio. It ensures that picture quality, graphics and sound are as good as the reception equipment. The 'super-professionalism' of the various service departments is seen as an important ingredient of quality programming.

Another aspect of professionalism is *commitment*. Especially in educational programming, the relatively low budget, the short time available for production and the need to do justice to the various professional services available to the producer, create a special working environment. To weld together in a very short space of time perhaps over a hundred different professionals into one team committed to doing their best for 'the programme' requires total commitment from the producer.

> The utter absorption of the producer in his show – a commitment more complete than I have encountered anywhere else – is the product of cumulative pressures . . . This absorption demands emotional reinforcement and expressive demonstration. No kind of detachment is really permissible; commitment has to be – and be seen to be – sincere and binding . . . He must, above all, it seems, 'believe in' his show (Burns, 1969).

This results, according to Burns, in the development of a strong 'in-group' feeling. The programme is the only thing that matters. Those concerned with the programme, who are helping to create it, are 'in'; everyone else is 'out'. Within the BBC system, programme production results in considerable job-satisfaction for many of those directly involved. There is a genuine pride in the product and, for the producer in particular, a close, sometimes fierce, identification with the programme. It is 'his (or her) baby'.

However, the need to control and respond to the requirements of highly professional service departments, the development of 'in-group' feelings and the producer's close personal identification with the programme, again force total concentration on the product, the programme itself. These pressures are particularly acute for educational producers, who have lower budgets and shorter production times than general broadcasters. Thus, with the best will in the world, relations with external agencies, pre-production research into audience needs and post-production follow-up of learning effectiveness, are inevitably pushed to the periphery of a producer's activities. In a broadcasting organisation, total commitment and absorption in the production process is essential if the programmes are to have quality. Destroy the commitment and you destroy the product. This is one reason why educational television produced outside of broadcasting organisations rarely compares with the quality of broadcast programmes. It is the pressure of working within a professional broadcasting organisation and the professionalism of the services available to programme makers which generates and sustains the commitment of producers to their programmes.

Autonomy and self-regulation are characteristics of most professions. In Britain, broadcasting organisations are meant to be independent of State interference regarding programming. This does not mean that there is never pressure from government, individual ministers or political parties, and the extent to which such pressure is successful varies constantly, depending on the subject, the current financial state of broadcasting organisations and the extent to which broadcasting is under public scrutiny. Nevertheless, most British producers believe that they have a good deal of personal freedom in the design and production of programmes, and that their independence is essential for quality programming.

This freedom though is not unconstrained. Some commentators, such as Elliott (1972) and the Glasgow University Media Group (1976), argue that the freedom of producers is illusory. Producers, they claim, are the unwitting carriers of the ideology of the ruling elite in British society, a view which has increasing support now within the Labour Party. One does not have to share this Marxist viewpoint to be aware that there are constraints placed on the freedom of producers by the broadcasting organisations themselves. These can be explicit, as in the guidelines on documentaries mentioned earlier. More frequently, the constraints are less explicit, but nevertheless real. They have to be 'read' or picked up by production staff; they must learn what is 'on' and 'not on', what can be done and what cannot. Those who continually misread the signs tend to get shunted out of sensitive areas of programming or into more remote areas of the BBC empire, or they themselves become frustrated and move out of mainline broadcasting altogether.

Internal control is exercised across the whole field of broadcasting, including educational programmes. The BBC for instance is prepared to exercise such control, even with regard to educational material for which another institution, the Open University, has formal responsibility regarding academic content, if the senior management in the BBC believes that the programmes are out of line. Some programmes on the Open University Drama course were refused transmission, after production, at a very late stage of course development. Genet's *Le Balcon* was refused transmission altogether, and two others were moved from their original 'prime time' in the middle of a Sunday morning, to a very early transmission slot on a Saturday, because they were too sexually explicit. (Offending early rising Jews was evidently preferable to offending Christians who were not at church.)

The *way* control was exercised in this instance is also pertinent, as the comments of the academic in charge of course production reveal:

Some programmes I was involved in making have been subjected to scrutiny and discussion at the very highest level in the BBC. They've all been involved – the Head of Open University Productions, the Controller of Educational Broadcasting, the Controller of BBC2, right up to the Board of Governors. And all this was completely unknown to me – the Course Team Chairman – or the producers who actually made the programmes . . . The distressing thing is that the programme scripts went through the normal vetting procedure; the programmes were made and approved. Then at this much later stage, because of a feeling *now* that there were some scenes which would offend certain sexual or moral codes, and would not be suitable for a mass audience the whole thing has suddenly become very nasty. Perhaps with Annan about to report, the BBC management is very sensitive about its image . . . In the present case, no criteria for censorship were offered, and the process by which decisions are made, and the people who make the decisions, accordingly cannot be called into account. In the present system, the University has no ultimate control over the broadcast components of its courses (from Gallagher, 1977d).

Despite eight years close co-operation between the BBC and the Open University, and an extensive system of joint committees, each case is apparently judged on its merits within the BBC. Second, this was a rare event; it is very unusual for any Open University programme once made to be rejected by the BBC because the BBC/OU Productions Department is as aware as any other of what is and is not acceptable. It does demonstrate though that the BBC has the last word on what should be shown, even in the unique Open University relationship, and control is determined by the BBC's interpretation of what is acceptable in general broadcasting terms, rather than by academic considerations.

Whatever one might think of the procedure in this case, there can be no argument about a public broadcasting organisation's *right* to act in this way. It is obliged by law or its charter and by its need to survive in a not altogether friendly political environment to exercise control over programming. It cannot under the present rules of the game abdicate its responsibility in this respect. In the current social and political context, the question is not *whether* the BBC or the independent television companies should exercise such control, but *how*. Broadcasting organisations jealously preserve their control over even educational programming to avoid unnecessary conflict with government or the public. If there is to be trouble, broadcasters would prefer to choose their own ground. At the same time, their independence makes it difficult for other agencies to work co-operatively with them. Broadcasting organisations believe they have the right to make ultimate decisions on what and how topics will be presented. However, the organisation and presentation of knowledge is also one of the major concerns of educators. They too feel they have a right to determine what and how subject material should be taught. Under the present structural and legal arrangements for broadcasting in Britain, conflict and tension between the professional position of broadcasters and educators seems inevitable. Again, therefore, what is remarkable is not that situations such as the censorship of Open University drama programmes should arise but that situations like that have occurred so rarely over fourteen years.

Professionalism is also marked by the importance given to judgements made by other professional colleagues: 'Only a specialist can judge the work of another specialist' (Burns, 1969). Thus broadcasters see themselves as being in the best position to judge the value of educational broadcasts, as the following comment from a BBC/Open University producer indicates:

Success is mainly judged by the reaction of one's colleagues. They're the people who really count. You can tell by the atmosphere in the studio, and the amount of drunkenness in the bar afterwards; by the number of people who congratulate you or avoid you over the next few days . . . One tries to get the programmes viewed by colleagues quite soon after the production, and their reaction is terribly important. Course team reaction can be important too, though sometimes it's less helpful. So we tend to make programmes for our peers and superiors (from Gallagher, 1977d).

Comments from another BBC/Open University producer will illustrate how this confidence and expertise are built up within the profession:

An experienced producer, with twenty years behind him, can look at a programme and say 'It'll work' and sure enough he'll have his 10 million viewers, and his reviews in the paper next morning say that it works . . . you're bound to be standing on the shoulders of the giants and they are saying 'it's bad', 'it's good'. How do they know it's bad? They say 'It's bad, because you don't do it that way. Isn't it better to do it this way?' And suddenly, when you do it this way, it works (from Gallagher, 1977d).

The dangers of over-dependence on peer-group assessment in the field of educational broadcasting are obvious. Producers are physically separate from their audience, and unless real efforts are made to collect reliable research information or to get out and meet a wide cross-section of the target audience, peer-group assessment could be way out of line with the actual responses of the audience. Perhaps even more dangerous is building up an incorrect 'image' of the target audience when making programmes. The use of producers, superiors, peers and other members of the public – even the BBC lift operator – as a surrogate audience has been frequently noted (e.g. Hood, 1967; Burns, 1969; Elliott, 1972). The more the target audience differs from the circle of contacts and personal experience of the producer, the greater the risk that programmes will fail to meet audience needs. Particularly in developing countries, where producers tend to come from a more wealthy and educated elite, the psychological distance between producer and audience is very large.

Burns (1969) suggests that the great reliance by broadcasters on peer-group assessment is partly due to a fear of populism, a fear of having to pander to the lowest common denominator of public taste and intelligence; and partly due to the need to protect themselves from undue political pressure regarding programming, a form of collective defence against charges of bias or inaccuracy.

Another factor is that audience research has often not proved helpful. The figures giving total numbers viewing or even the more detailed appreciation ratings are too crude to inform producers about the appropriateness of the day-to-day decisions they had to make when making the programme. Research results often arrive well after the programme has been made; nothing can be done about it, and the producer anyway is fully involved in another programme. However, this still does not explain the resistance of many broadcasters to *formative* evaluation, research into audience responses *before* the programme is finalised. Even when one allows for the extra costs and the inconvenience to production scheduling, one is still left with the feeling that producers trust their own and their colleagues' instincts far more than any research evidence. They feel they don't *need* research; their expertise is sufficient because their training and their superiors have encouraged them to believe so.

Educational television and radio programmes thus are not produced in a vacuum, but are embedded in a rich professional broadcasting culture in which there are deeply ingrained ways of thinking about and doing things. There are good reasons for the development of a particular professional culture or ideology. The need for audience appeal, ideals of public service, independence and internal control, commitment and perfectionism, attitudes to the audience and above all ideas about how programmes should be judged, all spring from British public broadcasting organisations' need to survive in a tough technological, commercial and political world, while at the same time maintaining their integrity and professional self-respect. This broad ideology permeates all aspects of programming, including education.

THE LIMITS OF PROFESSIONALISM

There are many advantages in educational programmes being produced by professional broadcasting organisations. For instance, the ability to produce large quantities of programmes of high quality within an agreed budget to firm deadlines was of immense value in the early development of the Open University. In addition, BBC producers helped encourage the academics into ways of working that were absolutely necessary for producing the first Open University courses on time. Producers in the BBC are expected to plan well in advance and to meet tight and firm deadlines. When Open University course production began in 1969, few academics were similarly disciplined. The broadcast production schedule provided unavoidable milestones in course development, points at which discussion about the 'ideal' course unit had to give way to the production of actual material. Producers' demands for decisions about programme content forced the academics to move the production of the whole course along, and in no small way enabled the University to deliver its first courses on schedule to 25,000 students, only two years after the first staff were appointed (even if in the process one lady academic emptied her gin and tonic over a producer's head when he continued to bully her about deadlines in the bar).

The constant flow of programme material also depends on a highly professional approach. The BBC has produced over 3,000 television programmes and a similar amount of radio and audio material for the Open University since it was established. There are virtually no instances when a scheduled programme was not ready for transmission. For educational broadcasting to have a widespread educational effect, a substantial flow of material is necessary, and experience in a number of institutions in Britain and overseas indicates that not all agencies are able to meet this requirement.

There is likely to be initial audience resistance if educational broadcasts are perceived as having lower professional standards than general broadcasts but, more to the point, if producers and their specialist colleagues feel the programmes they are making do not meet professional standards, their morale will drop. The effects of this are apparent in a number of non-broadcast television units in educational institutions, where there is a lack of commitment and a lackadaisical attitude to production.

Part of the excitement in working for a public broadcasting organisation is that the potential for achieving programme ideas is enormous. Once an idea is accepted, the resources available for implementing that idea are immense, which means that many of the unique advantages of television for education can be exploited. Producers have been trained to identify and fully exploit the unique characteristics of television and radio, and can then ensure that these features are incorporated into educational series. Their experience also enables them to attract and hold large audiences, even for educational programmes. 'Botanic Man' had the highest weekly audience figures in the London region; even some Open University programmes, when broadcast at reasonably popular times, have had audiences in excess of 800,000, and at one time the Open University early morning transmissions were attracting bigger audiences than commercial television's new breakfast television programmes according to BARB figures. If professional broadcasting can attract large audiences to educational programming, then it is extremely valuable.

But professionalism in broadcasting is not enough and in some ways it can run counter to the needs of education. For the broadcaster, the focus of the judgement is in the *programme* – how good is it by professional standards? For the educator, the focus of attention is the *learner* – what effects has the programme had? For broadcasters, their main function is to produce programmes. For an educator, though, programmes are merely means to an end. Educators are more concerned with the receiver of the programme, the student or pupil, and the whole environment and context in which learning takes place. Usually, television and radio will be only one small part of a much broader learning context.

Secondly, an important aspect of educational effectiveness is the attempt to relate cause and effect – the learning experience to the learning outcome. Educational experience is not randomly chosen. The changes desired in the learner are not meant to be random either. Teachers deliberately choose certain educational experiences because they believe that these are more likely to bring about the desired effects. Educators want some say in the choice of desired effects and of how these effects will be achieved. Educators therefore want to determine *what* students learn, what topics will be dealt with, and *how* they learn (by rote-learning, problem-solving, direct experience, etc.). Most educators will claim that these are fundamental pedagogic issues – part of their ideology – which should not be surrendered to broadcasters. When educators judge a programme then, it will be in terms of the kind of learning experiences offered by the programme and its likely or actual effect on the learners.

Thirdly, another important aspect of educational effectiveness is the choice of alternatives. Could the same or better results be achieved by using alternative methods? The level of decision may vary, from a national government to a classroom teacher, but the issue is the same. For the government, should we use resources for broadcasting or textbooks? For teachers, is this the best way of using the pupils' time? Decisions on possible alternatives to the use of broadcasting have to be based on information which stems from a range of sources, and not just from the broadcasting organisations.

Some broadcasters would not dispute the right of independent educators to determine content and its treatment in educational programmes (so long as it does not infringe the constitutional requirements of broadcasting, such as being obscene, biased and so on). However, since the production of broadcasts is a highly complex and skilled process, combining technological, creative and artistic skills, they would argue I think that educational broadcasting requires an *equal* partnership between broadcasters and educators working together as a team. This in fact is the basis of an increasing number of educational broadcasting enterprises, as we have seen.

However, creating a partnership does not necessarily result in equal contributions to the production process. There is evidence to suggest that even in partnerships, control remains largely in the hands of the producer because of the technological complexity of the process. Furthermore, feedback on the actual effectiveness of programmes on the audience is still needed, even within a partnership.

Thus broadcasting organisations tend to consult too little and too late with other agencies because of the professional pressures required to produce quality programmes on time, resulting in over-concentration on the programme itself at the expense of the context in which it is likely to be used. Little is done to discover the specific learning needs of target audiences and the effects of programmes because producers rely mainly on peer-group judgement and advice when making programmes, and it is the more senior professional broadcasters who determine promotion and career development, and not the researchers. Certain popular formats are found in educational programmes because criteria applied to general programming are carried over to educational programmes and because some producers see educational programming as a stepping-stone to a career in more prestigious departments of broadcasting.

In summary, then, broadcasters have their own standards and criteria of success. Broadcasters do not use the same criteria as teachers and, in particular, their career development is governed by different standards from the educational world. Broadcasters' criteria for success are developed as part of a rich professional ideology, established in general broadcasting but also permeating the work of educational broadcasters. These professional standards have particular implications for the way content is treated, for attitudes towards the audience and for relationships with those outside the broadcasting organisations with whom they may have to work. Teachers also have their own professional ideology. In their everyday activities they place more emphasis on certain areas of 'content' or knowledge than others, are more concerned with individuals than with mass audiences, and in particular are concerned with the process of learning; whereas producers inevitably place more emphasis in their everyday work on the process of producing materials for learning, i.e. on the programme itself. Although the ultimate purpose of teachers and educational broadcasters may be the same, there are fundamental differences in their approach to achieving that purpose. In pointing to these differences, I do not wish to infer that the criteria broadcasters use for judging programmes are inferior to those used by teachers, but the differences do need to be recognised because they are deep-rooted and not easily reconciled.

9

The impact of new technology
on educational broadcasting

For the last twenty years, educational broadcasting in Britain has enjoyed a relatively stable and comfortable existence. That security and tranquillity is quite suddenly being shattered as a result of major technological and political developments. New information technology is going to change educational broadcasting in ways that were inconceivable only five years ago. What exactly these changes will be is not easy to predict, but fundamental changes there certainly will be.

RADIO AND CASSETTES

A great deal of publicity is being given to 'high technology' in education, particularly microcomputers and video-discs. There is a danger though that these developments are diverting attention away from the effects of equally powerful *low-cost* technology. Audio recording is not new in education, nor glamorous, but the development of cheap, easy-to-use audio-cassette equipment has already had a major impact on the use of educational broadcasting, both in schools and adult education.

For many years, schools have used tape-recorders to record school radio broadcasts. In Chapter 3, we saw that nearly all schools now have audio recording equipment. Recording is ubiquitous, and the ability to record has been much enhanced by the introduction of combined radio-cassette machines. Recording became even more significant in 1983 when the BBC switched secondary school radio broadcasts from afternoon to night-time transmission. This move, resulting from the wish of the BBC Radio 4 Controller to offer popular programmes to a wider audience on the VHF (FM) bandwidth, requires recordings to be made in schools automatically at night-time using time-switches. This change has been implemented despite initial opposition from the BBC's own Educational Broadcasting Council. In 1982 less than 25 per cent of secondary schools had electronic time-switches, and night-time transmission requires local education authorities to spend over £200,000 on extra equipment. It entails centralised planning of recordings in advance, and a pilot showed that there was a high failure rate in overnight recording due to teachers not correctly operating the automatic recording equipment (Educational Broadcasting Council, 1983). The BBC radio producers, the Educational Broadcasting Council and the local education authorities all thought that the move would reduce the use of radio in secondary schools. At the time of writing, it is not known whether these predictions will come true. However, in Norway and Sweden, an alternative system works very effectively. Most local education authorities have set up an audio-visual unit in one of their local teachers' centres. Radio, and increasingly television programmes, are recorded off-air by a full-time technician in each centre. Schools are sent a catalogue of programmes from which they request the programmes that they need. The service is relatively cheap to run and there is virtually no failure rate in recording, with all programmes available to all schools. Indeed, there is no real need to broadcast radio at all, since all programmes could be mailed on tape at very low cost to the local centres (Bates, 1979).

At the Open University, the impact of audio-cassettes on radio has been dramatic, with radio transmissions in 1983 dropping to less than thirteen hours a week, and over 500,000 cassettes being mailed to students. Furthermore, more than a third of the students who listen to the radio programmes that remain do so on recordings. In 1982 91 per cent of Open University students had audio-cassette players. Just under half of the radio recordings are made off-air by students themselves but the majority (58 per cent) are heard from cassette tapes ordered by students through an audio-cassette loan scheme which has been in operation since 1977. Students wanting to hear a radio programme on cassette may obtain up to four programmes at a time by sending a request card to the University's headquarters. In 1981 42,000 programme recordings were requested, and the loan scheme increased the average listening rate by 6 per cent to 44 per cent, at an average cost to the University of 28 pence per programme request (including staff and copying costs). It is clear that even when made originally for radio transmission, programmes available on cassette are more helpful for students than when broadcast. On a five-point scale (with 5 = very helpful), the mean helpfulness rating for broadcast radio in 1979 and 1980 was 3·42. When the same material was used on cassette, the helpfulness rating was 3·79 (Bates *et al.*, 1982a; Grundin, 1980).

However, there is a big difference, both in production style and educational effectiveness, between programmes made originally as radio programmes, and programmes created from the beginning for use specifically in a cassette format. Course designers can make full use of the stop–start and review facility, and the hidden nature of the next part of the tape to be played can also be exploited. Thus students can be talked through diagrams, tables or formulae in a text, can stop the tape and carry out activities, and return to the tape for correct answers or comment. Cassettes combined with text allow the simultaneous use of sound and vision, with freedom for the students to move from one medium to another in their own time, and with the ability to rewind and repeat as necessary. Thus students have full control over their use of the medium.

Cassettes can be used for a variety of educational purposes for which radio is less suitable or convenient: practice leading to mastery of a technique (such as solving equations); commenting on diagrams, charts, tables or text; talking students through a home experiment (leaving their hands and eyes free); backing up or commenting on the television programmes; recordings of conversations, interviews, language use and discussions, which can be replayed several times for the purpose of analysis; and many other uses (see the Appendix for a full list). Durbridge (1981a) has designed an audio-cassette package which demonstrates various ways in which audio-cassettes can be used in a home-learning situation.

Academic staff at the Open University like audio-cassettes because they can easily integrate them with the texts as they design their courses. They can take a recorder home and rough out ideas as they develop the text, whereas with a radio programme, with its continuous and uninterrupted flow, it is impossible to develop such close integration between sound and print. The final cassette tape still benefits from being 'produced' to ensure good sound quality and to avoid mistakes or ambiguity in the script, but academics generally feel that they have much more control over the cassette script than with radio.

The Open University students also like audio-cassettes. In a majority of courses where audio-cassettes have been used, students rank them as the most useful course component after the correspondence texts, and in a few courses, they have been ranked even higher than the texts. The features that appeal to students are their convenience, the control they have over them and their informality. Students frequently comment that listening to an audio-cassette is like having a personal tutorial in their own room with the course author, a quality that appears to be lacking in most radio programmes no matter how skilfully they are made (Durbridge, 1981b).

Lastly, cassette distribution is remarkably cheap in large quantities compared with radio transmission costs, which themselves are not expensive (the Open University was charged about £225 an hour in 1980). A C60 cassette (holding the equivalent of three 20-minute radio programmes) can be copied, packaged and sent to a student as part of the course materials for less than fifty pence (excluding academic design time and initial production costs). Even including copying and clerical costs, it is generally cheaper for the Open University to mail cassettes to students than to pay radio transmission costs for two transmissions of each programme, when there are less than 1,000 students on a course. Cassettes, though, become increasingly more expensive than radio as student numbers increase beyond 1,000.

The initial choice of media for the Open University was made in 1967. Since then, audio-cassettes have been the University's most successful media innovation. Audio-cassettes are more widely used and more effective than computer-assisted learning, video-cassettes, telephone teaching, or even television and radio. It is surprising then that few other institutions have exploited this cheap, convenient and effective teaching medium. The Open University's success has been due to course teams *not* using audio-cassettes as lectures (text is better for that), but instead tightly integrating them with the printed material.

VIDEO-CASSETTES

The pattern regarding audio-cassettes and radio is repeating itself with video-cassettes and television to some extent, although there are important differences. As with audio recorders, a video-cassette player in a school gives more flexibility to the teachers in their use of broadcast materials. However, there are far fewer video-cassette machines in schools, although the numbers are rapidly increasing. While the proportion of *primary* schools with video-cassette machines in Britain doubled from 1980 to 1981, this brought the number up to only 25 per cent, and few schools had more than one, which meant that they could not play back and record at the same time. Nearly every *secondary* school had a video recorder in 1981 (96 per cent), but the average number per school was only two, not really enough to give the ease of access and flexibility required in secondary schools. Hayter (1974) concluded that an increase in video recording and playback equipment would do more than anything to increase the effectiveness of schools television. It is significant that the increase in equipment over the last five years has been paralleled by an increase in the overall use of television, particularly in secondary schools. Nevertheless, there is still not enough equipment yet in schools to justify the transfer of schools television to night-time transmission although, technically, it is easier to record television than radio off-air because of the in-built clock on most video-cassette machines.

The Inner London Education Authority used to distribute its own programmes, and those of the broadcasting organisations, via a cable system to all the schools in its area. Because of the high cost of renting the lines from the Post Office it closed down its cable service in 1979, since when it has distributed its programmes on video-cassettes. By 1981 over 75 per cent of the primary schools in the ILEA area had bought video-cassette machines, largely due to a deal worked out between ILEA and a commercial rental company which gave the schools large discount prices. ILEA schools pay a nominal rental for the hire of each cassette loaned from their television service.

Nothing is more volatile at the time of writing than the expansion of home ownership of video-cassette machines. At the end of 1983, nearly 30% of all households in Britain had video-cassette machines in their homes, and sales are roughly doubling each year. Furthermore, according to the BBC Audience Research Department figures video-cassette machines are just as likely to be found in lower income as in more wealthy households. The rate of growth of video-cassette access is greater in Britain than in any other country. By 1986 it is expected that half the homes in Britain will have a video-cassette machine (*Screen Digest*, 1983).

This rapid growth is due to several reasons. Machines can be rented for as little as £10 per month, and there are many High Street shops and back-street dealers from which video-cassette programmes, including feature films, can be hired at little cost. Because many of the broadcast programmes are still of high quality, it is also worth while recording these at home, especially since the range of choice at any one time is limited to four channels in the current absence of a widespread cable TV system.

In 1981 11 per cent of Open University students had access to video-cassette recorders in their homes and another 8 per cent (mainly teachers) had easy access to recorders elsewhere. By the end of 1982, 20 per cent of Open University students had access to machines in their home and another 22 per cent convenient access elsewhere (Grundin, 1983).

The advent of video-cassette technology has caused often bitter arguments within the Open University, although now its advantages are generally recognised by the academic staff. The Open University experimented as early as 1974 with a video-cassette replay service to students in its South region. Eventually, the University set up a modest loan scheme on a national basis in 1982. The University's reluctance was due to the fact that any video distribution system becomes an additional cost to broadcasting since although the *quality* of times has deteriorated, the *amount* of transmission, and hence its cost, has remained the same. Video distribution costs – like those for audio-cassettes – therefore have to be found from the University's academic budget, at the expense of alternative academic programmes, such as new courses or more research, and not from the part earmarked for the BBC.

The loan scheme in 1982 was limited to thirty-seven courses with low student numbers (less than 600) and courses without repeat transmission times. The scheme was designed to cope with a limit of 20,000 programme requests in the year. In 1983 the scheme was expanded to cover eighty-four courses, all with less than 850 students. Students obtain copies of programmes by sending in a request card to the University's headquarters. A small stock of each programme recorded in advance has been made and any demands over that basic stock are met by making extra copies. The cassettes are mailed directly to the students' homes. Students in 1982 and 1983 could either watch at home (on their own machines) or on machines placed in local study centres or colleges. Cassettes are returned by students after use, and stored for re-use. In this way, 20,000 cassette copies can be added each year to the stock, thereby increasing the number of student requests that can be met within a relatively stable budget from year to year. The full cost of the scheme, including the rental of over 240 machines in regional study centres, was £150,000 in 1982.

An evaluation of the first year's operation (Brown, 1983) showed that, in general, the scheme had been successful. Programmes with a single transmission and a cassette loan facility had higher viewing rates (by about 5 per cent) than comparable courses with two transmissions. The availability of programmes on video-cassette made it easier for students to integrate television with the rest of their studies and increased students' perception of the helpfulness of the programmes. There was also a high demand for cassettes from non-students, mainly from tutors for use in group sessions. However, few students used the machines located in study centres. The equipment appealed mainly to non-students since fifty-seven machines were stolen from study centres in the first year! Rental for study centre machines accounted for over half the cost of the scheme (£80,000), so, in response to yet another round of government cuts, there will probably be no national provision of replay machines in study centres in 1984. Regions will be left to make their own arrangements (if any) from their own budgets. It is expected though that demand for loan copies will increase as more students get their own machines.

Indeed, many more students make their own recordings than borrow through the video-cassette loan scheme. Home recording increased viewing on post-foundation courses by 8 per cent in 1983 (52 per cent on transmission, 60 per cent overall – Grundin, 1983).

The Open University faces a difficult situation over the next five to ten years, until most students have access to a video-recorder. It takes two years to plan an Open University course, then it runs for about eight years. Courses are now being planned which will be running in 1993. Some course teams are anxious to design video-programmes which will exploit the educational advantages of cassette facilities, such as the ability to stop, carry out an activity, rewind and review, or pause on a still-frame. It is the lack of student access to video-cassette machines rather than the costs of physical distribution which makes the University cautious about producing programmes which can only be used on a cassette machine. Calculating the costs of physical distribution of video-cassettes is complicated, and at the time of writing hypothetical, but it appears that it will actually be cheaper to mail video-cassettes to students than to pay for two transmissions when there are less than 500 students on a course, provided cassettes are returned and re-issued each year. This allows for costs of cassette copying, clerical staff, post and packing, and a 10 per cent loss or replacement annually. Four programme equivalents would be transferred to an E-120 cassette (two hours playing time) and mailed to students with their course material. Students would return the cassettes at the end of their course. Over an eight-year course life, the distribution cost would be as little as £1 per student per programme equivalent (provided the student paid the return postage). Consequently, the University has decided the following policy for all new courses from 1985:

(1) Programmes on courses with less than 300 students will have no transmissions but will be distributed on video-cassette to students' homes.
(2) Programmes on courses with between 300 and 1,000 students will have one television transmission and can also be borrowed on video-cassette through the loan scheme.
(3) Programmes on courses with more than 1,000 students will have two transmissions but will not be available through the loan scheme.
(4) Individual course teams may deviate from this policy if they can make a special case.

The aim of the policy is to encourage course teams to design programmes from the outset using either a broadcast *or* a video format but not confusing the two. It is also hoped that this will encourage a number of course teams to experiment with the design of video-cassettes, to build up experience about the best way to use the format. The policy at the same time limits the number of students who will *have* to use a video-cassette machine to about 6,000, possibly requiring about 3,000 students still without access to machines to get one (less than 5 per cent of the undergraduate population).

In the long term (i.e. by 1990), it is possible that only programmes on the foundation courses and two or three large second-level courses will be broadcast at convenient times. Programmes on courses with more than 300 students are likely to be made in a video format, but broadcast once during the night for automatic off-air recording, with a loan scheme back-up. On courses with less than 300 students, the cassettes will be mailed directly to students.

Why does the University believe that there is such a difference between broadcast and video formats? The first Open University course to be designed for use on video-cassettes was EM235, 'Developing Mathematical Thinking', presented for the first time in 1982. It was aimed at teachers and the programmes were planned to be viewed in groups at local teacher centres or schools already equipped with video-replay machines. In fact, about half the students watched in groups, with the rest watching at home on their own. The programmes were designed differently from broadcast programmes, although they were transmitted for off-air recording. Each twenty-five-minute programme consisted of a series of segments, each lasting from two to seven minutes, observing children carrying out mathematical operations. After each segment it was planned that the tape should be stopped and followed by group discussion of the segment. Suggested questions for discussion were contained both in the programme itself and in the accompanying broadcast notes.

An evaluation of this course (Durbridge, 1982) showed that students in groups used the programmes differently from students watching individually. Individual students used the replay facility more, while group students found that the discussion after each segment provided sufficient recall. Individual students were less confident about their interpretation of the material than group students and tended to concentrate on details rather than on more general points. Students in the group situation were sometimes anxious about using the equipment, not always being familiar with it, or were more self-conscious about stopping, starting or replaying the segments when others were present.

This course is perhaps unusual, being designed for group work, and great care must be taken in generalising to video programmes designed for individual use. It does, however, demonstrate that there are different design features of video programmes if the potential of the medium is to be exploited, and their structure and format will differ from broadcast programmes, just as audio-cassettes that exploit their medium differ from radio programmes. This principle has by no means permeated to all producers. Many programmes made by ILEA since 1979 still look like broadcast programmes, with a continuous, uninterrupted format, nor does the Open University's own drug therapy course, made for general practitioners, really exploit the cassette medium. Cassettes were used mainly because they would not be seen by the general public and consisted of a series of interviews between doctors and patients, but with no explicit instruction to stop or interrupt the tape.

While video-cassette programmes require different production formats from broadcasts, the design features of *audio*-cassettes will not always be appropriate for *video* production. The production requirements of a video programme are much more demanding technically and in terms of manpower. This means that recording of material, and its editing, is separate from the preparation of the texts to which it relates, and makes it more difficult at the design stage to develop the very close integration between text and programme that is possible with audio-cassettes, although careful advance planning and editing of both programme and text can go some way towards this. Nor can students so easily integrate video programme and text simultaneously, because they cannot watch video and read the text at the same time. Taking notes during a video sequence is much more difficult than during an audio sequence and tends to lead to concentration on detail rather than on principles or general points. In practice, this means that video sequences will tend to run for longer without interruption, with interrogation of the material taking place *between* segments, with some replay to assist. Particularly where students are having to share equipment – either a machine at a study centre, with other students waiting to use it, or at home, with the television set wanted by the rest of the family – it will be more difficult for students to spend a great deal of time working repeatedly through the cassette. This is less of a problem with audio-cassettes. It is clear that in the next few years there will be scope for a great deal of experiment and innovation to identify suitable video-cassette formats for education.

The most important aspect of both audio- and video-cassettes is the control over the medium that they offer the learner compared with broadcasts. It is worth looking more carefully at this comparison since it highlights some of the unique characteristics of television, as well as certain weaknesses of broadcasting as an instructional medium. Table 16 lists the control characteristics of *broadcast* television. A comparison with Table 17, which lists the control characteristics of recorded materials, brings to the fore some of the differences between broadcasts and cassettes.

In comparing these two tables, it would be an advantage to have an audio-cassette so that you could look at the framework while I comment upon it! It will be seen, though, that it is difficult for a learner to integrate or relate broadcasts to other learning materials because of the need to catch the broadcast at a set time and the impossibility of stopping or interrupting a programme at a specific point. If ideas or thoughts are stimulated during a broadcast, learners run the risk of either losing the thread of the programme or being unable to follow through their own ideas. Some producers at the Open University have argued that one of the values of a broadcast is its ability to teach learners to think 'on the run', and

TABLE 16

CONTROL CHARACTERISTICS OF BROADCASTS

Broadcast characteristics	*Learner implications*
Fixed schedules	Fixed time to view
Scarcity of time (hence only one or two transmissions)	Limited response to material
Ephemeral	Non-repeatable; non-retrievable (except by memory)
Continuous	Thinking 'on-the-run'
Holistic (i.e. a single unit)	Reflection, analysis, restructuring, relating to other materials, all difficult
Aimed at 'average' target viewer	No room for individual differences in pace
'Rich' in meaning	Interpretable in different ways and at different levels – but only a limited range of interpretation permissible in time available for any *one* student

TABLE 17

CONTROL CHARACTERISTICS OF RECORDED MATERIAL (CASSETTES)

Recorder characteristics	Learner implications
Available when required	Convenient
Rewind/fast forward facility	Repetition; mastery learning; search
Stop/start facility	Integration with other media; activities integrated with cassettes; more room for individual variation
Non-continuous/segmented	Reflection, analysis, restructuring easier

that this is an essential everyday skill. We have found little evidence that broadcasts do this, and some may well argue that education is more concerned with teaching students to think carefully, rather than quickly.

With either a broadcast programme or a cassette, each individual member of the target audience is sent the same material. No matter how specialised the target audience, each individual will vary in ability to learn from the programme. Programme makers have to make assumptions about the 'appropriate' level, but there will always be a majority of the audience who will not find the pace quite right in terms of their own learning needs. With recorded material, provided that the level of the material is not too wide off the mark, it is possible for learners over a range of abilities to repeat the material until they have mastery over it. Furthermore, with a recording, learners can stop to reflect on the material, analyse it or restructure it, as it best suits them.

Salomon (1979) has pointed out that television is particularly *rich* in the quantity and variety of information it conveys. It uses a wide variety of symbol systems – sounds, pictures, colour, movement. Television is also highly *ambiguous* in the way it conveys meaning. This results from the techniques used in production – camera angles and movement, editing procedures, manipulation of structure – and from the richness of the information television conveys. Because of its ambiguity, television material lends itself to a wide variety of interpretations from each individual viewer, many different interpretations being equally valid. This means that each viewer will abstract different meanings from the same programme. Television should therefore be valuable for developing creative or 'open-ended' thinking because it forces learners to impose their own construction of meaning from the programme material. If such a hypothesis is correct, it makes it all the more important that learners have the opportunity to explore television material more fully than is possible with a single, unbroken transmission.

Broadcasts thus appear to be much weaker instructionally than cassettes in terms of integration with other material, ease of recall, mastery learning, deep thinking and possibly creative thinking. By their very nature, broadcasts tend towards stimulating more superficial levels of response compared with cassettes or books.

I have left the most controversial, and potentially most challenging, implications of cassettes until last. Cassettes could free educators from the dominance that broadcasters have exerted over the design and distribution of educational audio-visual materials. Until recently, distributing audio-visual material widely through formats other than broadcasting has been unrealistic because of the high costs of distribution on alternative formats, such as film or open-reel video tape, and because of the lack of playback equipment in schools or homes. On the other hand, the distribution of broadcasts has been largely seen as a 'free' service from the user's point of view. The increasing accessibility of video-cassette machines and the relatively low costs of distributing video-cassettes, are changing that situation. With broadcasting, the broadcasting organisations set the priorities, select content, determine style and decide production and technical standards for what they broadcast. In practice, they only transmit material that they themselves have originated.

Video-cassettes can change all that. It is now realistic for other agencies – universities, colleges, local authorities, voluntary organisations, even schools – to commission, produce and distribute effective video material for the specialised audiences that broadcasters have been unable to serve adequately in the past. Costs will depend very much on what kind of programme is required and on whether full or marginal costs are charged. There is, however, a good deal of spare production capacity, particularly in the public education sector, so marginal costing is often realistic. Highly effective, professionally-made half-hour educational video-cassettes can be produced for between £8,000 and £20,000, depending on the nature of the material. Cheap programmes which nevertheless are very effective in certain contexts if carefully designed can cost as little as £2,000 to produce. This should be compared with a full production cost of around £35,000 or an average of £8,000 for a programme budget (i.e. excluding fixed staff costs and overheads) for a BBC/Open University television programme.

You get what you pay for, of course. BBC/Open University programmes often include overseas filming, expensive computer graphics or animation, glossy drama productions, or complex and originally designed physical models. However, for many educational purposes, such expensive facilities are just not necessary. It depends on what the teacher wants to do.

The implications of lower production costs and relatively low-cost non-broadcast distribution are far-reaching. Because video distribution costs are related to the number of cassettes to be distributed, video programmes for very small minority audiences become a real economic possibility, provided that there is a framework through which they can be marketed. Secondly, educators can make programmes in the style, pace and format which *they* believe to be important. There are obvious dangers that the full potential of television will not be developed by people who are not professional broadcasters. On the other hand, there are many able and trained production staff outside broadcasting organisations willing to work to a clear educational brief. Also, those who regularly deal with specialist groups are likely to be better judges of their needs than professional broadcasters. There will still probably be a shortage of educators with the talent to exploit the advantages of television on cassette, but the technology does open up the market to those who want to try.

Over the next few years, I foresee rapid expansion of an educational video production and distribution industry in parallel to broadcasting. This in itself is unlikely to lead to the end of educational broadcasting. Broadcasters still have two strong advantages: their programmes are available to schools and the general public at no extra direct cost; and they have a wealth of resources, experience and a powerful reputation behind them. Non-broadcast video is likely to serve rather different needs from those of broadcasters. Nevertheless, there will be areas of overlap, and where the broadcasters do not meet the needs of their target groups, they are likely to lose audiences to enterprising video producers. A number of agencies are now gearing themselves up for production and distribution of non-broadcast educational video. ILEA in particular has a large stock of cassette programmes available for hire by other local authorities, as does the recently established Educational Video Index.

It is unlikely that the commercial television companies will move into producing their own non-broadcast educational video material, but the BBC might, through BBC Enterprises. (Indeed, it has already issued a non-broadcast video-disc on reading.) More likely is that educational broadcasting will be moved to night-time transmission for off-air recording, or be abolished completely, to free the air-waves for extended morning television in order to compete with cable and satellite competition. If the broadcasting organisations do start extensively producing non-broadcast material for education, it will raise some interesting legal and financial issues. Will they reflect the true cost of making the programmes, or will they merely charge copying, marketing and distribution costs? The *true* cost (including production) is likely to be too high for schools. On the other hand, if the price of cassettes does not reflect the true cost, would broadcasting organisations be open to the charge of using licence-holders' money or profits from advertising to undercut independent, non-broadcast production companies?

Whatever happens, it will be interesting over the next few years to see whether there will be such an expansion of non-broadcast educational video as predicted, and if so, how the broadcasting organisations will respond to the challenge.

VIDEO-DISCS AND INTERACTIVE VIDEO

There are different manufacturers' formats for video-discs and a variety of models within each format but, nevertheless, the principle of video-disc technology is relatively simple to grasp. The more advanced systems using laser technology allow up to 54,000 single still-frames, with full colour, to be stored on one side of a disc. Each frame can be individually identified and accessed almost instantaneously. The rate at which these frames can be played can be varied across a wide range of speeds, from stepping through single frames, through slow motion, up to normal or even fast speeds. Two high-quality independent sound tracks capable of synchronisation with the pictures when played at normal motion speed (25 frames per second) are also available.

These features allow a combination of moving and still pictures to be played linked to stereo or two independent sound-tracks. The systems allow for slow-motion, frame-by-frame presentation, fast motion, fast or slow forward or reverse search, or still-frame presentation, with no picture jitter at all on still-frame, each feature under the direct control of the viewer. More significantly, full computer control over the video-disc player is possible, either using an 'in-board' computer (i.e. one built into the video-disc player) or an 'out-board' microcomputer linked to the video-disc player through an 'interface', i.e. a processor or computer programme that allows the microcomputer electronic assess to the video-disc player's controls. With the right interface, it is possible to link up low-cost domestic video-disc players with low-cost micro-computers, and to combine graphics or keyboard symbols from the computer with sound and pictures from the video-disc, on the same television set, with pictures from both sources either overlaid, or presented in sequence.

Because the laser-based systems use light to read the disc, there is no mechanical contact. Therefore disc life and quality are not likely to be affected by constant use. Picture and sound quality, even on the cheaper players, is better than on video-cassette machines, although as yet commercial video-disc machines cannot record, only play back. The low-cost and simpler domestic models retail at around £400, with the more advanced commercial machines costing £1,200.

Video-discs certainly provide more sophisticated and better quality video and audio facilities than video-cassettes, but it would be a mistake to think of video-disc systems as merely a more advanced form of video-cassettes in terms of educational functions. We shall see that video-disc technology is a distinct teaching medium in its own right, with a unique potential for education, and its own unique requirements for design and production.

Because access, control of speed and search facilities are more refined on video-disc machines, they allow learners even greater control over video materials. Furthermore, by linking video-discs to microcomputers, learners can *interact* with the video-disc and the computer. This means that the computer can provide feedback to learners on what they have learned from the disc and can guide learners through appropriate 'routes', so that the learning experience is more individualised and suited to each learner's needs.

Video-*cassettes* can also be linked to computers in this way, but less efficiently than video-discs. Video-cassettes do not have individual frames like video-discs, so on all but the highest-cost machines, it is difficult to get completely still pictures. While it is possible to lay electronic pulses as markers along a video-cassette tape, thus enabling each point on the tape to be identified and accessed, this cannot be done so accurately and cleanly as with a video-disc. It also takes time for video-cassettes to wind backwards and forwards to the point to be accessed, whereas video-disc access is virtually instantaneous. Nevertheless, a microcomputer linked to a video-cassette machine can do many of the things that a video-disc can do, if less elegantly (see, for instance, Laurillard, 1982).

At the time of writing, very few educational video-discs have been made, so the educational potential of interactive video is still to be explored. The reason for the interest is that interactive video combines two well-established learning media, video and computer-assisted learning, in the hope that it will bring together the advantages and overcome the deficiences of both.

So far, three rather different ways of using video-discs in education seem to be emerging. The first is to use video-discs to provide a superior form of control and access. Thus a 'normal' television programme can be made available on disc format, with perhaps a second sound-track added. The learner can then use the still-frame, slow motion and fast search facilities as required. A refinement would be the provision of an index at the start of the disc so that the learner can go immediately to the section of most interest. Such discs can be useful for showing model procedures, such as the correct positions or movements for gymnasts or golfers and the correct procedure for stripping down a car engine, or for showing animals operating in their natural habitat. The BBC has produced a video-disc of this kind on British garden birds, with linked bird song on one track, and a commentary by David Attenborough on the other. No computer control is needed for this kind of programme but it is possible for those who purchase such a disc to add their own computer control relatively easily. In this way, tests, feedback and suitable routing through the disc dependent on test responses, can all be added through a linked computer.

Alternatively, video-disc and computer control can be designed together as the video-disc is being planned. The resulting package can be extremely complex, both to design and to work through as a student. Student responses via the computer need not be limited to selecting from an array of multiple-choice answers, but can involve feeding in data, or more complex problem solving. Very sophisticated programmes are possible in this form. For instance, a video-disc made at the University of Nebraska provided training on instrument reading for flying light aircraft. After a short period of instruction, the learner is given a set of instrument readings, then has to make decisions about operation of the plane's controls in order to bring the plane in to land. Dependent on the action chosen, the disc shows the position of the plane relative to the earth. This is done by the computer processing the student's answer and selecting the appropriate part of the disc for such an action. Learners can in this way be provided with very realistic simulation exercises with the consequences of their decisions becoming painfully clear! The computer programme that accompanies such a disc can either be physically separate, on cassette or on a computer disc, or it could be contained on the video-disc itself and 'dumped' from there into the computer when played. Computer programmes stored on video-discs, though, can be used only on the type of computer for which the programme was designed. The first commercial interactive educational video-disc, on teaching physics, was made at the University of Nebraska and marketed in 1982 by John Wiley.

There is a third way of using video-discs which is just beginning to be explored in an educational context. Video-discs can provide an efficient and substantial data-base, with information stored in a variety of ways: as computer data, still-colour pictures, moving pictures, or text. Video-discs could therefore be used as a resource base, which the learner searches or uses for a particular purpose. For instance, in training historians, or archaeologists, a whole set of materials could be archived on disc – pictures of archaeological sites and artefacts, historical documents, short, dramatised extracts from historical events, archive film and so on. Students could be asked to work through this material, drawing conclusions and testing hypotheses, with students to some extent imposing their own structure on the organisation of the data. A teacher could use the video-disc material to show a sequence of pictures as desired to students. The first such 'archival' video-disc commercially marketed featured the satellite photographs of Jupiter and Saturn.

These are merely glimpses of the potential for education of video-discs. But what are their implications for educational broadcasting? Although the cost of making the master for discs from the final edited tape is not expensive (around £2,000) given the cost of production, video-disc production seems to require broadcast-quality technical standards and sophisticated editing techniques which, unlike video-cassette production, are likely to be found mainly in production centres concerned with broadcasting. Secondly, to exploit the advantages of video-disc, programme production costs are likely to be towards the more expensive end of the scale. Broadcasting organisations thus are well placed to exploit video-disc technology, at least technically.

The design requirements of interactive video-discs and their implications for broadcasting organisations, though, are critical. Where programmes are to be designed from the outset to be used in an integrated way with computer control, difficulties are likely to arise. The structure of the video-disc, the choice of responses required from learners, the extent to which learners will be free to choose their own paths through the material, what paths are permissible or desirable, the number of difficulty levels to be built into the disc, the balance between computer and video graphics, and the design of the computer programme, all have major educational implications and go far beyond the normal brief of an educational television producer. It would be a fundamental mistake to consider that this type of production is merely a mild extension of the normal television production process, with the computer programming contracted out as an afterthought almost. This kind of disc requires a team approach, involving teacher, television producer, computer programmer and instructional designer/evaluator, working as equals from conception to final credits. This inevitably slows up the production process, limits the producer's freedom and increases the cost of production. It will be interesting to see whether broadcasters will be willing to enter into this more complex form of video-disc design and, if so, under what conditions; or whether they will prefer to stick to the safer form of video-disc design, where the disc can stand alone without being tied to pre-determined computer control (see Fuller, 1983; 1984, for more details of designing video-discs for educational use).

How realistic is it to expect video-discs or interactive video to become widespread in education? Video-discs have only just come on the market and their commercial viability as a consumer product has yet to be proved. There are at the time of writing few commercial discs available for sale in Britain and it is not yet possible to record off-air on to disc. Video-*cassettes* are in the process of becoming well-established, at least in Britain, as a consumer product in direct competition with discs. It may be many years before home ownership of video-discs becomes widespread. However, a microcomputer can easily be linked to a video-cassette, in this way replicating many of the functions of video-discs. Furthermore, institutional use of video-discs is a more realistic possibility. The Open Universtiy has already produced a video-disc for teaching students at summer school. Particularly for industrial training purposes, where very high-cost technology is being used, such as in nuclear power stations, air-traffic control, or oil-fields, the relatively high cost of interactive video-disc production is irrelevant when set against the phenomenally high cost or disastrous consequences of mistakes made in real circumstances.

The use of video-discs in schools is less certain. The cost of a video-disc machine is not out of the question, but given the slow growth of video-*cassette* machines with far greater amounts of suitable programme material, I do not see schools rushing to get disc technology. Even more of a problem will be the cost of discs if they have to cover their full production costs. It is difficult to imagine a well-designed interactive video-disc costing less than £25,000 to produce. To retail at £10 a disc, at least 3,000 discs would need to be sold to recoup costs, and this is a high target for the school market given that there are less than 6,000 secondary schools in Britain. It is likely therefore that video-discs will have a more specialised and restricted use than video-cassettes, at least over the next ten years, but where they are used and well designed they could prove to be extremely valuable.

While the combination of video and computer-assisted learning may bring together the advantages of both, it is as well to remember what Bernard Shaw once said to a lady suggesting an experiment in genetic engineering: 'But what if it has *my* looks and *your* brains?' After all, there is only one medium more expensive in education than television – and that is computer-assisted learning. Without careful design and choice of appropriate situations for its use, an interactive video-disc could easily turn out to be a horribly ugly and expensive baby.

CABLE AND SATELLITE

Cable and satellite developments are also likely to have some impact on educational broadcasting, although less immediately than video-cassettes or even video-discs. Should anyone be reading this book in 1988, or beyond, they will no doubt obtain some perverse satisfaction in seeing how wrong my predictions have turned out to be, but, for reasons which I shall explain, I suspect that there will be no significant expansion of cable for educational purposes much before 1990, although no doubt there will be a number of significant experiments. Similarly, the first UK direct broadcast satellite (DBS) will not be launched until 1986, and while there will be four DBS television channels available from around that time, none will offer educational services.

Cable and satellite could have major implications for education, but given the slowness with which they are likely to develop in the United Kingdom I shall limit myself to a very brief outline of their potential and limitations and the likely consequences for educational broadcasting.

There are four basic characteristics of cable television that are significant for education: the ability to provide a large number of channels – from thirty to a hundred, dependent on the technology – thereby theoretically increasing choice of service; the possibility of two-way communications through the cable system; the possibility of local programming; and the ability to 'filter' or 'select' viewers electronically (i.e. pay-per-view, or certain programmes available only to those who have paid a subscription). Satellite television can provide national coverage but, due to international regulations, Britain is limited to only five channels (putting us in the same category as Monaco, Luxembourg and the Republic of Ireland).

A study of the implications of cable developments for the Open University (Bacsich *et al.*, 1983) suggested the following *potential* advantages of cable for education: better transmission times, more time available for educational television; channels dedicated solely to educational use; access to more potential students; more specifically targeted programming; increased interaction and student participation; improved facilities for local programming by local institutions; more choice of educational programming; easier access to television for teachers; more scope for experiment; multiple sound-tracks or radio channels.

These are all possible, but whether they are likely depends very much on political and financial decisions yet to be finalised. At the time of writing, though, it seems most unlikely that these benefits will be realised in Britain, and, in fact, cable developments are more likely to have negative educational effects. For instance, even the most optimistic forecasts predict that less than 50 per cent of the United Kingdom population will be on the cable by the end of the century. Given the current unbridled commercial basis on which cable is to expand, the first and most profitable areas to be cabled up will be the outer suburban areas and commercial centres of large cities. Rural communities and the poorer inner city areas are less likely to be cabled up quickly, yet this is where the educational need and lack of provision is the greatest.

Currently it seems that there will be no statutory obligation for British cable operators to carry educational or community programmes, unlike practically every other major developed country with cable systems. Nor are there plans yet to ensure the establishment of a nationally linked cable network. Current proposals are based on the establishment of independent local systems. This does not guarantee local programming, though. At least one commentator, John Howkins, of the International Institute of Communications, predicts that London-based communications companies will make up 'packages' of programming which will then be sold to local stations. The lack of a national network is a severe limitation for the Open University, but if there is spare capacity for local programming this would provide opportunities for other educational institutions to negotiate deals with stations in their own area.

The key question, though, is who will pay for the educational services on cable, and how? Some stations, just to earn 'brownie points', may allow local colleges to use spare studio capacity and an otherwise unused channel to provide low-cost programming free of charge. More likely, companies such as Rediffusion Ltd will put together an educational package of programmes, using whatever existing material it can obtain at nil or low cost from current educational providers, such as those universities, colleges and local education authorities that have their own production facilities. Some courses may be mounted on a 'pay-per-view' basis, or made available only to students who enrol. Enrolled students could be given an electronic code or key which would enable them to access the relevant programmes.

It is difficult, though, to see coherent educational offerings of any quality being offered in these ways. Educational broadcasts and Open University programmes are strongly protected by copyright, and it is unlikely that such material will be released free of charge for use by cable operators. The real issue is who is going to pay for the costs of creating original educational material for use on cable. It is unlikely that students will be able to pay the sort of charges that would be necessary to recoup 'true' production costs. At the time of writing there is no lobby for education among the political debates on cable, and the educational and voluntary agencies seem to be too diverse and unco-ordinated to sort out any agreed policy.

One of the major attractions of cable for education frequently claimed by politicians is its potential for two-way communication, allowing the viewer to interact, respond or participate in the viewing event. This is the sort of claim that needs to be taken with a good pinch of salt. There are major financial and technical obstacles that limit the likelihood of cable being a truly two-way communication system for some time. There are two types of cable that can be laid. *Co-axial* cable (similar to the current TV aerial cable found in most homes) is the basis of virtually all current systems but, for practical purposes, co-axial systems tend to be limited to a maximum of thirty to forty channels in one direction. Co-axial cable is not really suitable as a two-way communication system. *Fibre-optic* cable has much greater capacity and is a realistic proposition for two-way communication. However, it is still a largely untried technology in a fully operational sense and it will probably be more expensive than co-axial cable to lay.

Secondly, two-way communication will depend crucially on the configuration or design of the cable system. Co-axial cable uses a 'trunk and branch' system, i.e. a central 'trunk' cable running down a street with 'branches' off to each house. The street cable itself is probably a branch of a more central trunk running through the town. Even with fibre-optic cable laid in a trunk and branch configuration, 'backward' communication from the home could only follow the same route as the downward signal, i.e. back to the 'head-end', the local station. It would not be possible to communi-cate across branches, i.e. with neighbours in the street, or the local college on the other side of town, unless this communication was relayed from the head-end. If all communications have to go through the head-end, this obviously limits the amount of com-munications that can be handled, even with a hundred channels.

The alternative, only possible with fibre-optic cable, is a configuration similar to that of the public service telephone system. This has been named a 'star' system since each house would be linked directly to a central (automatic) switchboard, which in turn would also be linked up with other switchboards. This would allow any one point to communicate directly with any of the others, as with the current telephone system but using much wider bandwidths, including even television transmission 'outwards' as well as inwards. Fibre-optic cable would be essential for such a system. Also, a national grid or satellite-linked system would also be necessary for cross-connections between different cable systems (another difficulty for 'trunk and branch' and co-axial systems). Unfortunately, because of the amount of switching gear required, a 'star' system would be much more expensive to introduce.

For these reasons, interaction is most likely to be limited to *user typing*, i.e. keying-in instructions along the lines of PRESTEL responses, enabling home banking and possibly some computer-assisted learning responses, through a local viewdata system. In other words, it would give little more than is currently available through PRESTEL. Until a national fibre-optic 'star' system is established, it will still probably be more practical to use the public telephone network for voice interaction or even telewriting.

These technical considerations indicate quite clearly the kind of framework required for education from any national policy for cable development: statutory obligation on cable operators to carry at least one educational and community channel; a policy which will encourage cable operators to provide services in areas of greatest educational need – i.e. inner city and rural areas – as well as in commercially attractive areas; cable systems based on fibre-optics technology; 'star' cable configurations; and a national grid or a satellite-linked system for cable allowing inter-communication between all cable users.

Unfortunately, at the time of writing, most of these developments are unlikely for some time given the 'free market' policy of the present Conservative government. The use of cable for educational purposes, therefore, is likely to develop very slowly and to be very piecemeal, as indeed will cable be generally. The original reason for setting up cable systems in North America was to provide decent signals for the many areas not covered by adequate off-air transmission, but in Britain most homes can receive high quality, off-air broadcast transmissions. Secondly, there is no guarantee that an increase in channels will lead to an increase in the range or quality of programmes available. Anyone who has switched from channel to channel on cable systems in America cannot fail to have noticed the similarity of programming on each channel. It is significant that the BBC plans to use one of the new statellite channels merely for repeating old BBC programmes. Leaps in technology are not necessarily accompanied by leaps in imagination. The growth of video-cassette machine ownership, the ease of hiring video-cassettes for a small fee from the local corner shop and the opportunity to record high-quality broadcast programmes, are all real threats to the competitiveness of cable television. Most of all, laying the cables, connecting up homes, providing extra programming and linking cable systems together, will be extremely expensive and financially risky. There is likely to be a great deal of caution exercised, therefore, before there is a major expansion of cable services.

For all these reasons, I am very sceptical of cable being of any significant value for education in the 1980s and early 1990s, despite its potential. The main danger of cable developments is that, despite their slow growth, they will put yet more pressure on channel controllers in the broadcasting organisations to remove educational programmes from transmission. *Only* the national broadcasting organisations are in a position during the 1980s and 90s to provide a *national* educational television service. Cable would be a very poor alternative.

TELETEXT AND VIEWDATA

Teletext systems such as CEEFAX (BBC) and ORACLE (ITV) which broadcast 'frames' or 'pages' of information that can be called up at any time by the viewer, have at the moment only two real educational advantages: they are useful for up-dating information, such as news headlines and weather forecasts; and the service is free (once a suitable television receiver is acquired). Their educational limitations though are considerable. The number of pages that can be accessed is limited, in 1983 to around eight hundred, and since each teletext page holds far less information than a printed page, the total amount of information that can be accessed is very small indeed. Because of the inherent nature of the technology, teletext information tends to be geared to maximum audiences with common interests (e.g. the weather), and to deal primarily with information that can be easily condensed and up-dated (e.g. sports news). There is no possibility of two-way communication, and a viewer can have irritating time delays while waiting for pages called up. Teletext services have been used, however, for transmitting computer programmes ('telesoftware') to schools, which are received on a standard aerial and 'dumped' into a BBC (Acorn) microcomputer, again offering a free, if limited, distribution service.

Viewdata systems based on the telephone, such as PRESTEL in Britain, ANTIOPE in France and TELIDON in Canada, have a much wider range of features which may prove more useful in education, but not to the extent of having much impact on broadcasting. Viewdata systems also have major educational limitations. In theory, the number of pages that can be accessed is limited only by the size of the computers that store the pages. However, like teletext systems, the technology limits the amount of information that can be displayed per page. Also, because of the cost of creating and accessing viewdata pages, information again tends to be presented in a condensed and simplified form. Viewdata systems, also like teletext, have no sound. The lack of synchronised sound and pictures is a major disadvantage, as too is the lack of movement, compared with broadcasting. Lastly, the way viewdata systems structure information is still unsatisfactory: searching through the branching structure for the information one needs is a tedious business – especially if it was never there in the first place. This technology structures knowledge in a way that is unhelpful for learning. Attempts to base systems on keywords may improve access and structuring, but it is hard to see how the system can ever have the flexibility and richness of an educational television programme.

There have been some experiments, particularly in Canada, to create teaching materials for use on viewdata systems. TV Ontario located Telidon terminals in 120 primary schools throughout the province, and asked teachers to create their own programmes by sending in specifications to TV Ontario where skilled Telidon advisers created the frames and stored them on the mainframe computer. Teachers could then call up on the telephone not only their own programmes but also all the other programmes so created. However, despite the superior picture quality compared with Prestel, the quality of the programmes that I saw was poor, being limited to testing recognition skills ('Identify the flags', etc.). There was of course no sound, and very primitive animation. Pupils appeared restless and easily distracted without the sound facility.

It may be too early yet to judge but it seems there are inherent problems with using systems such as teletext or viewdata extensively in education for teaching purposes, although they may have their use as a data-base or for general informational purposes. If they do have their values, they are more likely to complement than compete with educational broadcasts.

MICROCOMPUTERS AND MICROCOMPUTER DEVELOPMENTS

It is the microcomputer which is likely to have the greatest long-term impact on educational broadcasting, as on many other aspects of our lives. Microcomputers will enable individual teachers to create their own audio-visual teaching materials quickly, easily and economically, and will enable the individual learner to interact in a wide variety of ways with such audio-visual materials, which can be tailor-made to the individual's needs. This material is likely to be highly motivating both for the teacher and the learner. To do this, teachers will not need to be highly skilled in using computers, and the learner need not have any programming expertise to study in this way. Furthermore, this is not a Utopian dream: such a situation could be widespread in British education by the early 1990s. The ability to create one's own audio-visual materials on microcomputers will not eliminate altogether the need for educational broadcasting but it will require educational broadcasting to be used more precisely.

What evidence do I have for such a bold claim? First, it is important to distinguish between two educational roles for microcomputers. The first is to use them to develop knowledge and skills in computers and computing, since these will be essential requirements for children and many adults in the coming years. But the microcomputer has also the potential to be a very powerful teaching aid in its own right.

Currently, this potential has not been realised, because of technical limitations. Designing computer-assisted learning (CAL) programmes is at the moment extremely time-consuming, requires a good deal of computer power, and needs a sensitive combination of high-level computing and teaching skills. Effective CAL programmes tend to be expensive to produce in terms of the actual use made of them. The learner is generally limited to responses via the keyboard, and the range of responses in this mode is also limiting. Another very real limitation of CAL is the lack of adequate sound, particularly the teacher's voice. This means that CAL programmes have a heavy reliance on textual and simple graphical presentation, although animation is also available at a price. Creating good quality, effective graphics and animation requires a lot of programming time and can be difficult to achieve on the lower-priced microcomputers. The major limitation, however, at present is the need for teachers to become skilled programmers. Many have neither the time nor the inclination to do this, and in terms of what CAL can currently offer on microcomputers, they are probably correct in assuming that the results are not worth the effort. Those who have proved skilful in this area have tended to produce packages which are used by other teachers – resulting in a degree of centralisation of teaching which in practice limits the use of such materials ('It's good, but not quite what I want').

But all that is changing. By the late 1980s 'peripherals' (accessories) to standard microcomputers, and special packages of programming which can be loaded into a microcomputer so that it can be operated easily in a certain way, will allow teachers to create their own sophisticated audio-visual materials very simply and without needing computer programming skills. Similar developments will also allow audio-visual material to be sent down a telephone line and for learners at home to communicate back with a teacher and other learners, both with voice and visually.

It is possible to predict fairly accurately what a low-cost microcomputer-based audio-visual teaching system will look like, partly as a result of experience gained from using a prototype system called CYCLOPS at the Open University and in schools. CYCLOPS digitally converts simple colour-video graphics – handwriting, text, diagrams and very simple animation – into sound codes. These graphics can be very easily generated using a combination of a standard computer keyboard and an electronic light-pen, which writes on a standard television screen, or an electronic writing-pad which also displays graphics on the TV screen. Still images from a video-camera can be similarly coded. Because the video signals are converted into a sound code, they can be stored on audio-cassette or transmitted down standard telephone lines, then decoded back into a video signal. Using either standard stereo audio-cassettes or two telephone lines, full sound can be synchronised with the visuals (see Read, 1981, for technical details).

The crucial point is that audio-visual materials can be created very simply and quickly this way without any need for computer programming skills. The system has been successfully used in the Open University for three years for running distance audio-visual telephone tutorials. Students and tutors may be scattered across as many as seven different locations at any one time. Each person though is able to communicate with everyone else taking part, both visually and orally, using a standard teleconference bridge (see McConnell and Sharples, 1983, for a full account and evaluation of this project, funded by British Telecom). The same equipment has been used in schools. Three teachers with no previous experience of using computers created their own CYCLOPS materials for use by individual children in their classes using the audio-cassette facility.

It proved possible in this way to develop very quickly highly motivating and interactive audio-visual materials (see Bates *et al.*, 1982b, for an account of this project, funded by the Microelectronics in Education Programme). CYCLOPS is basically a 'peripheral' system for a standard microcomputer since its 'core' can be made available as a cartridge or a ROM to be added to a standard microcomputer.

While it may not be the CYCLOPS system that eventually gets used, by the late 1980s microcomputer-based audio-visual teaching systems will be common in schools. A probable configuration will consist of a standard television receiver, a stereo-cassette player and microphone, a light-pen or an electronic writing-pad, and a standard microcomputer. This will incorporate a CYCLOPS-type facility, either built into the microcomputer itself, or as an add-on accessory, and a connection to the public telephone system. Most of this equipment is already available in schools in Britain at the time of writing. For instance, in 1983, 98 per cent of British secondary schools were equipped with a microcomputer (Educational Broadcasting Council, 1982). The additional components – the light-pen and the CYCLOPS-type cartridge – will cost approximately £50 each, and in the future, facilities similar to CYCLOPS are likely to be built into a microcomputer as a standard feature. Microcomputers will also increase in power and reduce in price over the next few years.

With such a facility, teachers can create their own teaching materials. They can draw on the screen and add text via the keyboard. They can also use standard graphics facilities in the cartridge or the microcomputer itself, to create shapes such as triangles, squares and circles, and to 'fill-in' these shapes with different colours. They can also create certain forms of animation. The facility enables a teacher to build up pictures or frames which are then transferred to a standard audio-cassette. Each picture or frame can be coded and stored, enabling editing to be carried out simply and easily by the microcomputer. When all the pictures have been assembled, edited and correctly ordered, the teacher can add the sound-track using the microphone and the audio-cassette player. As well as the teacher's or the pupils' voices, music or special effects can be added. The computer controls the length of time each frame is displayed to enable sound-track and picture to be synchronised. The programme can be tested on one or two learners, then amended as necessary. Using the connection with the telephone system, programmes can be exchanged with other schools, ordered from a central bank or used for distance teaching. Teachers can learn how to use the system either by following a simple manual or by loading on a cassette containing a training programme. It is likely to take teachers two or three hours to learn how to use the system, after which time they will have no difficulty in creating their own materials.

Learners will load the audio-cassette and work through the programme very much in the same way they would work through an audio-cassette or video-cassette. In addition, though, they can use the light-pen or keyboard or microphone to give answers to questions on the tape, and their responses can be recorded (using a second tape-recorder) together with the original programme, for later inspection by the teacher if so desired. CAL features can also be added, with feedback given on keyboard responses, and the tape can be directed to appropriate sections according to the learner's responses.

The technology to do this is already here and will be introduced to schools and colleges in the mid 1980s. We will have to wait and see whether teachers will want to create their own materials in this way or whether they will prefer to use materials prepared more professionally by others, probably marketed by publishers. Such developments, however, have obvious implications for broadcasters since microcomputer programmes of this kind will have a number of advantages over video materials. They will be much cheaper and easier to produce and distribute than video-cassettes. They will be much more interactive and specific to the needs of individual teachers and learners, especially if created by teachers themselves. But there will also be disadvantages. It is likely that a majority of teachers will prefer high-quality, off-the-shelf material that is readily and easily available. The 'cottage-industry', teacher-generated computer materials cannot currently match the quality of professionally produced broadcasts, or even non-broadcast video-cassettes. Even with the advanced CYCLOPS-type facilities, computer-generated materials will still lack many of the features of video, no matter how professional the computer design. There will still be need for film or tape of overseas situations, for portraying human interactions, for presenting the world in a fully representational manner, for the more personal aspects of seeing a human face, for seeing things as they happen. Microcomputer-based programmes will not eliminate the need for video. They will, however, provide teachers with a convenient and cheaper alternative. Video programmes will therefore have to compete against other highly effective media for the limited time of teachers and learners. If video is to compete successfully, broadcasters and video producers will need to identify and exploit to the full the unique advantages of their medium.

THE KEY DEVELOPMENTS

The main developments likely to impact directly on educational broadcasting are cassettes (audio and video) and microcomputers. Both will develop independently of and in parallel with broadcasting, and are likely to reduce to some extent the use of educational broadcasts, particularly in schools. Cable and satellite may have a further negative effect, increasing pressure on broadcasting organisations either to transfer educational programmes to inconvenient or impossible times or, for financial reasons, to drop educational programmes altogether. Cable is unlikely though to offer an effective alternative for education. The main overall effect on broadcasters will be the need to identify and exploit the unique educational advantages of broadcasting, since a range of highly effective audio-visual alternatives are now becoming available to teachers and learners.

10

The future of educational broadcasting

I have tried to answer certain questions. What is the role of educational broadcasting? What can it do better than anything else? How effective is it? What is needed to make it effective? Will there be a need for educational broadcasting in the future? In this final chapter I will try to pull together the answers to these questions.

VARIETY

Broadcasting is a major form of educational publishing. It provides, in Britain at least, a massive amount of educational material which by and large increases the nation's stock of educational resources, since it is funded separately from the education budget. The length of this book is in part testimony to the extremely wide range of purposes, target groups and contexts for which broadcasting has been used, both in the formal and non-formal education sectors. Furthermore, television and radio are heavily utilised in British schools.

To some extent, though, the variety of educational broadcasting merely reflects the wide variety of educational needs in the public at large. For broadcasting to succeed, it must actually *meet* those needs, not only by providing programmes but also by enabling real learning to take place. This requires learners' needs to be accurately identified in each of the many contexts in which educational broadcasting is used. It also requires choice of appropriate programme formats to meet those learning needs, which will vary from context to context; too often, programme formats have been chosen irrespective of learning needs.

SUCCESSES

Differences within a medium are far more important than differences between media. Thus a well-designed television programme is more likely to be effective than a poorly designed book, while a poorly designed television programme will be far less effective than a well-designed lecture. Given the talent and resources that have gone into educational broadcasting, it is not surprising that there are numerous examples of extremely effective uses of broadcasting in education, in all sectors. Many children from poorer homes have learned pre-reading skills before attending school from programmes specially designed for the purpose; teachers in schools in Britain use television and radio extensively, and there is evidence of television and radio helping in the development of language skills and pupils' understanding of other races; broadcasting has been used effectively for in-service teacher training (in many countries) and for recruiting to personal tuition large numbers of adults with reading difficulties; television has proved to be a unique and valuable resource for multi-media distance education, and has been used as a catalyst for the reform of whole national school curricula, resulting in major improvements in academic performance; broadcasters have initiated badly-needed educational developments which conventional educational agencies had hitherto ignored or neglected; most of all, broadcasting has brought education to many who otherwise would not have had it.

WEAKNESSES

However, on balance, broadcasting has tended to be a marginal educational activity. For it to be used successfully, very demanding conditions have to be met, and meeting these has often proved to be impossible. Within the formal education sector, more recording and playback equipment, improved training of teachers and major changes in the way lessons and curricula are designed, are all necessary if television and radio are to be used as effective learning resources rather than as a weak form of enrichment. Broadcasting's real potential for meeting special needs in schools has been largely unexploited because the broadcasters are not expert in these areas and have not used their advisers to the full. In developing countries, while the introduction of direct teaching by broadcasting has led to improved educational provision, it has had little impact on their wider political, economic and social problems, which can really be resolved only by radical political, economic and social reforms. While broadcasting has helped a little then, it is no substitute for more radical action.

In non-formal education the huge educational potential of *general* broadcasting is chained within the prison of copyright and royalty restrictions. Furthermore the shunting of educational broadcasts to minority channels and unsocial hours limits their effectiveness. This is a particular difficulty for basic adult education which needs access to its target audience through the more popular channels. Broadcasting has generally proved ineffective educationally in non-formal education unless combined with substantial non-broadcast support services. Although in recent years there has been an increase in truly co-operative projects between broadcasters and other agencies providing the support services, too often partnerships, where they have existed, have been unequal ones, with broadcasters setting the agenda and timing and the other agencies scrabbling in the wake.

In distance education, the role of broadcasting has never been central in terms of teaching, and in recent years difficulties with transmission arrangements, small student target groups, the ephemeral nature of broadcast material and technological developments in non-broadcast audio-visual media, have all combined to promote a shift away from broadcasting to other media, even in those few distance education institutions which use broadcasting extensively.

The basic problem is that broadcasting is a weak instructional medium. It is difficult for students to master skills or acquire deep understanding through broadcasting alone, and difficult for teachers to integrate broadcasting with other learning activities.

BROADCASTING AS A PROFESSION

In judging effectiveness one must ask: 'By whose criteria?' Broadcasting as a profession has its own standards and criteria for judging success, and these criteria have been developed as a result of organisational and institutional pressures unique to broadcasting. Professionalism in broadcasting allows the potential or richness of the medium to be fully exploited, but at a price. Producers have a different approach to teachers. Educators see viewers and listeners as students for whom a broadcast is only one, relatively minor event in a much broader learning context; for a producer, the programme is the centre of attention. This is not to argue that broadcasters' criteria and approaches are better or worse, more right or more wrong, than those of teachers. However, educational broadcasters, many of whom started out as teachers, are to some extent caught between these different professional ideologies, and one will therefore find a spectrum of approaches in any educational broadcasting department. On balance, though, I believe that the technological pressures of creating broadcast programmes, the full-time commitment of educational producers to programme making, and the organisational milieu in which they work, clearly identify them as broadcasters rather than teachers.

FUTURE TRENDS

There are several clear trends emerging in media development, each of which will have implications for educational broadcasting.

Educators have more audio-visual media to choose from. Broadcasting is therefore facing increasing competition from other sources for teachers' and learners' time. Both broadcasters and teachers then will need to identify and fully exploit the unique teaching strengths of broadcasting if it is to continue to be used. Broadcasting can no longer be considered a comprehensive teaching medium in its own right.

Media are converging. Technological developments are bringing together print (via word-processing), the telephone, the computer and video, into integrated systems that combine the strengths of each medium. Such developments have major implications for professional boundaries. Broadcasting skills will not necessarily carry over to the design of computer-assisted learning programmes, nor to overall instructional design. Indeed, computer programming and television production require very different approaches and ways of thinking, and tend to attract different kinds of people. Thus training and skills in one area may inhibit an individual's ability to work in another. Successful integrated teaching will require a genuine team approach, drawing on the separate skills of different professions and the expertise of the teacher. Currently, the existence of independent, professional broadcasting organisations, with their own career structure and methods of rewards separate from the educational system, is a major obstacle to a fully integrated team approach. Broadcasting is not a superior instructional medium to which others must pay obeisance. For this reason, I see independent non-broadcast, multi-media production companies who contract consultant staff willing to work together as equals, becoming increasingly more influential in education during the 1980s and early 90s. It will be a measure of their flexibility if broadcasting organisations are willing to enter into such arrangements as one amongst equals. If not, they will find they are losing audiences to such independent non-broadcast companies.

Because of the rapid expansion in the range of media available to educators, there is an urgent need for practical guidelines on media selection and use. This is an old chestnut in educational technology.

Many attempts have been made in the past by academics to develop theories of media selection, based primarily on pedagogic considerations. All have failed miserably to come up with a theory that can be applied in practice. The difficulty is in finding a practical set of guidelines which can at the same time take account of all the different contextual factors found in education. Also, most previous attempts have concentrated almost entirely on pedagogic factors. Although these are important, so too are factors such as cost, accessibility, convenience for both learners and teachers, and academic control. Further development of this issue is beyond the scope of this book; it is sufficient here to note that educators are now being forced to choose between a wide range of media, and this will require the unique characteristics of broadcasting to be clearly differentiated from those of other media if a rational choice is to be made.

Current developments in media allow for alternatives very different from the mass media model of education fashionable in the 1960s and 1970s, a model which led to such radical but different innovations as the Open University and the El Salvador ETV school reform. More diverse, smaller and less centralised models are now possible. This could mean a move away from large national systems of audio-visual production and distribution for education, to more diversity of provision and more local initiatives. There will be much greater opportunities for 'do-it-yourself' production of audio-visual materials by teachers, or for buying audio-visual materials from sources other than broadcasting organisations. New media allow local schools and colleges to develop their own on-campus, and, more significantly, off-campus multi-media courses at reasonable cost. With enrolments of full-time students steadily dropping in a number of countries, local, off-campus teaching using low-cost audio-visual media will become increasingly important. This development will affect not only the use of educational broadcasting but even more so large centralised distance teaching systems, such as the Open University.

The spread of technology, particularly to the home, is likely to increase educational differences within society. Not everyone will be able to afford to be connected to a cable system *and* to erect a dish aerial for satellite transmission *and* to buy or rent a video-cassette machine *and* a video-disc machine *and* a computer *and* a telephone, nor will everyone be able to afford the purchase of the software (cassettes, discs, programmes) that will carry the educational material. What we will see is a much greater variety of technological equipment in people's homes with potential educational uses. Those in most need of further education and training –

the unemployed and the less well educated, who tend to have lower incomes – are the least likely to benefit from home learning through the new media since they are likely to have a more limited range of home equipment. How does one get through to *these* people, to promote the opportunities for further education and training that are available outside the home? Here surely remains a vital role for broadcasting since, together with the postal service, broadcast television and radio will for many, many years be the only media that can reach into every home.

FUTURE ADVANTAGES OF BROADCASTING

Where do these developments leave broadcasting? I believe there are several major reasons why broadcasting should continue to play a major role in education.

Access

Broadcasting reaches the parts that other forms of education do not reach (to adapt a larger advertisement). In the United Kingdom and North America, 98 per cent of homes have television sets, and 97 per cent one radio set at least (the average UK household has 2·5 radio sets – one for every man, woman and child! In the USA the figure is nearer two per person). About 80 per cent of the United Kingdom population watch television at least some time during each day, and just over half (56 per cent) listen at least once a day to the radio. The average time each adult spends watching television in Britain is between two to three hours per day. In many developed countries, more than half the population will be watching television at the same time during some parts of an evening.

Access to television and radio in developing countries is less universal, particularly regarding television. According to Katz and Wedell (1977), there was less than one radio set for every ten people in fifty-four developing countries in 1976, despite a massive and continuing expansion of radio ownership over the previous twenty years in such countries. Nevertheless, there is now only a handful of countries without any form of broadcast television service (twelve in 1976). There is no country in the world without widespread geographical coverage by radio, and in all but the poorest countries, a high proportion of households have at least one radio receiver. Many bars and cafes in poor urban areas have television sets, and in Latin America and the Middle East, television coverage is widespread. Neither television nor radio demand literacy skills, and for most countries these media offer the most effective way of accessing the bulk of the population.

Recruitment to education

Broadcasting has the capacity to reach people who are uninterested in or disenchanted with conventional educational provision, even if local courses are available. There is a good deal of accidental or unplanned viewing and listening. At certain times – in particular early evening and weekend mornings in Britain – millions of people will be randomly accessing television; not switching on because they know a particular programme is on at that time, but just waiting to see what comes on. Broadcasting can therefore play the role of recruiting agent for education, either attracting and holding the audience through the intrinsic interest of the programmes themselves, or leading viewers to pursue the subject further, through purchasing accompanying books, contacting agencies, or enrolling in local classes or correspondence schools.

Convenience

For working adults, time is at a premium. Study has to be fitted into their leisure time, outside working hours. For many people then, it is attractive to be able to study in the comfort of their own homes, without the cost and inconvenience of travel to schools or colleges which may be miles away.

Motivation

Broadcasting clearly has the ability to make education interesting and enjoyable, when it is used well. It provides a break from the normal school routine. For adult learners, independent study, especially starting back to study for the first time, requires considerable motivation. Through the variety of techniques used to appeal to audiences, broadcasting can provide a real stimulus to learning.

Consciousness-raising

Broadcasting can help to raise general awareness of problems or situations about which the general public were previously ignorant or apathetic. Thus, as well as the primary target group for a set of programmes, there is often a secondary target audience: the general public, local or national politicians, leaders of industry, whose awareness of a problem may be raised by the programmes. It is claimed for instance by some broadcasters that the British television programme 'The Chips are Down' was mainly responsible for alerting the British government to the real significance of micro-chip technology. This may say more about the British government than about broadcasting if it is true, but certainly casual viewers can have their awareness raised by such programming.

Comparative cheapness

Broadcasting can be the cheapest way to get large quantities of audio-visual learning materials to large numbers of people scattered throughout the country. This is particularly important for schools. Even if schools have an abundant provision of video-recording and playback equipment, broadcasting and local recording is the cheapest way to distribute large quantities of audio-visual material. This applies also to computer-based audio-visual media which can be broadcast within a radio bandwidth ('telesoftware').

Improving the general cultural milieu

Educational broadcasting can be multi-purpose, not only in raising awareness but also in presenting an alternative source of pro-gramming to that available on the general service, an alternative sometimes desperately needed. For those who otherwise would be left with a choice between Nationwide, Crossroads and a rock music programme, an Open University programme on the economics of oil-pricing can provide a welcome alternative. (However, Open University programmes are now no longer shown in the early evening, having been replaced by old black and white films.) The cultural argument for educational programmes only holds if the programmes are comprehensible to a general public and available at times when most people are able to watch them.

NEEDED IMPROVEMENTS

Having set out some of the special advantages of broadcasting for education, there is still much that needs to be done to make it more effective:

Increased access to general programming for educational purposes

It should be permissible to record selected *general* broadcast programmes and series, so that they can be used in schools and colleges and for adult education courses. This means easing copyright and royalty agreements on general programmes for strictly non-profit, educational purposes. Support materials for schools and adults using pictures and materials from selected general programmes and other sources should also be prepared, either by the existing publication departments in broadcasting organisations, or by external agencies with particular interest in the series. Broadcast announcements before and following the programmes should be made indicating the availability of support materials and permission to record for educational purposes. The value of such general programmes and series would be enhanced if there was liaison between the production team and appropriate educational agencies or voluntary organisations from an early stage. Easing copyright and royalty restrictions would not mean loss of income for artists and performers in general programmes since at the moment no income is generated by educational users, unless programmes are available for purchase, which many are not.

Production of integrated, multi-media packages

Serious consideration needs to be given to the appropriateness of current broadcast provision to schools. Continuous broadcast programmes of a set length are not necessarily the best way to use television or radio. Self-standing programmes, even when recorded on cassette, are difficult to integrate with other teaching activities. More useful to teachers will be integrated multi-media packages with varying combinations of print, video, microcomputer material and audio-cassettes. This requires broadcasters to join with other agencies in the design of such components, as equal members in a team.

Improved teacher training in media

Improved and extended training of teachers in the use of media is becoming desperately urgent. Saunders (1980) carried out a thorough study of training for use of broadcasting in schools provided by eleven initial teacher-training centres and a variety of in-service courses in five counties in the south of England. She found that training was on the whole inadequate and misdirected. Teachers after training frequently used broadcasting incompetently and un-imaginatively, yet broadcast material is if anything being used more than ever. Cassettes offer greater opportunities for more effective use as integrated components in a carefully planned curriculum. The range of media available is rapidly widening, and teachers will need to know not only how to use the different media available but when and why they should use each medium. Teacher training in this area needs to be more widely available and better designed.

Improved co-operative arrangements

This is perhaps the most important and certainly the most difficult area for improvement. Robinson (1982) provides an excellent account of the development of partnership. His account shows increasing co-operation and a genuine willingness on the part of educational broadcasters to work with other agencies. The BBC and the IBA have for many years had advisory panels for schools and adult education. There are examples in this book of highly successful co-operative ventures. But nevertheless there are wide-spread criticisms of broadcasting arrangements from other agencies wishing to make full use of the promotional opportunities of broadcasting. Too often other agencies are consulted too late after all the major decisions have been made by the broadcasting organ-isation. Too often the approach of broadcasters is paternalistic and condescending. This kind of criticism can be found from teachers, programme advisers, voluntary agencies and even from academics at the Open University where the partnership arrangement is formalised. Such tensions are inherent in the way broadcasting is structured, financed and controlled.

Broadcasting organisations in Britain have full control over both production and transmission, with the exception of Channel 4. While Channel 4 will take programmes produced by independent companies, it retains full editorial control over what it will broad-cast. Only the BBC, and the IBA through the commercial com-panies, and Channel 4, have the right to broadcast television programmes. Even if another agency is willing to pay for production and transmission, it cannot insist on the right to broadcast. Effec-tively, the State has allowed broadcasting to be placed in the trust of professional broadcasters who represent no one except themselves. This may be preferable to political control but it is surely not the only alternative. The consequence is that voluntary agencies or educational institutions who wish to use broadcasting as a means of communication in a manner of their own choosing cannot do so in Britain. Broadcasting organisations may decide to do 'something' in an area of interest to a voluntary agency or educators, but when and how that something is done is entirely at the discretion of the broadcasters. Under such circumstances, broadcasters can *only* be paternalistic and condescending to other agencies, no matter how well-meaning or courteous they may be.

There is of course no justification for changing the present arrangements if most people are satisfied that they are working well. Few educators, though, are really happy with the present arrangements, I believe. Broadcast frequencies are a national asset. This is recognised in the powers of the Home Secretary, who allocates the frequencies and regulates broadcasting. These frequencies no more belong to Granada Television or the BBC than does the River Thames or the M1. They are held in trust for all of us by the broadcasting agencies, and if the arrangements are no longer satisfactory, they should be changed.

What could be done to ensure a more equal partnership between broadcasting and education? Probably very little in the current political climate. The power of the broadcasting organisations is too strong and the will of the people and the interest of Parliament too weak. The simplest method would be for the government to set up a statutory body which would have powers to set educational and social action priorities for broadcasting, and to require from the broadcasting organisations certain minimal arrangements – such as adequate transmission facilities. In practice, such a body would operate through a set of committees very similar to the existing advisory bodies established by the broadcasters themselves. In any case, the membership of the current advisory councils needs to be extended or a new council established, to ensure representation of the interests of voluntary agencies which are inadequately represented at the moment. The advantage of a statutory body is that members would be appointed independently, and, more importantly, it would be in a position to insist on the use of certain transmission facilities for educational and social action purposes.

THE DECOMMITMENT TO PUBLIC SERVICE BROADCASTING

State regulation of educational broadcasting will be anathema to many in Britain, particularly in the broadcasting world. The realistic alternative, though, is the end of educational broadcasting altogether. The whole concept of public service broadcasting is under serious attack in Britain, due mainly to increased competition from unregulated video-cassette use and new cable and satellite services. John Birt, programme director of one of Britain's biggest independent television companies, London Weekend Television, was reported by *The Guardian* in September, 1983, as saying:

> The new area of competition is likely to mean that the scope for scheduling programmes of minority appeal during peak time will be limited. Indeed, soon there may be no case for it all. . . .

He went on to argue that another £50 million a year should be spent on peak viewing programmes, while less popular slots such as current affairs, the arts, sport, religion and education should be 'pruned'. While these comments are contained in a discussion paper and are not policy (yet), it highlights the problems likely to be caused through increased competition from cable, satellite and cassettes. Public service no longer appears to be fashionable. Populism, commercial profit and the maximisation of audience ratings seem to be the main concerns. Working through some of the accounts of projects and research reports, I had the feeling that the only reason why some broadcast organisations do anything in the area of educational and social action programming is to prevent other agencies from gaining access to broadcasting frequencies. Maybe everyone in the long run would be happier if broadcasting organisations withdrew completely from specific educational activities. However, this would not only be a very real loss to education but also a clear indication of the decline in social responsibility in British broadcasting.

Broadcasting and education make an uneasy alliance. While often sharing common aims, broadcasters and teachers have different perspectives. Education is at the best of times a difficult and an ill-defined process; the values of broadcasting are not identical to those of education. Nevertheless, do we really want to see broadcasting become nothing more than a continuous variety show? If not, then vigorous efforts will be needed to protect educational broadcasting, and major changes will be necessary to ensure that it is used effectively in education.

Appendix

A summary of functions proposed in successful course team bids

Broadcasts can be considered as having two distinct aspects: the actual content of the programme, in terms of the topics or concepts contained in the programme; and the way in which this content is used, by either the teacher or the students. The latter might be called the intended teaching function. *Experience in the use of broadcasting at the Open University suggests that television and radio are particularly appropriate for certain teaching functions. Some of these are listed below.*

GENERAL

There are several functions particularly appropriate to both television and radio which nevertheless are so general that they would apply to *all* programmes in the OU context:

  (1) to increase students' sense of *belonging*; *identification* of and with course designers; making the teaching *less impersonal*;
  (2) to *reduce the time* required by students to master content from reading alone;
  (3) to *pace* students; to keep them working regularly; to break inertia of beginning to study in evening;
  (4) to *recruit or attract new students* (either to the University or to specific courses); to interest general viewers in subject matter;
  (5) to establish *academic credibility* of course to 'outside' world.

SPECIFIC

In a situation though of scarce resources, course teams are expected to propose more specific teaching functions for television and radio. Some of these functions are associated with courses in some faculties more than others and these are indicated in the margin.

Television

(1) To demonstrate experiments or experimental situations, particularly:

   (a) where equipment or phenomena to be observed are *large, expensive, inaccessible, or difficult to observe* without special equipment;

   (b) where the experimental design is *complex*;

   (c) where the measurement of experimental behaviour is not easily reduced to a single scale or dimension (e.g. human behaviour);

   (d) where the experimental behaviour may be influenced by *uncontrollable but observable variables*.

                                               Science/ Technology/ Psychology

(2) To illustrate principles involving *dynamic change or movement*.

(3) To illustrate abstract principles through the use of specially constructed *physical models*.

(4) To illustrate principles involving *two-*; *three-*; or *n-dimensional* space.

(5) To use *animated, slow-motion, or speeded-up film* or video-tape to demonstrate changes over time (including computer animation).

(6) To teach certain advanced scientific or technological concepts (such as theories of relativity or quantum theory) *without* students having to master highly advanced mathematical techniques, by using instead animation, physical models, televisual representation or two-, three- or n-dimensional space, and of dynamic change or movement.

                                               Maths/ Science/ Technology

(7) To substitute for a *field visit* (e.g. to a factory, museum, archaeological or architectural site, geographical location etc.). Field visits may be used for a number of purposes, for example:

   (a) to provide students with an accurate, comprehensive visual picture of the site, or to provide an overall visual context or environment for certain phenomena, in order to place their study in *context*;

   (b) to demonstrate the *relationship* between different elements of the particular system being viewed (e.g. machinery, pro-

                                               All faculty areas

duction processes, ecological balance);

(c) to observe differences in scale and process *between laboratory and mass-production* techniques;

(d) to assist students to differentiate between different *classes or categories* or phenomena *in situ*.

(8) To bring to students *primary resource material*, or *case-study material*, i.e. film or recordings of naturally occurring events which, through editing and selection, demonstrate or illustrate principles covered in the units. This material may be used in a number of different ways, for example:

(a) to enable students to recognise naturally occurring categories, symptoms, phenomena, etc. (e.g. teaching strategies, mental disorders, examples of certain kinds of human interaction etc.);

(b) to enable students to *analyse* a situation, using principles or criteria established elsewhere in a unit; or to *test* students in this way;

(c) to enable the course team to demonstrate ways in which more abstract principles or concepts established elsewhere in a unit have been *applied* to the solution of 'real-world' problems, where visualisation of the application in its total environment is necessary to understand the way the principle has been applied, and the difficulties encountered.

Social Sciences/ Educational Studies/ Technology

(9) To demonstrate *decision-making processes*:

(a) by filming or observing the decision-making process as it occurs;

(b) by dramatisation;

(c) by simulation or role-playing.

(10) *To change student attitudes*:

(a) by presenting material in a *novel* manner, or from an unfamiliar viewpoint;

(b) by presenting material in a *dramatised* form, enabling students to identify with the emotions and viewpoints of the main participants;

+ Arts

(c) by allowing the students to *identify* closely with someone in the programme who overcomes problems or himself changes his attitudes as a result of evidence presented in the programme or televised exercise.

(11) Through performance, to demonstrate methods of techniques of *dramatic* production, or different *interpretations* of plays and novels.

(12) To *analyse* through a combination of graphics and sound, the structure of *music*.

(13) To bring students examples of films or television programme, where *the critical study and analysis of film or television itself* is the subject material of a course.

> Arts/ Social Sciences

(14) To teach *sketching, drawing or painting techniques* (e.g. the sketching of three-dimensional engineering components, the construction of fresco, the drawing of perspective, etc.).

(15) To demonstrate the way in which *instruments or tools* can be played or used; to demonstrate the *skills of craftsmen* and their relationship with the materials and tools which they use.

> Arts/ Technology/ Social Sciences

(16) To *record specifically* events, experiments, species, places, people, buildings, etc., which are crucial to the content of units, but may be likely to disappear, die or be destroyed in the near future.

(17) To explain or demonstrate *practical activities* that students are to carry out themselves (e.g. home experiments, interviewing, project work).

(18) To *condense* or *synthesise* into a coherent whole a wide range of information which would require considerable length in print, and which in print would not provide the richness of background material necessary for students to appreciate fully the situation.

> All faculty areas

Radio and audio-cassettes

In general, radio has a clear *cost* advantage over cassettes for courses with more than 750 students per annum; otherwise cassettes have clear *educational* advantages over radio, with one or two exceptions described below. Audio material intended for distribution on cassette *only* will usually require a different production *style* and *format* than audio material designed for radio transmission, although teaching functions may be similar.

More appropriate for cassettes (cost factors being equal) (i.e. *not* appropriate for radio):

(1) To analyse or process *detailed visual material*. This visual material may take the form of mathematical equations or formulae, reproduction of paintings, graphs, statistical tables, 'real' objects such as rock samples, technical drawings, architectural drawings, maps, etc. (The purpose of the cassette is to 'talk' students through the visual material.)

(2) To enable students through repetition to obtain *mastery* in learning certain skills or techniques (e.g. analysis of language, language pronunciation, analysis of musical structure and technique, mathematical computation).

(3) To *analyse* or critically review *complex arguments*, or carefully structured logical arguments.

Appropriate for cassette or radio (cassettes are still likely to have educational advantages over radio, but radio would not be inappropriate for the factors listed below):

(1) To bring to students *primary resource material*, i.e. recordings which, through careful editing and selection, can demonstrate principles covered in the units. This material may be used in a number of ways, for example:

   (a) recordings of *naturally occurring events*, e.g. political speeches, children talking, concerts or performances, talks previously recorded for other than OU purposes (e.g. Reith lectures), eyewitness interviews at historical events;

   (b) to provide students with a *selection of sources* of evidence to analyse.

(2) To bring to students the views or knowledge of *eminent people* who can condense in an interview the essential points of an argument or opinion, or who can be edited afterwards to provide the essential points, which otherwise in written form may have been more complex or lengthy.

(3) To *record specially* the voices of people who have not been recorded before but whose contribution to the course would provide a unique experience (e.g. famous poets reading their own work, civil servants talking – perhaps anonymously – about their role in decision making).

(4) To *change student attitudes*:

   (a) by presenting material in a *novel* manner, or from an unfamiliar viewpoint;

   (b) by presenting material in *dramatised* form, enabling students to identify with the emotions and viewpoints of the main participants.

(5) To provide the student with a *condensed argument* in lecture form which may:

   (a) *reinforce* points made elsewhere in the course;

(b) introduce *new* concepts not covered elsewhere in the course;

(c) provide an *alternative* view to that presented in the correspondence text and/or television programmes;

(d) *analyse* material contained elsewhere in the course, especially in specially written broadcast notes or television programmes;

(e) *summarise* the main points of the block or course as far as it had gone, providing integration and orientation;

(f) draw on quotation, recorded information, interviews, etc., as *evidence* in support of (or against) the argument.

(6) To enable students to perceive that *different points of view* exist, and observe ideas being challenged, through discussions and interviews.

(7) To provide students with *performances* of music, drama, poetry, for appreciation.

More appropriate for radio (cost factors being equal):

(1) To provide *remedial tutorials*, or some other form of tutorial based on feedback.

(2) To provide *corrections*, where print re-make budgets are limited, or where print cannot reach students quickly enough.

(3) To relate course material to current events (e.g. news stories, recent natural hazards, social, environmental, political or industrial developments), emphasising the *relevance* or *application* of principles or concepts covered by the print material.

(4) To *up-date* course material, to take account of events during the life of the course.

(5) To provide *external criticism* or *alternative viewpoints* to course material in second or subsequent years of presentation as a result of exposure of course material to public view.

(6) Radio can be used where only *one hearing* of the material would generally be considered *sufficient*. This might cover a number of circumstances:

(a) an introduction, summary, or overview of a unit or block;

(b) a discussion, where the *raising* of issues and counterviews is considered to be more important than the actual arguments themselves;

(c) where an *experience* – such as a performance of music, a dramatisation, a poetry reading – is considered to be of more value than an intellectual analysis of concepts, or the provision of information;

(d) a single argument or story, again where analysis of the argument or story is less important than *familiarising* the student with the argument or story, or *reinforcing* ground covered elsewhere in the course.

Prepared for the Broadcast and Audio-Visual Subcommittee by A. W. Bates

Bibliography

Abell, H. C. (1968) *Farm Radio Forum Project: Ghana 1964–65*. Paris: UNESCO.

Agrawal, B. C. (1981) *SITE Social Evaluation*. Ahmedabad: Space Application Centre.

Ahrens, S. *et al.* (1975) *M231, 'Analysis'*. Milton Keynes: Open University (Broadcast Evaluation Report, No. 1).

Arena, G. *et al.* (1977) *Economic Analysis of Educational Television in Maranhao, Brazil*. Paris: UNESCO.

Arnove, R. (1976) *Educational Television: A Policy Critique and Guide for Developing Countries*. New York: Praeger.

Bacsich, P. *et al.* (1983) *The Implications for the Open University of Recent Cable and Satellite Developments*. Milton Keynes: Open University (IET Papers on Broadcasting, No. 213).

Ball, S. and Bogatz, G. A. (1970) *The First Year of 'Sesame Street': An Evaluation*. Princeton, N.J.: Educational Testing Service.

Bates, A. W. (1975) *Student Use of Open University Broadcasting*. Milton Keynes: Open University (IET Papers on Broadcasting, No. 44).

Bates, A. W. (1979) *Appropriate Media and Methods for Distance Education in Norway*. Trondheim: Trondheim Technological University.

Bates, A. W. (1980) *The Planning and Management of Audio-Visual Media in Distance Learning Institutions*. Paris: International Institute for Educational Planning.

Bates, A. W. (1981a) 'Towards a better research framework for evaluating the effectiveness of educational media.' *British Journal of Educational Technology*, Vol. 12, No. 3.

Bates, A. W. (1981b) 'Some unique characteristics of television and some implications for teaching and learning,' *Journal of Educational Television*, Vol. 7, No. 3.

Bates, A. W. (1983) 'Adults learning from educational television: the Open University experience', in Howe, M. J. A. (ed.) *Learning from Television*. London: Academic Press.

Bates, A. W. and Gallagher, M. (1977) *Improving the Effectiveness of Open University Television Case-Studies and Documentaries*. Milton Keynes: Open University (IET Papers on Broadcasting, No. 77).

Bates, A. W. and Robinson, J. (1977) *Evaluating Educational Television and Radio*. Milton Keynes: Open University Press.

Bates, A. W. *et al.* (1982a) *Radio: the Forgotten Medium?* Milton Keynes: Open University (IET Papers on Broadcasting, No. 185).

Bates, A. W. *et al.* (1982b) *CYCLOPS in Schools: A Small Pilot Study*. Milton Keynes: Open University (IET Papers on Broadcasting, No. 200).

BBC (1979) *Annual Review of BBC Audience Research Findings: No. 5.* London: BBC.

BBC (1981) *BBC Enterprises Film and Video Catalogue.* London: BBC Enterprises.

Beardsley, J. (1975) 'The Free University of Iran' in McKenzie, N. *et al.* (eds) *Open Learning.* Paris: UNESCO.

Beck, T. K. (1979) 'Widening "Sesame Street"', *Journal of Educational Television*, Vol. 5, No. 2.

Belson, W. (1952) '"Topic for Tonight": a study of comprehensibility', *BBC Quarterly*, Vol. 7, No. 2.

Bernal, H. *et. al.* (1978) *Acción Cultural Popular.* Bogatá: Acción Cultural Popular.

Björkland, K. (1977) 'Delta Project in teacher training' in Polish National Commission for UNESCO *Report of the International Seminar on Experience Gained from the Polish System NURT.* Warsaw: Polish National Commission for UNESCO.

Blumler, J. G. and Katz, E. (1974) *The Uses of Mass Communications: Current Perspectives in Gratifications Research.* London: Sage.

Bogatz, G. A. and Ball, S. (1972) *The Second Year of 'Sesame Street': A Continuing Evaluation.* Princeton, N.J.: Educational Testing Services.

Bon, A. (1977) 'Educational television in teachers' training in France', in Polish National Commission for UNESCO *Report of the International Seminar on Experience Gained from the Polish System NURT.* Warsaw: Polish National Commission for UNESCO.

Bonzon, S. (1979) 'Cotabato Now' in Dikshit, K. A. *et al. Rural Radio: Programme Formats.* Paris: UNESCO.

Booth, J. (1980) *A Different Animal: Local Radio and the Community.* London: IBA.

Brown, D. (1980) 'New students and radio at the Open University', *Educational Broadcasting International*, Vol. 13, No. 1.

Brown S. (1981) *T101 '2 + 6' Evaluation: Final Report on First Year Broadcast Presentation.* Milton Keynes: Open University (IET Papers on Broadcasting, No. 187)

Brown, S. (1983) *The 1982 Video-Cassette Loan Service.* Milton Keynes: Open University (IET Papers on Broadcasting, No. 215)

Burns, T. (1969) 'Public service and private world', *Sociological Review Monograph*, Vol. 13.

Cassirer, H. (1959) 'Audience participation new style', *Public Opinion Quarterly*, Vol. 23.

Cassirer, H. (1977) 'Radio in an African context: a description of Senegal's pilot project' in Spain, P. *et al.* (eds) *Radio for Education and Development: Case Studies.* Washington, D.C.: The World Bank.

Cawston, R. *et al.* (1972) *Principles and Practice in Documentary Programmes.* London: BBC (mimeo).

Cepeda, L. E. (1982) 'Radio ECCA: Canary Islands' in Kaye, A. and Harry, K. (eds) *Using the Media for Adult Basic Education.* London: Croom Helm.

Champness, B. and Young, I. (1980) 'Social limits on educational technology', *European Journal of Education*, Vol. 15, No. 3.

Coldevin, G. O. (1980) 'Broadcasting development and research in Kenya', *Journal of Educational Television*, Vol. 6, No. 2.

Coleman, J. S. *et al.* (1966) *Equality of Educational Opportunity*. Washington, D.C.: United States Office of Education.

Cook, T. D. *et al.* (1975) *'Sesame Street' Revisited*. New York: Russell Sage Foundation.

Cooney, J. A. (1968) 'Television for pre-school children: a proposal', cited in Cook, T. D. *et al. 'Sesame Street' Revisited*. New York: Russell Sage Foundation.

Croton, G. (1980) *'Let's Go . . .': An Account of the BBC's Mental Handicap Project, 1976–1979*. London: BBC.

Croton, G. and Pascoe, C. (1981) *BBC Programmes on Mental and Physical Handicap, 1970–1980*. London: BBC.

Cuff, A. (1976) *A Study of the Use of Modern Language Broadcasts for Schools*. London: IBA.

Curran, J. *et al.* (1977) *Mass Communication and Society*. London: Arnold.

Darveau, J. G. *et al.* (1979) 'Synthèse des recommendations tirées de l'expérience Tevec' in Ministère de l'Education, Quebec *Documents Etudes et Recherches* 2–12. Québec: Ministère de l'Education.

Dodds, T. (1972) *Multi-Media Approaches to Rural Education*. Cambridge: International Extension College.

Durbridge, N. (1981a) *The 'Durbridge Box': Examples of Audio-Cassette Use in the Open University*. Milton Keynes: Open University (training pack).

Durbridge, N. (1981b) 'The use of audio-cassettes' in Bates, A. W. *et al. Radio: the Forgotten Medium?* Milton Keynes: Open University (IET Papers on Broadcasting, No. 185).

Durbridge, N. (1982) *Developing the Use of Video-Cassettes in the Open University*. Milton Keynes: Open University. (IET Papers on Broadcasting, No. 208).

Educational Broadcasting Councils for the United Kingdom (1979). *Social Studies, 11–14*. London: BBC.

Educational Broadcasting Councils for the United Kingdom (1982) *Surveys of Viewing and Listening in U.K. Schools: Annual Reports, 1981–82*. London: BBC.

Educational Broadcasting Councils for the United Kingdom (1983). *The Night-Time Feasibility Study*. London: BBC.

Edwards, R. (1974) *Fool's Lantern or Aladdin's Lamp? The Use of Educational Television with Slow Learning and Handicapped Children*. London: IBA.

Eicher, J. C. and Orivel, F. (1980) 'Cost analysis of primary education by television in the Ivory Coast', in *The Economics of New Educational Media: Vol. 2, Cost and Effectiveness*. Paris: UNESCO.

Elliott, P. (1972) 'Mass communication: a contradiction in terms?' in McQuail, D. (ed.) *Sociology of Mass Communications*. Harmondsworth: Penguin.

Elliott, S. (1979) *'Dizzy' Questionnaire*. London: IBA (mimeo)

Findahl, O. and Höijer, B. (1978) *How Important is Presentation? A Review of Experimental Research*. Stockholm: PUB, Sveriges Radio.

Fiske, T. and Hartley, J. (1978) *Reading Television*. London: Methuen.

Fortosky, D. (1982) *Distance Education and Technology at the University of Saskatchewan: Options for the Future*. Saskatoon: University of Saskatchewan (Ph.D. thesis).

Friend, J. *et al*. (1980) *Radio Mathematics in Nicaragua*. Stanford, Ca.: Institute for Mathematical Studies in the Social Sciences, Stanford University.

Fuller, R. (1983) *Using Inter-Active Video-Discs in Open University Courses*. Milton Keynes: Open University (IET Papers on Broadcasting, No. 218).

Fuller, R. (1984) 'Video-discs' in Bates, A. W. (ed.) *The Role of Technology in Distance Education*. London: Croom Helm.

Gallagher, M. (1977a) *Broadcasting and the Open University Student*. Milton Keynes: Open University (IET Papers on Broadcasting, No. 80).

Gallagher, M. (1977b) *D302, 'Patterns of Equality', TV1*. Milton Keynes: Open University (Broadcast Evaluation Report, No. 22).

Gallagher, M. (1977c) *D302, 'Patterns of Inequality', TV2*. Milton Keynes: Open University (Broadcast Evaluation Report No. 23).

Gallagher, M. (1977d) 'Organisations and occupations: Unit 11', in *Mass Communication and Society: DE353*. Milton Keynes: The Open University Press.

Girardin, M. (1982) 'Télépromotion Rurale: Rhônes-Alpes, Auvergne, France' in Kaye, A. and Harry, K. (eds) *Using the Media for Adult Basic Education*. London: Croom Helm.

Glasgow University Media Group (1976) *Bad News*. London: Routledge and Kegan Paul.

Glasgow University Media Group (1980) *More Bad News*. London: Routledge and Kegan Paul.

Glikman, V. and Corduant, J. P. (1977) 'RTS/Promotion and BBC Further Education: a comparison between two adult education organisations', in Bates, A. W. and Robinson, J. (eds) *Evaluating Educational Television and Radio*. Milton Keynes: Open University Press.

Goldsen, R. (1976) 'Literacy without books: the case of "Sesame Street"', in Arnove, R. (ed.) *Educational Television: A Policy Critique and Guide for Developing Countries*. New York: Praeger.

Great Britain: Committee on Higher Education (1963) *Higher Education*. London: HMSO (the 'Robbins Report').

Great Britain: Department of Education and Science (1967) *Children and their Primary Schools*. London: HMSO (the 'Plowden Report').

Great Britain: Department of Education and Science (1973) *Adult Education: A Plan for Development*. London: HMSO (the 'Russell Report').

Great Britain: Department of Education and Science (1978) *Special Educational Needs*. London: HMSO (the 'Warnock Report').

Great Britain: Department of Education and Science (1983) *Future De-*

mand for Higher Education in Great Britain. London: HMSO (DES Report on Education No. 99).

Great Britain: Home Office (1977) *Report of the Committee on the Future of Broadcasting*. London: HMSO (the 'Annan Report').

Grundin, H. U. (1978) *Broadcasting and the Open University Student: the 1977 Survey*. Milton Keynes: Open University (IET Papers on Broadcasting, No. 97).

Grundin, H. U. (1980) *Audio-Visual and Other Media in 91 Open University Courses: Results of the 1979 Undergraduate Survey*. Milton Keynes: Open University (IET Papers on Broadcasting, No. 149).

Grundin, H. U. (1981) *Open University Broadcasting Times and their Impact on Students' Viewing/Listening*. Milton Keynes: Open University (IET Papers on Broadcasting, No. 171).

Grundin, H. U. (1983) *Audio-Visual Media in the Open University: Results of a Survey of 93 Courses*. Milton Keynes: Open University (IET Papers on Broadcasting, No. 224).

Gulbenkian Foundation (1979) *Broadcasting and Youth*. London: Gulbenkian Foundation.

Gunter, B. *et al.* (1982) 'Remembering broadcast news: the implications of experimental research for production technique', *Human Learning*, Vol. 1.

Gunter, J. and Theroux, J. (1977) 'Open broadcast educational radio: three paradigms', in Spain, P. *et al.* (eds) *Radio for Education and Development: Case Studies*. Washington, D.C.: The World Bank.

Hall, B. L. and Dodds, T. (1977) *Voices for Development: The Tanzanian National Radio Study Campaigns*. Cambridge: International Extension College.

Hall, P. (1980) 'Adult education and the media – "Your Own Business"', *Adult Education*, Vol. 53, No. 3.

Hall, S. (1982) *Social Integration 1: Children's Television, D102, TV19*. Milton Keynes: Open University/BBC-Open University Productions.

Hargreaves, D. (1980) *Adult Literacy and Broadcasting*. London: Frances Pinter.

Haviland, R. M. (1973) 'Survey of provision for adult literacy in England', cited in Jones, H. A. and Charnley, A. H. (1978) *Adult Literacy: A Study of its Impact*. Leicester: National Institute of Adult Education.

Hawkridge, D. and Robinson, J. (1982) *Organising Educational Broadcasting*. London: Croom Helm.

Hayter, C. J. (1974) *Using Broadcasts in Schools: A Study and Evaluation*. London: BBC/ITV.

Heidt, E. V. (1978) *Instructional Media and the Individual Learner*. London: Kogan Page.

Hill, R. (1981) *An Evaluation of 'Insight'*. London: IBA.

Hood, S. (1967) *A Survey of Television*. London: Heinemann.

Hood, S. (1972) 'The politics of television', in McQuail, D. (ed.) *Sociology of Mass Communications*. Harmondsworth: Penguin.

Horneij, R. (1975) *The Development of 'Start': An English Course for Adults*. Stockholm: Swedish Educational Broadcasting Company.

Howe, M. (1983) *Learning from Television*. London: Academic Press.

Hunt, A. (1981) *Language of Television: Uses and Abuses*. London: Eyre Methuen.

Independent Broadcasting Authority (1979) *Audience Research Department Research Summary, 8th March*. London: IBA (mimeo).

Ingle, H. T. (1974) *Communication Media and Technology: A Look at their Role in Non-Formal Education Programmes*. Washington, D.C.: Academy for Educational Development.

Ingle, H. T. (1976) 'Reconsidering the use of television for educational reform: the case of El Salvador', in Arnove, R. (ed.) *Educational Television: A Policy Critique and Guide for Developing Countries*. New York: Praeger.

International Institute for Adult Literacy Methods (1974) 'Radio's predominant role in literacy drive', *Literacy Work*, Vol. 4, No. 1.

Internationales Zentralinstitut für das Jugend- und Bildungsfernsehen (1979) *School Radio in Europe*. London: K. G. Saur.

Jacquinot, G. (1977) *Image et Pédagogie*. Paris: Presses Universitaires de France.

Jamison, D. and McAnany, E. (1978) *Radio for Education and Development*. London: Sage.

Jamison, D. and Yoon Tai Kim (1977) 'The cost of instructional radio and television in Korea', in Bates, A. W. and Robinson, J. (eds) *Evaluating Educational Television and Radio*. Milton Keynes: Open University Press.

Japanese International Co-operation Agency (1975) *A Television System for Afghanistan*. Tokyo: Japanese International Co-operation Agency.

Jay, A. (1972) *Corporation Man*. London: Cape.

Jones, H. A. and Charnley, A. H. (1978) *Adult Literacy: A Study of its Impact*. Leicester: National Institute of Adult Education.

Kanocz, S. (1975) 'Part-time higher education using radio: an example from the Federal Republic of Germany', in McKenzie, N. *et al.* (eds) *Open Learning*. Paris: UNESCO.

Katz, E. and Wedell, G. (1978) *Broadcasting in the Third World*. London: Macmillan.

Kaye, A. (1976) 'The Ivory Coast Educational Television Project', in Arnove, R. (ed.) *Educational Television: A Policy Critique and Guide for Developing Countries*. New York: Praeger.

Kaye, A. and Rumble, G. (1980) *Distance Teaching for Higher and Adult Education*. London: Croom Helm.

Keegan, D. (1980) 'On defining distance education', *Distance Education*, Vol. 1, No. 1.

Keegan, D. and Rumble, G. (1982) 'Distance teaching at university-level', in Rumble, G. and Harry, K. (eds) *The Distance Teaching Universities*. London: Croom Helm.

Kemelfield, G. (1972) *The Evaluation of Schools Broadcasts: Piloting a New Approach*. London: Independent Television Authority.

Kern, L. (1976) *Basing Assignments on Broadcasts*. Milton Keynes: Open University (IET Papers on Broadcasting, No. 66).

Kuznetsov, V. (1975) 'Correspondence education in the Soviet Union', in McKenzie, N. *et al.* (eds) *Open Learning*. Paris: UNESCO.

Lallez, R. (1972) *The TEVEC Case: An Experiment in Adult Education Using the Multi-Media System*. Paris: UNESCO.

Larimore, D. (1977) 'Appalachian educational satellite project', in Polish National Commission for UNESCO *Report of the International Seminar on Experience Gained from the Polish System NURT*. Warsaw: Polish National Commission for UNESCO.

Laurillard, D. (1982) 'The potential of inter-active video', *Journal of Educational Television*, Vol. 8, No. 3.

Lee, R. *et al.* (1978) 'The pre-testing of "Let's Go . . .": a BBC television series for the mentally handicapped', in Bates, A. W. and Gallagher, M. (eds) *Formative Evaluation of Educational Television Programmes*. London: Council for Educational Technology.

Lewis, R. (1983) *Meeting Learners' Needs Through Telecommunications: A Directory and Guide to Programmes*. Washington, D.C.: American Association for Higher Education.

Lyle, J. (1982) 'The original case-studies reviewed' in Hawkridge, D. and Robinson, J. (eds) *Organising Educational Broadcasting*. London: Croom Helm.

McAnany, E. G. (1976) *Radio's Role in Development: Five Strategies for Use*. Washington, D.C.: Academy for Educational Development.

McAnany, E. G. and Mayo, J. (1979) *Communication Media in Education for Low Income Countries: Implications for Planning*. Paris: International Institute for Educational Planning.

McConnell, D. and Sharples, M. (1983) 'Distance teaching by Cyclops', *British Journal of Educational Technology*, Vol. 14, No. 2.

McCormick, R. (1982) 'The Central Broadcasting and Television University, People's Republic of China', in Rumble, G. and Harry, K. (eds) *The Distance Teaching Universities*. London: Croom Helm.

McCron, R. (1981) 'Social action programming', *Educational Broadcasting International*, Vol. 14, No. 3.

MacLeod, S. (1981) 'Is there hope?', *Times Educational Supplement*, June 12th.

McQuail, D. (1972) *Sociology of Mass Communications*. Harmondsworth: Penguin.

Maddison, J. (1974) *Radio and Television in Literacy*. Paris: UNESCO.

Manuelian, A. (1980) 'Technology as a stimulus to new educational structures: a university distance teaching federation in Eastern France', *European Journal of Education*, Vol. 15, No. 3.

Masland, L. and Masland, G. (1976) 'Some cross-cultural implications of educational television: the Samoan ETV project', in Arnove, R. (ed.) *Educational Television: A Policy Critique and Guide for Developing Countries*. New York: Praeger.

Mason, E. J. (1954) 'Writing a radio serial', *BBC Quarterly*, Vol. 9, No. 1.

Masterman, L. (1980) *Teaching About Television*. London: Macmillan.

Matsui, J. (1981) *Adult Learning Needs, Life Interests and Media Use: Some Implications for TV Ontario*. Toronto: TV Ontario.

Matthews, T. (1978) *'Parosi': A BBC Contribution to Language Learning in the Asian Community*. London: BBC.

Mayo, J. *et al*. (1975) 'The Mexican Telesecundaria: a cost-effectiveness analysis', *Instructional Science*, Vol. 4, No. 3/4.

Mayo, J. *et al*. (1976) *Education with Television: The El Salvador Experience*. Stanford, Ca.: Stanford University Press.

Morris, E. and Gregory, F. (1976) *TV, The Family School*. Atlanta, Ga.: Avator Press.

Neurath, P. M. (1960) *Radio Farm Forums in India*. Delhi: Government of India.

NHK (1969) *Survey and Study of Educational Broadcasts: 1960–68*. Tokyo: NHK.

Oliveira, J. B. A. (1979) 'The ETV project of Fundaçao Maranhense de Televiso Educativa', in Melmed, A. (ed.) *The Organisation and Management of Distance Media Systems: Some New Directions*. Palo Alto, Ca.: Edutel.

Oliveira, J. B. A. and Orivel, F. (1982) 'The Minerva project in Brazil', in Perraton, H. (ed.) *Alternative Routes to Formal Education: Distance Teaching for School Equivalency*. Washington, D.C.: The World Bank.

Olson, D. and Bruner, J. (1974) 'Learning through experience and learning through media', in Olson, D. (ed.) *Media and Symbols: The Forms of Expression*. Chicago: University of Chicago Press (The 73rd NSSE Yearbook).

Open University (1982) *Guide to the Associate Student Programme, 1983*. Milton Keynes: Open University.

Palmer, E. L. (1972) 'Formative research in educational television: the experience of Children's Television Workshop', in Schramm, W. (ed.) *Quality in Instructional Television*. Honolulu: University Press of Hawaii.

Palmer, E. L. *et al*. (1976) ' "Sesame Street": patterns of international adaptation', *Journal of Communications Research*, Spring.

Pease, M. (1983) 'The early years', *Media Project News*, January.

Perry, W. (1976) *The Open University*. Milton Keynes: Open University Press.

Polsky, R. M. (1974) *Getting to 'Sesame Street'*. New York: Praeger.

Porter, P. (1978) *Television with Slow Learning Children*. London: IBA.

Porter, P. (1982) 'Matching educational television to the learning needs of handicapped children', *Journal of Educational Television*, Vol. 8, No. 1.

Postman, N. (1983) *The Disappearance of Childhood*. London: W. H. Allen.

Puszczewicz, B. (1977) 'The Radio-Television University for Teachers in Poland', in Polish National Commission for UNESCO *Report of the International Seminar on Experience Gained from the Polish System NURT*. Warsaw: Polish National Commission for UNESCO.

Read, G. (1981) *CYCLOPS: A Versatile Graphics System*. Milton Keynes: Open University.

Reeves, B. (1982) ' "Just the Job": Westward TV/NEC, United Kingdom' in Kaye, A. and Harry, K. (eds) *Using the Media for Adult Basic Education*. London: Croom Helm.

Reinhold, M. (1980) 'Just the Job', *Journal of Educational Television*, Vol. 6, No. 2.

Reith, J. (1949) *Into the Wind*. London: Hodder and Stoughton.

Robinson, J. (1982) *Learning over the Air*. London: BBC.

Rogers, E. *et al*. (1977) 'Radio forums: a strategy for rural development', in Spain, P. *et al*. (eds) *Radio for Education and Development: Case Studies*. Washington, D.C.: The World Bank.

Rogers, J. (1977) *Adults Learning*. Milton Keynes: Open University Press.

Rumble, G. and Harry, K. (1982) *The Distance Teaching Universities*. London: Croom Helm.

Rybak, S. (1980) *Learning Languages from the BBC*. London: BBC.

Rybak, S. (1983) *Learning Languages by Radio and Television: The Development of a Support Strategy for Adult Home Learners*. Brighton: Brighton Polytechnic (CNAA Ph.D. thesis)

Salkeld, R. (1979) *'What Right Have You Got?'* London: BBC.

Salomon, G. (1979) *Interaction of Media, Cognition and Learning*. London: Jossey-Bass.

Salomon, G. (1981) *Communication and Education*. London: Sage.

Salomon, G. (1983) *Using Television as a Unique Teaching Resource for OU Courses*. Milton Keynes: Open University (IET Papers on Broadcasting, No. 225).

Saunders, U. C. (1980) *Training for Effective Use of Schools Broadcasting*. Southampton: University of Southampton (M.Ed. thesis).

Schmelkes de Sotelo, B. (1977) 'The radio schools of the Tarahumara, Mexico: an evaluation', in Spain, P. L. *et al*. (eds) *Radio for Education and Development: Case Studies*. Washington, D.C.: The World Bank.

Schools Broadcasting Council (1972) *Listening and Reading: I and II*. London: BBC.

Schools Broadcasting Council (1976) *Schools Broadcasts and Primary English and Reading*. London: BBC.

Schools Broadcasting Council (1977) *'Merry-Go-Round'*. London: BBC.

Schools Broadcasting Council (1978) *A Survey of Project Work Undertaken by 6–9 Year Old Children*. London: BBC.

Schools Broadcasting Council (1979) *Assemblies in Primary and Secondary Schools*. London: BBC.

Schramm, W. (1972) *Quality in Instructional Television*. Honolulu: University Press of Hawaii.

Schramm, W. (1977) *Big Media, Little Media*. London: Sage.

Schramm, W. *et al*. (1967) *The New Media: Memo to Educational Planners*. Paris: UNESCO.

Schramm, W. *et al*. (1980) *Bold Adventure: The Story of Television in American Samoa*. Stanford, Ca.: Stanford University Press.

Screen Digest (1983) 'World video population at 30 million', *Screen Digest*, May.

Sissons, L. (1974) *'Living Decisions in Family and Community'*. Edinburgh: University of Edinburgh (Dip. Adult Education dissertation).

Skandar, O. (1977) 'Use of radio and television for teacher training in the light of Algerian experiences', in Polish National Commission for UNESCO *Report of the International Seminar on Experience Gained from the Polish System NURT.* Warsaw: Polish National Commission for UNESCO.

Spain, P. L. (1977) 'The Mexican Radioprimaria project', in Spain, P. L. *et al.* (eds) *Radio for Education and Development: Case Studies.* Washington, D.C.: The World Bank.

Spencer, K. and Clarke, A. (1981) 'A BBC television series for the mentally handicapped', *Educational Broadcasting International*, Vol. 14, No. 3.

Steedman, J. (1975) *Evaluating Schools Television: A Programme for ROSLA Pupils from the Granada Series 'Decision'.* London: IBA.

Stephens, M. (1976) *'Living Decisions in Family and Community'.* London: BBC.

Stringer, D. (1979) *'Make It Count'.* London: IBA.

Swift, B. (1980) *Outcomes of Open University Studies: Some Statistics from a 1980 Survey of Graduates.* Milton Keynes: Open University (mimeo).

Taylor, N. (1979) *Some Aspects of the Use of Television in the Open University of the United Kingdom.* Milton Keynes: Open University Conference on the Education of Adults at a Distance, Paper No. 66.

Thompson, G. (1979) 'Television as text: Open University case study programmes', in Barrett, M. *et al. Ideology and Cultural Production.* London: Croom Helm.

Tough, A. (1968) *Why Adults Learn.* Toronto: Ontario Institute for Studies in Education.

Trenaman, J. (1967) *Communication and Comprehension.* London: Longmans.

Tucker, J. D. (1979) *Television for Certain Handicapped Children – Phase 1.* London: IBA.

Tunstall, J. (1970) *Media Sociology.* London: Constable.

UNESCO (1980) *Statistical Yearbook, 1980.* Paris: UNESCO.

Vaughan, D. (1976) *Television Documentary Usage.* London: British Film Institute.

Vellekoop, L. (1982) 'Open School, Netherlands', in Kaye, A. and Harry, K. (eds) *Using Media for Adult Basic Education.* London: Croom Helm.

Vernon, P. (1950) 'The intelligibility of broadcast talks,' *BBC Quarterly*, Vol. 5.

Ware, E. (1983) 'Television Audience Research', *Media Project News*, July.

Waniewicz, I. (1981) 'The TVOntario Academy', *Educational Broadcasting International*, Vol. 14, No. 2.

Wenham, B. (1983) *The Third Age of Broadcasting.* London: Faber and Faber.

White, R. (1976) *An Alternative Pattern of Basic Education: Radio Santa Maria.* Paris: UNESCO.

Wright, A. (1980) *Local Radio and Local Democracy.* London: IBA.

Yacoub, S. M. *et al.* (1973) *The Impact of Farm Radio Forum on the Diffusion of Innovations in Lahore and Gujrat Districts of West Pakistan.* Beirut: American University of Beirut.

General Index

(Tables are given in italic)

abstract thinking, 173–6
ACCESS, Alberta, 133, 148, 169
Accion Cultural Popular (ACPO), 86
accountability, 95, 136
activities, learners', 21, 22, 75, 89, 149, 172, 174, 178, 205, 211
adult literacy: Adult Literacy Resource Agency (ALRA), 108, 110, 112, 113; appropriate programme formats, 96–7; BBC Adult Literacy Campaign, 76, 80, 86, 94, 102, 106–115; Broadcast Support Services, 80; literacy rate in Great Britain, 69; literacy rate world-wide, *70*, 71; radio schools, 87
advertising techniques, 74, 83, 104, 185, 186
Afghanistan, 13–15, 58, 59, 84
Africa, 78, 85, 86 *see also* name of individual country
AGB Research Ltd, 4.
Agency for Instructional Television, 17, 18, 64
Alaska, 87
Algeria, 29
Allama Iqbal Open University, 29, *143*, 168
ambition, 187–8
American Samoa, 24, 25, 26, *57*, 60
Angola, *70*
ANIK-C, 149
Annan Committee on the future of broadcasting, 4, 159, 181–2, 196
ANTIOPE, 226
Appalachian Educational Satellite Project, 31–2, 87
Arts subjects, 127, *131*, 171–2 *see also* name of individual subject
Athabasca University, 140, 141, *142*, 169
ATS-3, 32
ATS-6, 31
attention, 52, 53, 176, 186
attitude change, 49–50, 91–2, 93
ATV, 121

audience appeal *see* entertainment
audience characteristics: adult literacy students, 96–7, 114; basic adult education students, 96–9, 102; children, 114–5; distance higher education students, 96, 150, 164, 171; foreign language students, 101–2; levels of commitment, 99–101, 182; occupation/educational status, 173, 179; producers' attitudes to, 181, 198, 201; programme formats and, 96–7, 98, 173, 232; *see also* non interested learners; open learners; structured learners
audio-cassettes and tapes, 128, 134, 141, 142–3, 144, 148, 167, 177, 203–6, 211–3, 228, 229, 230, 231
audio-visual centres, 204
Audio-visual Media Research Group, Open University, 10, 175
Australia, 23, 24, 145
auxiliaries, 84
awareness: adult literacy, 110, 112; casual viewers, 238–9; disadvantaged minorities, 93

balance, 189, 191–2
balloons, communications, 56
basic adult education, 68, 69–71, 76–8, *130*, 234; *see also* adult literacy; numeracy; social skills
battery-operated television sets, 25, 60
BBC: adult literacy, 76, 108–115; audience research, 4, 207; BBC 1, 2, 116; BBC 2, 1, 2, 157, 175, 196; BBC Enterprises, 47, 215; Board of Governors, 196; CEEFAX, 225; computer literacy, 127, 128; continuing education broadcasting, 6, 78, 122–9, 135–7, 152–6; cooperative arrangements, 241; disadvantaged groups, 102; Educational Broadcasting Councils, 6, 10, *17*, 34, *36*, *38*, 39, *40*, 43, 203, 229; education officers, 6; foreign

BBC: adult literacy – *cont.*
  language broadcasting, 101–2;
  general broadcasting, 169; in
  America, 129; licence fee, 3, 47, 138;
  local radio, 3; Open University
  Productions (BBC/OUP), 7, 123–9,
  130–1, 140, 141, 159, 168, 169–70,
  182, 192–3, 195–6, 197, 214; overseas
  (external) service, 3; Radio 1, 3, 115,
  116, 171; Radio 2, 3, 115, 116, 171;
  Radio 3, 3, 116, 171, 172; Radio 4, 3,
  116, 171, 172, 203; satellites, 2, 5,
  225; Schools Broadcasting Council,
  37, 43; schools radio, 6, 20, *21*, 34–5;
  schools TV, 6, 20, *21*, 34–5, 37–9;
  social skills, 77
Besançon, University of, 148
bias *see* balance
Brazil, 24, 26, *57*, 63, *70*, 78
breakfast television, 1, 200
British Association of Settlements, 110
British Columbia, 148–50
British Columbia Institute of
  Technology, 148, 149
British Columbia University, 148
British Telecom, 228
Broadcasters Audience Research
  Board (BARB), 4, 154, 200
broadcast notes, 167, 177
Broadcast Support Services, 80

cable television, 1–2, 5, 17, 82, 129,
  137, 149, 207, 221–5, 231, 243
Cadbury Trust, 112
campesinos, 72, 86, 87, 88
Canada: adult education broadcasting,
  132–3; adult learning, 71; distance
  teaching universities, 140, 141, *142*,
  169; Fogo Island, 80–1; Knowledge
  Network, 148–50; radio farm forums,
  85; rural broadcasting, 87; satellites,
  86–7; Tevec, 89; university extension
  departments, 145; viewdata, 226; *see
  also* TV Ontario
Canadian Broadcasting Corporation,
  132
Canary Islands, 78
Capital Radio, *17*
careers education, 32, 37, *38*, *40*
Carnegie Foundation, 129
Catholic Church, 72, 86–8
CEEFAX, 225
censorship, 195–7
Central Office of Information (U.K.),
  115
Centre National De Documentation
  Pédagogique (CNDP), 134, 135, 137
Centre National De Télé-enseignement
  (CNTE), 139–40
Centres De Télé-enseignement

Universitaire (CTUs), 145, 147–8,
  150
Channel 4: continuing education, 123,
  136; effect on BBC, 157; finance, 3;
  'Make it Count', 76–7; minority
  programming, 128; open access,
  81–2; origin, 1; out of school
  children's TV, 6; programme control,
  241; social purpose programming, 6,
  80; vocational training, 136
channel identity, 116
chemistry, *38*
Chicago TV College, 132
children's programming, 73–5, 103–5,
  119
Children's Television Workshop
  (CTW), 73, 105, 112, 114, 115, 133
China, 140, *142*
Chinese Central Television University
  (CCTU), 140–1, *142*, 150
City Colleges of Chicago, 132
class differences *see* socio-economic
  differences
classroom observation, 193
college TV courses, 132
Colombia, 41, 86
colour television, 35
commercial television: American, 104,
  185–6; U.K. *see* Independent
  Television Companies (ITV-UK)
commitment, learners', 98, 99–101, 117
community development/education,
  71–2, 80–2, 89, *124*, 126, *131*, 136
comprehension, 172–3, 175, 178, 179
computers: BBC microcomputer, 127,
  128, 225–6; computer assisted
  learning (CAL), 206, 217, 221, 224,
  227–8, 235; CYCLOPS, 228–9, 230;
  feedback, 133; literacy, 127;
  microcomputers, 203, 227–30;
  programmes, 2; telesoftware, 225,
  239; video-cassettes and, 217;
  video-discs and, 217, 218, 219
concreteness, 173–4, 175, 179
conditions for success: basic adult
  education, 112–8, 234; continuing
  and distance higher education, 179,
  234; schools radio, 41–2, 44, 233;
  schools TV, 45–7, 50–2, 53–5, 65–6,
  233
continuing education, 6, 122–37, 152–3,
  155–6, 160, 179; *see also* basic adult
  education; disadvantaged; social
  purpose programming control
  groups, 41, 42, 56
control of programming, 194–7, 201,
  205, 214–5, 241–2
controversy, 188–9
cooperation: between broadcasting
  organisations, 129; in distance higher

education, 146–51; limits of collaboration, 137, 181, 196, 201, 235, 241–2; necessity for basic adult education, 117, 234; necessity for multi media projects, 240; with correspondence colleges, 78, 93, 134; with educationalists, 113; with local colleges, 132; with local education authorities, 76, 113; with Open University, 196; with voluntary agencies, 80, 92, 134
co-production, 133
copyright, 7, 47, 65, 121, 223, 233, 240
Corporation For Public Broadcasting, 129
correspondence education, 78, 93, 99, 128, 134, 139, 155
Costa Rica, *142*
costs and finances: Adult Literacy Campaign, 112; advertising, 3; audio cassettes, 144, 204, 206; average cost per transmission, 170; average cost per TV programme, 170, 214; BBC schools/CE, 133, 182; broadcast TV compared with video, 154, 209, 214; cable TV, 221, 222; conventional education, 58–9; cost effectiveness, 179; cost per user, 170; expenditure on adults, 70; expenditure on pupils, 70; farm forum, 87; fixed costs, 168–9, 216; production, 135, 158; 147; licence revenue, 3; marginal costs, 169, 214; principles of costing, 168–7, 216; production, 135, 158; radio compared with cassettes, 144, 206; 'Sesame Street', 74, 105, 112–3; transmission, 30, 135, 144, 206; TV Ontario, 133; unit costs, 159, 170; video cassettes, 208, 209, 214; video discs, 217, 219, 220
credit awards *see* examinations and assessment
cultural standards, 119–20, 190, 239
current affairs, 20, 119, 127, *131*, 183, 191
curriculum, schools, 18–21, 23–7, 46, 47, 76, 78, 233
curriculum reform/development: adult education, 94, 102, 111, 113, 117; distance higher education, 146; limits of, 105; pre-school, 113; schools, 24–7, 55–63, 233
CYCLOPS, 228–9, 230

dance and movement, 37
decision making, 50–1, 77, 162–3, 187
Delhi, 31, 89
Delta project, 30–1
Denmark, 77, 134
Department of Education and Science

(U.K.), 7, 108, 127
Deutsches Institut Für Fernstudien (DIFF), 146, 147
developing countries: access to broadcasting, 237–8; adult education, 70–1; cultural dominance, 105; curriculum reform, 23–7, 55–63, 233; direct teaching, 23, 65–6, 233; distance higher education, *142–3*; education about, 80; enrichment, 19, 21; producer alienation, 198; reasons for educational broadcasting, 13–15; rural programming, 82–91; *see also* name of individual country
Dijon, University of, 148
Direct Broadcast Satellite (DBS) *see* satellite TV
direct teaching (didactic): adult education (USA), 132; developing countries, 23–7, 55–63, 65–6, 233; distance higher education, 96, 140, 172, 175; pre-school, 74, 104; reading (UK), 43–4; structured learners, 98; *see also* style of programmes
disadvantaged: amount of programming, 128, *130*, 135–6; basic adult education, 76–8, 106–115, 116–7, 123, *124*, 126; enrolment, 99–101; impact of new technology, 236–7; inner city children, 103–5; minority programming, 91–3, 123, *124*, 126; size of problem, 69–71; viewing and listening patterns, 115–7
discipline, 63
disc jockeys, 115
discovery learning, 74
distance education, 67, 137–51, 234 *see also* Open University
documentaries, 20, 51, 119, 120, 174–9, 182, 188, 191–2
Dominican Republic, 78
drama, 79, 82, 83, 92, 119, 161, 173, 178, 179, 182, 188, 195–6, 197
drop-out, 56, 152–6
Dutch Open School, 77, 86
Dutch Open University, 140, *142*, 144

Ecuador, 83, 84
education, programmes on, *125*, 127, *131*, 174, 210–211
Educational Broadcasting Council *see* BBC
Educational Video Index, 215
education officers, 6, 19, 45, 55; *see also* BBC, Educational Broadcasting Councils, Schools Broadcasting Council
Egypt, *70*
elderly, 123, *124*

El Salvador, 24, 26, 56, *57*, 58, 60, 61, 62, 63, 236
English, *36*, 37, *38*, 43–5, 46, 78, 99–101, 134, 161
enrichment, 18–20, 21, 41–8, 56, 62, 65, 98, 190, 233
enrolments: adult literacy, 110; basic education, *100*; conventional universities, 69–70; Entente de l'Est, 148; Funkkolleg, 147; language courses, *100*; Open Learning Institute, 148; Open Universities, *142–3*, 154; schools, 56
entertainment technique: adult learners, 98, 117, 176, 238; audience appeal, 183–9; career development, 182–3; children and, 73, 105, 112; educationally disadvantaged, 97, 112, 114; news programmes, 120; rural programming, 82, 83; social action, 79; young adults, 93
equipment, 5–6, 7, *35*, 43–5, 65, 233, 236–7
ethnic minorities, 48–50, 91–2, 105, *124*, *130*
ETV Maranhao, 24, 26, *57*, 58, 62–3
Everyman's University, 141, *142*
examinations and assessment: continuing education, 99, *100*; distance higher education, 97, 139, 145, 146, 148, 165–6, 179; school equivalence for adults, 78, 136; use of broadcasting in exams, 164, 165–6
experimental projects, 59–60, 90

family, 74, 75, 111, *124*, *131*
Federal Republic of Germany, 30, 34, 59, 135, 141, *143*, 146–7
Federation Interuniversitaire Des Centres De Téléenseignement de L'Est, 147–8
Fernuniversität, 141, *143*, 144, 147
Fiji, 145
Finland, 134
Finnish immigrants, 92
Fogo Island, 80–1
Ford Foundation, 112, 129
Foreign aid, 13–15, 26, 27, 58–60
Foreign Office (UK), 3
France, 29–30, 59, *70*, 89, 134–5, 136, 137, 139, 145, 147–8, 226
Free University of Iran, 140, *142*, 162
French, *36*, 42–3, 127, 153, 155
Funkkolleg, 30, 135, 146–7

Gaelic, 127
Gaspesie, 89
general broadcasting: audience needs, 98–9; British network policies, 115–7; comparison with school audience, 37;

copyright and, 47, 121, 233, 240; departments originating educational programmes, 94; educative programmes, 7–8, 68; influence on educational broadcast style, 19, 179, 182, 201–2; learning and thinking influenced by, 119–21, 186–7; local radio, 136–7; media literacy, 11–12; public broadcasting in North America, 104, 129, 149, 185; use in schools, 47; young children affected by, 104
general interest, *124*, 126, 128
General studies, *40*
Geography, 37, *40*
German, *38*, 127, 153
German Democratic Republic, 145
Glasgow University Media Group, 192, 195
Granada TV, 48, 50, 79, 126, 127, 242
Grenoble, 89
groups, 77, 85–8, 94, 99, *100*, 101, 109, 126, 128, 133–4, 139, 145, 146, 155, 208, 210–211
Gulbenkian Foundation, 92

handicapped children/adults, 52–5, 80, 92, 123, *124*, 128, *130*, 174
Hawkes Bay, 81
Health education and medicine, 82, 83, 85, 87, 90, *131*, 149, 186, 211
Hesse, 146
Hessischer Rundfunk, 146
History, *36*, 37, *38*, 127, *131*, 161, 219
Holland, 77, 79, 135, 140, *142*, 144
Home Office (UK), 5, 159, 242
Honduras, 87
Hong Kong, 19
Household skills, *124*, 126, *131*

ideology, 10, 181–202
INCE, 134
Independent Broadcasting Authority (IBA), 3, 5, 6, 10, 48, 50, 52, 65, 122, 182, 241
independent producers, 80–1, 241
Independent Television Companies (ITV-UK): adult literacy, 115; audience characteristics, 116; Channel 4 and, 81–2; competition with BBC, 183–4; continuing education, 122–3, 128, 136; control, 196; non broadcast material, 215; organization, 3; public service, 190; recruitment, 191; sales to America, 129; schools TV, 6, 34, *35*, 37, *38*
Independent Television Companies Association (ITCA), 4
India, 19, 31, 41, 59, 60, *70*, 85, 89–91, 145

Indian Space Research Organisation, 31
infant schools, 75
Inner London Education Authority (ILEA), 17, 207, 211, 215
integration of programmes, 166–7, 174, 179, 205, 211, 212, *213*, 235, 240
International Broadcasting Trust, 80
Internationales Zentralinstitut Fur Das Jugend-und-Bildungsfernsehen, 34
International Institute for Adult Literacy Methods, 76
International Institute of Communications, 222
IPN, 134
Iran, 76, 140, *142*, 162–3
Israel, 141, *142*
Italian, 127
Italy, 76
Ivory Coast, 24, 25, 26, 31, *57*, 60

Jamaica, 145
Japan, 41–2, 58, *70*, 135, 140
Japanese International Co-operation Agency, 13–15
Japan Prize, 112

Kentucky, University of, 31–2
Kentucky Educational Television (KET), 17, 132
Kenya, 29, 82
Knowledge Network, 148–50

Labour party, 138, 195
Labrador, 81
language teaching: development of language, 45, 53, 61, 75, 233; foreign languages, *36*, *38*, 39, 42–3, 101–2, 127, *131*, 152–4, 155–6; second languages for immigrants, 91–2; *see also* name of language
Latin America, 78, 85, 86, 87
learner control, 211–3, 218
learning gains, 41–2, 44, 45, 50, 58, 65, 103, 104, 120, 164, 173–4
learning needs *see* audience characteristics
learning resource, broadcasting as, 20–2, 42–8, 65, 108
learning skills, 164, 165–6, 175–6, 177–8, 179
legal rights, 77, 99–101
Leisure and hobbies, 71, 126, *131*
Leningrad, 140
L'Entente de L'Est, 147
listening figures *see* Research
Literature, 127, *131*
local education authorities, 6, 17, 45, 92, 109, 110, 113, 203, 214
local radio, 3, 82, 93, 108, 115, 116, 136

London University, 139
London Weekend Television, 243

Madureza, 78
magazine format, 20, 84, 92, 119, 135, 186
Malawi, 78
Manchester, 49
Manpower Services Commission, 93
Mathematics, 24, 25–6, 28, 30–1, *57*, 58, 61, 76, 161, 172, 210
Mauritius, 19
Media literacy/studies, 11–12, 127, *131*, 172–3, 176–8
media selection, 160–4, 235–6
Mediscreen, 80
Memorial University, St. Johns, 81, 145
mental effort, 172, 174, 177
Metz, University of, 148
Mexico, 24, *57*, 62, *70*
microelectronics, 127
Microelectronics In Education Programme, 229
Minerva Project, 78
Moscow Polytechnical Correspondence Institute, 140
Mulhouse, University of, 148
multi-media, 128, 134, 135, 136, 150, 156, 160–8, 179, 233, 236, 240
multiple audio channels, 31, 90
Music, 23, *36*, 37, 119

Nairobi, University of, 29
Nancy, 89, 148
National Centre for Educational Technology, Delhi, 31
National Council for Educational Technology, 44
National Extension College, 78, 93, 128, 155
National Film Board of Canada, 81
National Institute Of Adult Education, 108, 109, 110
National Radio-Television University For Teachers (NURT), 28, 31, *143*
Natural History, 47, *131*, 218
Nebraska, University of, 218
Nebraska Educational Communications Network, 17, 132
Newfoundland, 80–1, 82, 145
News, 84, 92, 115, 119, 120, 187, 191–2
new technology, 11, 163, 203–31
New York, 133
New York University, 132
New Zealand, 145
NHK (Japan Broadcasting Co.), 41–2, 135
Nicaragua, 24, 25, *57*, 58, 59, 60, 61, 62
Niger, 24, 26, 56, *57*, 59, 86
Nigeria, *70*

Norsk Fjernundervisning, 135
North America, 17, 136
Northern Open Learning, 121, 122
North-West Polytechnical
    Correspondence Institute, 140
Norway, 134, 135, 204
NOS (Holland), 77, 135
not-interested learners, 97
NRK (Norwegian Broadcasting
    Company), 135
numeracy, functional, 76–7, 113, 123
nursery schools, 75

objectives, 74–5, 104, 111, 113
off-air recording, 46–7
OFRATEME, 134
Ontario, 87, *see also* TV Ontario
open broadcasting, 83–5, 88, 94
'open' learners, 98, 172
Open Learning Institute, 148, 150
Open Tech, 136
Open universities, 140–5 *see also* Open
    University (U.K.)
Open University (U.K.): A101, 171;
    audience figures, 152, 153–4, 156–8,
    167, 200, 204, 209; audio cassettes,
    204–6; BBC role, 138, 195–6, 199;
    cable TV, 221–3; continuing
    education, *123*, 126–9, 136; cost per
    student, 70; CYCLOPS, 228–30;
    documentaries, 174–9; drop out, 214;
    language teaching, 127; M101, 167,
    172; multi media factors, 161–8;
    origins, 137–9, 236; production costs,
    168, 170; production loads, 61, 140,
    199; programme cost per student,
    170, 204; radio, 141, *143*, 144, 152–3,
    157, 171–3, 204, 206; regions, 126;
    resource allocation, 161, 163; role in
    educational broadcasting, 6–7;
    student characteristics, 96–7, 98,
    171–2; T101, 165, 172; teacher
    training, 28–9, 30; transmission costs,
    169, 170; transmission time, 140,
    156–8, 204; unique functions of
    broadcasting, 161–2; video cassettes,
    144, 158, 207–211; mentioned, 67,
    143, 146, 151, 239
ORACLE, 225
organisational factors, 151, 160, 167,
    235
Oswiata I Wychowanie, 28

pacing, 166
Pakistan, 29, 49, *143*, 168
parents, 24, 47, 75, 115, 127
participation in production, 81–2, 84,
    92
Pay-TV, 5
Philippines, 19, 24, 84

Poland, 28, 31, *143*
policy, broadcasting: basic adult
    education, 94–5, 115–7; continuing
    education, 135–7; schools, 64–6
political consciousness, 72–3, 85, 127,
    131
pre-school education, 69
Pre-school Playgroups Association, 126
PRESTEL, 224, 226
primary resource material, 20–2
primary schools, 34–8, 43–5
producers: autonomy, 170–1, 194–6;
    careers, 182–3, 202, 235;
    commitment, 193–4, 234–5; goals,
    193, 234; job satisfaction, 200; peer
    group assessment, 197–8, 201; role
    with video discs, 219–20; training,
    182, 191, 235; *see also*
    professionalism
production loads, 60–1, 158–9
production scheduling, 167, 179
professionalism, 181–202, 234–5
Public Broadcasting System (PBS),
    115, 119, 129, *132*
publicity, 108, 110, 115, 117, 129, 134,
    137, 138, 155
public service, 2, 190–4, 242–3

qualifications *see* examinations and
    assessment
quality in programming, 117, 119,
    183–94
Quebec, 89
quiz shows, 84

race relations, 48–50, 73, 233
radio animation groups, 86
radio campaigns, 85–6
Radio ECCA, 78
radio farm forums, 85, 86, 87
Radio Luxembourg, 2
Radio Mensaje, 84
Radioprimaria, Mexico, 24, *57*
Radio Quebec, 133, 148
radio schools, 24, 86, 87–8, 94, 105
Radio Sutatenza, 86
Radio Taramuhara, *57*
reading, 32, 37, 43–4, 76, 104, 215, 233
    see also adult literacy
realism, 176
recruitment to education, 88, 93, 99,
    108, 110, 111–2, 138, 200, 233, 238
Rediffusion Ltd, 222
Reims, University of, 148
relevance of programmes, 164–8, 179
religious assemblies, 37
research: formative, 51, 54, 55, 64, 66,
    74, 114, 117, 194, 198; general
    broadcasting, 4, 200; helpfulness
    ratings, 204, 205, 208; lack of, 10;

methodology, 39, 42, 45, 49, 51, 64, 103, 109, 152; producer attitudes to, 181–2, 198; summative, 74, 194; viewing and listening figures: basic adult education, *100*, *106–7*, 110, continuing education, 152–6, general broadcasting, 116, Open University, 156–7, 165, 167, 200, 208–9, schools TV/radio, 33–40; *see also* audience characteristics
rote learning, 62, 104
Royal Television Society, 112
RTS/promotion, 134
rural education, 60, 82–91
Russian, 102, 127

Satellite Instructional Television Experiment (SITE), 31, 59, 90
satellite TV and radio, 2, 5, 31–2, 60, 86–7, 90, 129, 133, 149, 221, 224, 231
school equivalent courses, 78, 148
school leavers, 50–2, 69–70
schools broadcasting, 16–27, 33–66
Schools Broadcasting Council *see* BBC: Schools Broadcasting Council
schools radio, 6, 16, *17*, 34–7, *40*, 41–2, 43–5, 286–7
schools television, 5–6, 8, 16, *17*, 34–5, 37–9, *40*, 41, 44–5
science, 28, 30, 31, *38*, 39, 161, 172, 218
Scottish TV, 126
SECAM, 60
secondary schools, 34–9, 42–3
Senegal, 86
series' length and levels, 152–6
Simon Fraser University, 148
Singapore, 19
Smith, W.H., 115
soap opera *see* drama
social action, 71–2, 78–82, 88, 242
socialising effects, 74–5
social purpose programming, 6, 71–2, 74, 90, 136, 242
social sciences, 161, 174, 178
social skills, 53, 61, 62–3, 76, 77–8
socio-economic differences: access to new media, 236–7; audience characteristics, 96–9; educational qualifications, 71; educational spending, 70; media use (U.K.), 115–7; pre-school, 69, 73, 75, 103, 105; role of broadcasting, 117–8; university entrance, 138; video cassette access, 207
South Africa, 141, *143*, 144
South Korea, 56, *57*, 60
Soviet Union, 139, 140, 145
Spain, *70*, 78, 141, *143*, 144
Spanish, 39, 102, 127, 128
special needs, 22–3, 48–55, 65, 233 *see*

also disadvantaged; handicapped
spot announcements, 83, 88
Sri Lanka, *143*
Strasbourg 11, University of, 148
structure, programme, 19, 21–2, 54, 65, 75, 120–1, 160, 174, 176, 178, 184–7, 210, 213, 219
'structured' learners, 97–8, 164, 172
study circles *see* groups
style, programme, 19, 23, 43, 48, 51–2, 53–4, 65, 83, 96–7, 98, 140, 149, 172, 174–9, 181, 182, 184, 189, 201–2, 204, 214, 232
Sukhothaithammathirat University, 141, *143*
support materials and services, 5, 7, 18, 25–6, 28, 31, 34, 43–4, 47, 59, 77, 80, 84–5, 86, 87, 88, 89, 92, 93, 94, 99, 108, 111, 121, 126, 128, 133–4, 135, 136, 139, *142–3*, 144, 147, 148, 155–6, 160, 177, 234, 240
Sveriges Radio *see* Swedish Educational Broadcasting Company
Sweden, 16, 30–1, 59, 92, 99, 133–4, 145, 204
Swedish Educational Broadcasting Company, 64, 133
Switzerland, 146

Tanzania, 85–6, 87
teacher advisors, 48, 51, 54, 55, 233
teacher roles, 17–27, 42–3, 47–8, 50, 61–2, 114, 197, 200–1
teacher training: broadcasting in, 25, 27–32, 66, 146, 233; training teachers to use broadcasting, 43, 45, 65, 233, 240–1
technical assistance *see* foreign aid
technological determinism, 2
technology, 127, 161, 172, 174
TELEAC, 77, 135
Téléformation, 135
telephone, 79, 93, 108, 110, 112, 113, 115, 126, 145, 149, 155, 206, 224, 228
Telesecundaria, Mexico, 24, *57*, 58, 62
Teletext, 225–6
Téléuniversité, Quebec, 140, *142*
TELIDON, 226
Tesco, 115
Tevec, 89
Thailand, 19, 24, 41, 141, *143*
Thames TV, 79, 122
thinking, 186, 187
Toronto, 133, 137
training in educational broadcasting, 59
transmission: balloons, 56; costs, 30; effect of course life, 159; effect on viewing and listening figures, 156–9, 208, 234; France, 134, 137; frequencies, 242; need for repeats,

transmission – *cont.*
159; networks, 115–7; night time,
203, 207, 210, 215; Open universities,
142–3; time, 60, 79, *106–7*, 111, 115,
117, 136, 141, 179, 243; timing, 166;
TV Ontario, 133
TRU, 133
Tübingen, 147
TV Academy (Ontario), 133
TV Ontario, 97, 133, 137, 148, 226
two way communication, 24, 32, 86–7,
139, 149, 221, 223–4, 228

unemployment, 72, 79, 93, 237
UNESCO, 76
unique characteristics of audio cassette,
205
unique characteristics of TV, 45, 53,
154, 160–4, 171, 177, 179, 187, 200,
212–4, 231, 235
United Nations Development
Programme, 14, 59
United States of America, 17, 18, 31–2,
41, 59, 64, *70*, 73, 74, 87, 103, 120,
121, 129, 132, 145, 185, 186, 224, 237
United States Agency For International
Development (USAID), 14, 19
Universidad Estatal A Distancia, Costa
Rica, *142*
Universidad Nacional Albierto,
Venezuela, *143*
Universidad Nacional De Educacion A
Distancia, Spain, 141, *143*, 144
university extension services, 145–6
up-market continuing education
programmes, 127–9, 135, 137
Urals Polytechnical Institute, 140

Venezuela, *143*
Victoria, University of, 148

video cassettes: audio cassettes
compared with, 206, 211; broadcast
TV compared with, 163, 212–4, 243;
cable and, 225; computers and, 217,
220, 230; effect on viewing figures,
158; France, 135, 148; general
broadcasts, 47; ILEA, 17, 207; in
curriculum design, 22, 47, 65; in
examinations, 166; in homes, 1, 207;
in schools and colleges, 6, 35, 48, 62,
65, 206; open universities, *142–3*,
144, 207–211; rural education, 89,
145
video discs, 1, 163, 203, 215, 216–21
video games, 2
viewdata, 224, 225–6
viewing figures *see* research
vocational training/development, 127,
131, 136, 148
volunteers and voluntary agencies,
79–80, 85, 92, 93, 108, 110, 112, 113,
117, 134, 214, 234, 240, 241, 242

Wales, 3
Welsh, 127
West Germany *see* Federal Republic Of
Germany
Westinghouse Corporation, 56
Westward TV, 93, 126, 127
Whitfield Committee, 65
Wisconsin, University of, 145
Wolsey Hall, 139
women's studies, 123, *124*, *130*
World Bank, 14, 19, 59

Yorkshire TV, 52, 76, 121, 126, 186
young adults, 92–3, *124*, 128, *130*
Yugoslav immigrants, 92

Zambia, 145

Author Index

Abell, H. C., 87
Agrawal, B., 90
Ahrens, S., 166
Arena, G., *57*
Arnove, R., 56

Bacsich, P., 221
Ball, S., 103, 114
Bates, A. W., 10, 16, *143*, 152, 157,
    159, 161, 168, 174, 204, 229
Beardsley, J., 162
Beck, T. K., 115
Belson, W., 173
Bernal, H., 86
Berry, C., 120
Birt, J., 243
Bjorklund, K., 31
Blumler, J. G., 171
Bogatz, G. A., 103, 114
Bon, A., 30
Bonzon, S., 84
Booth, J., 82, 84
Bouillon, C., 147
Brown, D., 171–2
Brown, S., 165, 208
Bruner, J., 165
Burns, T., 190, 192, 194, 197, 198

Cassirer, H. R., 85, 86
Cawston, R., 191
Cepeda, L. E., 78
Champness, B., 61
Charnley, A. H., 108
Chen, M., 74
Chesterton, G. K., 145
Clarke, A., 52, 53
Clifford, B., 120
Coldevin, G., 82
Coleman, J. S., 69
Cook, T. M., 103, 114
Cooney, J. G., 73
Corduant, J. P., 137
Croton, G., 54, 92
Cuff, A., 42–3

Darveau, J. G., 89
Dodds, T., 85, 89
Durbridge, N., 205, 210

Edwards, R., 52, 53, 54
Eicher, J. C., *57*
Elliott, P., 195, 198
Elliott, S., 121

Findahl, D., 120
Fiske, T., 12
Fortosky, D., 146
Friend, J., *57*
Fuller, R., 220

Gallagher, M., 157, 165, 167, 174, 178,
    183, 193, 196, 197
Girardin, M., 89
Glikman, V., 137
Goldsen, R., 104, 105
Gregory, F., 114–5
Grundin, H., 156, 157, 158, 159, 164,
    170, 204, 207, 209
Gunter, B., 120
Gunter, J., 83, 84, 88

Hall, B. L., 85
Hall, P., 181
Hall, S., 74, 75
Hargreaves, D., 80, 109, 114
Harry, K., *143*
Hartley, J., 12
Haviland, R. M., 69
Hawkridge, D., *57*
Hayter, G., 44–5, 206
Heidt, E. V., 160, 171
Hill, R., 52, 53
Höijer, B., 120
Hood, S., 189, 198
Hooper, R., 20
Horneij, R., *100*
Howe, M., 12
Howkins, J., 222
Hunt, A., 12

Ingle, H., *57*, 67

Jacquinot, G., 174
Jamison, D., *57*, 83, 86
Jay, A., 191
Jones, H. A., 108

Kadelbach, G., 146
Kanocz, S., 147
Katz, E., 15, 171, 237
Kaye, A. R., 25, *57*, 139, 145, 146
Keegan, D., 139, 145
Kemmelfield, G., 48–50, 55
Kern, L., 165

Lallez, R., 89
Larimore, D., 32
Laurillard, D., 217
Lecomte, G., 147
Lee, R., 54
Lesser, G. S., 74, 113
Lewis, R., 132
Lyle, J., 62

McAnany, E., 16, 83, 86, 87
McCormick, R., 140
McCron, R., 79–80
Macleod, S., 186
Maddison, J., 76
Manuelian, A., 147
Masland, G., *57*
Masland, L., *57*
Mason, E. J., 83
Masterman, L., 12
Matsui, J., 97–8
Matthews, T., 92
Mayo, J., 16, *57*
Morris, E., 114–5
Murdoch, R., 2

Neurath, P. M., 87

Oliveira, J. B. A., 63, 78
Olson, D., 165
Orivel, F., *57*, 78

Palmer, E. L., 74, 114
Pascoe, C., 92
Pease, M., 79
Perry, W., 137
Plowden, B., 69
Polsky, R. M., 113
Porter, P., 52–4, 174
Postman, N., 12, 185, 186
Puszczewicz, B., 28

Read, G. A., 228
Reeves, B., 93
Reith, J., 190

Rheinhold, M., 93
Robbins, 138
Robinson, J., 16, *57*, 99, 128, 241
Rogers, E., 85, 87
Rogers, J., 71
Rumble, G., 139, *143*, 145, 146
Russell, L., 69, 119
Rybak, S., 101–2, 152, 153, 155–6

Salkeld, R., 77, *100*, 102
Salomon, G., 166, 171, 172, 174, 176, 213
Sassoon, V., 186
Saunders, U. C., 240–1
Schmelkes De Sotelo, B., *57*
Schramm, W., 23–4, 25, 41, 42, 56, *57*, 60–1, 67, 85, 87, 183
Shaw, B., 221
Sissons, L., 102
Skandar, O., 29
Spain, P. L., *57*
Spencer, K., 52, 53
Steedman, J., 50–2, 55
Stephens, M., 77, 102
Stringer, D., 76, 113
Swift, B., 29

Taylor, N., 162
Theroux, J., 83, 84, 88
Thompson, G., 176
Tough, A., 71
Trenaman, J., 97, 164, 172–3, 175
Tucker, J. D., 52
Tunstall, J., 120

UNESCO, *70*

Vaughan, D., 184
Vellekoop, L., 77
Vernon, P., 173

Waniewicz, I., 133
Ware, E., 4
Warnock, M., 52
Wedell, G., 15, 237
Wenham, B., 1
Whelan, E., 54
White, R., 87
Wilson, H., 138
Wright, A., 82, 84

Yacoub, S. M., 87

Programme Index

Alles Klar (BBC TV), *38*
Archers, The (BBC Radio), 37, 83
Artists In Print (BBC TV), 127
Arts Foundation Course-A101 (BBC/OUP), 171–2
As Good As New (Yorkshire TV), 126
Ascent of Man (BBC TV), 132

Better Badminton (BBC TV), 126
Blue Peter (BBC TV), 75, 93
Botanic Man (Thames TV), 122, 200
Brush, Basil, 188

Camera (Granada TV), 126
Capricorn Game (BBC TV), 52
Chips Are Down, The (BBC TV), 239
Computer Programme, The (BBC TV), 127, 128
Computing In Everyday Life (France), 135
Consumer Decisions (BBC/OUP), 126
Cotabato Ngyon (Philippines), 84

Danish For Adults (Danish Radio), 77
Day, Robin, 188
Decision (Granada TV), 50–2
Delia Smith's Cookery (BBC TV), 126
Developing Mathematical Thinking: EM235 (BBC/OUP), 210–211
¡Digame! (BBC TV and Radio), 102, 128
Dizzy (ATV), 121
Drama: A307 (BBC/OUP), 195–6

Effective Manager, The (BBC/OUP), 127
Electronics (BBC Radio), *36*, 37
Electronics In The Home (France), 135
Energy In The Home (BBC/OUP), 126
English Programme, The (Thames TV), *38*
Ensemble (BBC TV and Radio), 153, 155
Experiment: Chemistry (Granada TV), *38*

Finding Out (Thames TV), *38*
First Years Of Life (BBC/OUP), 126

Get By In Spanish (BBC TV), 127
Going To Work (BBC TV), 37, *38*
Grange Hill (BBC TV), 75

Help! (Thames TV), 79
Helping With Spelling (BBC Radio), *107*
Horizon (BBC TV), 175
How We Used To Live (Yorkshire TV), *38*
Huckleberry Hound Show (USA), 105

Industrial Relations (BBC/OUP), 127
Insight (Yorkshire TV), 52, 53, 54

Jackanory (BBC TV), 74
Just The Job (Westward TV), 93

Know Your Rights (France), 135
Kontakte (BBC TV/Radio), 153
Krishi Darsan (India), 89

Le Nouvel Arrivé (BBC TV), 42
Learning From Television (BBC/OUP), 178
Let's Go . . . (BBC TV), 52, 54, 92, 93
Let's Move (BBC Radio), *36*, 37
Life on Earth (BBC TV), 47
Listen With Mother (BBC Radio), 74, 115
Listening And Reading (BBC Radio), 43–4, 46
Listening And Writing (BBC Radio), *36*
Living Decisions (BBC Radio), 77, 102, 116
Living With Technology – A Foundation Course-T101 (BBC/OUP), 165, 172
Long Search, The (BBC TV), 132
Look And Read (BBC TV), 37

Make It Count (Yorkshire TV), 76–7, 113
Mass Communications In Society-DE353 (BBC/OUP), 177
Mathematics – A Foundation Course-M101 (BBC/OUP), 166–7, 172

Maths Across The Curriculum (BBC/OUP), 127
Merry-Go-Round (BBC TV), *38*, 43
Moneywise (Scottish TV), 126
Move On (BBC Radio), *107*
Mr. Smith's Fruit Garden (BBC TV), 126
Mtu Ni Afya (Tanzania), 86
My World (Yorkshire TV), *38*

Nai Zindagi Naya Jeevan (BBC TV), 92
Near And Far (BBC TV), *38*
Next Move (BBC Radio), *106*
Not So Long Ago (BBC Radio), *36*

Ochen Pryatno (BBC TV), 102
On The Move (BBC TV), 80, 96, 97, *106*, 111, 112–5, 117
Open Door (BBC TV), 81
Our Neighbours (Granada TV), 48–50

Parosi (BBC TV), 91–2, 93
Past At Work, The (BBC), 127
Play It Safe (BBC TV), 126
Playschool (BBC TV), 74–5
Principles Of Counselling (BBC TV), 126
Public Office (Granada TV), 127

Reports Action (Granada TV), 79
Roadshow (BBC TV), 79

Scene (BBC TV), 37
Service For Schools (BBC Radio), 37
Sesame Street (USA, CTW), 73–5, 94, 102, 103–5, 112–5, 117
Shakespeare Perspectives (BBC TV), 127
Singing Together (BBC Radio), 37
Social Sciences; A Foundation Course-D102 (BBC/OUP), 178
START (Swedish Radio), 99, *100*, 101, 134, 137, 146

Stories And Rhymes (BBC Radio), *36*
Sunrise Semester (USA), 132
Supervisors (BBC TV), 127
Sur Le Vif (BBC Radio), 153

Take It Easy (Sweden), 134
Teaching Adults To Read (BBC Radio), *107*
Télépromotion Rurale (France), 89
Telescuola (Italy), 76
Telethon (Thames TV), 79
Television Club (BBC TV), 52
Television Programme, The (Westward TV), 127
Time and Tune (BBC Radio), 37
Trades Union Studies (BBC TV), 127
Training Dogs (BBC TV), 126
Twentieth Century History (BBC TV), 37

Urban Development-DT201 (BBC/OUP), 177

Village Action (Westward TV), 126
Voix De France (BBC Radio), *36*

Wainwright's Law (BBC TV), 126
Watch! (BBC TV), 37, *38*
Wegweiser (BBC Radio), 153
Werwinkel (Holland), 79
What Right Have You Got? (BBC Radio), 77, 99–101, 102, 116
Where There's Life . . . (Yorkshire TV), 186
Words And Pictures (BBC TV), 37

Yogi Bear (USA), 105
You And Me (BBC TV), 75
Your Move (BBC TV), *106*, 115
Your Own Business (BBC TV), 127, 181

Zaa Na Uwatunze (Kenya), 82, 83